Undoing Ethics

Natasha Whiteman

Undoing Ethics

Rethinking Practice in Online Research

Springer

Natasha Whiteman
Department of Media and Communication
University of Leicester
Leicester, UK
new9@le.ac.uk

ISBN 978-1-4614-1826-9 e-ISBN 978-1-4614-1827-6
DOI 10.1007/978-1-4614-1827-6
Springer New York Dordrecht Heidelberg London

Library of Congress Control Number: 2011943348

Printed on acid-free paper

Springer is part of Springer Science+Business Media (www.springer.com)

Preface

Are you feeling blue? the headline in the free daily newspaper *Metro*[1] asks. Beneath a large image of two blue aliens, the article describes how the '3D fantasy world of blockbuster film Avatar [...] has left some cinema-goers unable to cope with reality – and even feeling suicidal'. The writer reports how:

> On the fan forum site Avatar Forums, a topic thread entitled 'Ways to cope with the depression of the dream of Pandora being intangible' has received more than 1,000 posts. 'Ever since I went to see Avatar I have been depressed,' wrote a poster called Mike. 'Watching the wonderful world of Pandora and all the Na'vi made me want to be one of them. I even contemplate suicide thinking that if I do I will be rebirthed in a world similar to Pandora [where] everything is the same as in Avatar.' Another movie-goer called Elequin added: It's so hard I can't force myself to think that it's just a movie and to get over it, that living like the Na'vi will never happen. I think I need a rebound movie.

Typing 'Avatar Forums' into Google takes the curious reader directly to the bulletin boards of avatar-forums.com where the threaded discussion is played out in full. A notice at the top of the page reminds the visitor that they are currently 'viewing our boards as a guest which gives you limited access to view most discussions and access our other features'. It appears the usernames presented in the article have not been changed.

A number of similar stories are published on other news and media sites. A story on www.techradar.com[2] (which uses quotes but does not name users) is more openly disparaging of the members of the forums ('The web has been awash with slightly delusional fans [...]') and provides readers with a hyperlink direct to avatar-forums.com. A CNN article portrays the fans in a similar tone ('A post by a user called Elequin expresses an almost obsessive relationship with the film.') and makes reference to extracts from an interview with one of the site's members:

> Ivar Hill posts to the "Avatar" forum page under the name Eltu. He wrote about his post-"Avatar" depression after he first saw the film earlier this month.

[1] *Metro*, Wednesday, January 13, 2010.

[2] http://www.techradar.com/news/internet/avatar-s-3d-planet-leaves-moviegoers-depressed-and-suicidal--663355?src=rss&attr=all

> *"When I woke up this morning after watching Avatar for the first time yesterday, the world seemed … gray. It was like my whole life, everything I've done and worked for, lost its meaning," Hill wrote on the forum. "It just seems so … meaningless. I still don't really see any reason to keep … doing things at all. I live in a dying world."*
>
> *Reached via e-mail in Sweden where he is studying game design, Hill, 17, explained that his feelings of despair made him desperately want to escape reality.*[3]

On the forums of avatar-forums.com, opinion appears mixed about the coverage the site has received and journalists' use of content from the boards. Some members note their discomfort with the use of usernames and real names. One states that they would feel uncomfortable with their name being published in this way. Another responds 'yeah, I wonder if they had permission'. Another is concerned about their words being taken out of context, worried that it appeared that they were advocating suicide ('I just want to clarify that I am 100% sure that suicide will not achieve that'). Some remind users that the site is largely a safe haven with most members being people 'who won't exploit you on International media'. Others celebrate the fame the coverage has brought to the site (addressing the user Elequin, one thread begins 'you're famous now!').

The reporting of *Avatar* fans' online discussions described above raises a host of complex ethical issues. Discussion of a popular film on a publically accessible website might appear fair game, but if these were academic rather than journalistic interventions, the decisions made in the very public reporting of these postings would be controversial[4]. What might we make of the naming of websites and use of real usernames which deny anonymity to the *Avatar* fansites and their members? What about the use of verbatim extracts from posts, which has the same effect, as search engines enable easy identification of, and access to, the location of their origin? What about the issue of consent – apparently neglected here? The contrasting reactions of the posters described in the reports, expressing feelings of violation, anxiety, pride and also excitement, raise questions about the responsibility of the reporter to their subjects. They also suggest that members of the forums have very different ideas about the status of their activity (public? private?). At the same time, the negativity of the reporting, apparently based on outsider readings of the sites, with fans characterised as 'obsessive' and 'deluded', might be questioned. The reports also establish connections between online identities (Eltu) and the 'real' people beyond the screen (Ivar Hill), people who, in this example, appear to be under the age of 18. Finally, although the subject matter of these fansites may appear trivial, we also have the reporting of a potentially sensitive topic in discussion of depression and suicide.

Any student or researcher entering into such online environments for the purpose of research needs to be able to demonstrate that they have considered the ethics of their practice, their use of data and their relationship to the researched settings. No matter what the activity they are interested in, it is likely that they will be asked to account for the decisions they make and describe the strategies they have developed

[3] 'Audiences experience "Avatar" blues' Jo Piazza, CNN January 11, 2010 8:06 a.m. EST http://www.cnn.com/2010/SHOWBIZ/Movies/01/11/avatar.movie.blues/index.html

[4] And it is worth noting that the use of my entry into the site for the purposes of this preface itself raises ethical questions.

for managing the ethics of their work. The conflicting guidance on Internet research practice and the diverse nature and characteristics of different online environments can make this task difficult.

This book examines some of the challenges that researchers may face when researching online activity and the ways that existing guidance on research ethics can inform our responses to these. This is not, however, solely a book about 'Internet research ethics'. The development of the Internet has reinvigorated ethical debates, but many of the dilemmas and debates it presents to researchers are not new. For this reason, rather than just specialising to the Internet, the following chapters introduce a number of key ethical questions, aiming to expose and explore some of the continuities between the study of online and offline domains.

The book conceptualises the *doing* of research ethics as involving the production of an ethical stance in respect of key ethical issues and methodological decisions. This stance is established in relation to a number of different domains in which ethics is articulated/embodied (rather than involving self-evident notions of what actions might be 'good' or 'bad') and involves a consideration of the researcher's accountability to different audiences and interested parties. The chapters examine the ways such stances might be established and unsettled during research and the resources that might be used to inform this ongoing work.

Although I discuss the use of Internet-based tools for generating data (via the use of online interviews and surveys etc.), my primary focus is the ethics of online research that is based on methods of observation and participation. Of particular interest is the use of unobtrusive observation (so-called lurking) in online domains. In considering the key ethical questions that researchers using such methods face, the book also examines the way that ethics are codified, articulated, and experienced in academic and non-academic domains and in different contexts, from the research literature that researchers engage with, the varied online settings they may explore, and their personal and institutional contexts. The book aims to consider the ways that the articulation of ethics in these different contexts might inform each other. Whilst the following chapters do not provide a roadmap for the ethical conduct of online research, I hope that they provide a useful way of thinking about the reader's own position in respect of these issues.

Acknowledgements

There are a number of people that I would like to thank for their help and support in the writing of this book. Some provided encouragement, a few were kind enough to read draft chapters and provide invaluable comments and others have been willing to talk to me about ethics and research. I am extremely grateful for all their contributions to this text. Thanks in particular to Maria Touri, Caroline Pelletier, Joanne Metivier, Diane Carr, Meredith DiPietro, Will Gibson, Aleks Krotoski, Elizabeth Buchanan, Neil Selwyn, Martin Oliver, Andrew Brown, David Buckingham, the members of Paul Dowling's research students' group, my colleagues at the Department of Media and Communication at the University of Leicester and the editors of the *International Journal of Internet Research Ethics*. I am particularly indebted to Russell Dudley-Smith for his extremely helpful critical and educational engagement with this book as well as my earlier work on fans. Massive thanks also to Claudia Lapping who has helped me to clarify my ideas on many occasions. I am grateful for her patience in doing so, and for her rigorous and insightful feedback. Most of all, I would like to thank Paul Dowling, who was an outstanding Ph.D. supervisor and has contributed hugely to the development of my ideas. This book could not have happened without his enthusiasm for my work, his intellectual perspicacity and his generosity in reading and re-reading draft chapters. I value his friendship and always look forward to our conversations.

I am also grateful to my excellent friends Nicole Slavin and Kathryn Cullen for providing welcome distractions during the writing of this book.

Love and thanks to my family. Thanks in particular to my parents who have always encouraged and supported me. This book is dedicated to them.

Finally, thanks to Jamie.

My Ph.D. research, which is discussed in the following chapters, was funded by the Economic and Social Research Council.

Contents

Chapter 1
Ethical Stances in (Internet) Research

Abstract This chapter explores the ethical destabilisation that the development of the Internet and related new media technologies has provoked, an unsettling of ethical expectations and assumptions that is felt by both researchers and Internet users. Examining researchers' responses to the challenges of conducting research in online environments, the chapter considers how the idea of an 'ethical' Internet researcher has emerged in this work. It then explores moves towards localised and contingent research ethics in recent writing about online and offline research, and considers how these moves relate to the institutionalisation of ethical guidance and regulation of research in academic contexts. The chapter closes with an introduction to the author's study of two online fan communities – a study that underpins the discussion of ethics in the chapters that follow – and a description of the key ethical issues that were faced during the project.

Introduction: The Internet and Ethical Uncertainty

The development of the field of social science research methods can be characterised as involving the establishment of different ways of looking at the world. Whilst these methodological frameworks are very different and often contested, the referential 'world' to which they relate often appears reassuringly familiar and relatively stable. Common understandings of the world and researchers' responses to it have developed within different academic disciplines and within different traditions of inquiry. As John Law describes in *After Method* (2004), researchers' endeavours have involved the naturalising of certain assumptions about research, assumptions relating to 'what is most important in the world, the kinds of facts we need to gather, and the appropriate techniques for gathering and theorising data' (Law 2004, 5).

A similar naturalising move can be recognised in the articulation of research ethics guidance, where key principles have become embedded into expectations about what constitutes professional and ethical behaviour. Traditional methodological

N. Whiteman, *Undoing Ethics: Rethinking Practice in Online Research*,
DOI 10.1007/978-1-4614-1827-6_1, © Springer Science+Business Media, LLC 2012

debates have to some extent involved a stabilising of research methods and ethics, with certain understandings of what is ethical having become generally accepted. We are used to asking permission before entering someone's home to observe them, for example, and have become accustomed to the idea that we should ask participants for consent before involving them in research.

These ways of looking are by no means fixed, as heated debates about the methods and ethics of 'real-world' research continue. However, they tend to be based on relatively established understandings of the nature of the world. This includes broad assumptions about the characteristics of settings such as classrooms, homes and offices and the physically embodied people who inhabit them, as well as the dominance of certain positions (albeit not always shared) regarding the ways these settings/individuals can and should be approached. At the same time, the discussion of research ethics has settled into certain familiar arguments. For some, this has had a negative effect on the field, resulting in the academic discussion of research ethics becoming increasingly frustrating, entrenched into a regular patterning of familiar, irresolvable debates that tend to focus on certain infamous cases of ethical misconduct and particular methods (including experiments and covert research), whilst ignoring other methods and more everyday ethical quandaries (Bryman 2008).

The development and expansion of the Internet and related new media technologies unsettled some of the certainties that these assumptions, expectations, and discussions are based upon. As traditional debates were reignited by the need to respond to the characteristics of technologically mediated environments, researchers entered anew key discussions regarding the moral, legal, and regulative aspects of research ethics. Challenges to existing understandings of ethical behaviour in research surfaced as researchers engaged with the demands of researching the Internet, considering important questions about the status and use of data sourced from online environments, the responsibilities of the researcher to those participating in technologically mediated settings, and the extent to which – more broadly – existing rules of ethical practice should be extended to online research. As Baym and Markham (2009) have described, in their response to these questions, Internet researchers have engaged in a reassessment of 'basic principles and practices of qualitative inquiry', producing 'important critiques of a priori methodological certainties' (9). This has involved not only the development of new assumptions but also contestation arising from the thinking through of emerging methodological and ethical problems.

Of course, it is not just researchers who have experienced ethical dilemmas in relation to the Internet, or have been confronted with questions that 'lurk less visibly in traditional contexts'. Internet users also face distinct ethical challenges. In her 1996 paper on Internet research ethics 'What's wrong with the "Golden Rule"? Conundrums of conducting ethical research in cyberspace', for example, Christina Allen presented the following prediction regarding the future development of ethical behaviour on the Internet:

> [...] as more participants gain experience in these now novel modes of communication, diverse amalgams of values will begin to emerge. Many cyberspace sites are already developing innovative approaches to governance, conditions of membership and regulation of patterns of use, partially in response to what researchers 'do' with the information that is

> available. In other words, the cyberspace experiences that can contribute to ethical wisdom are just now developing.
>
> (Allen 1996, no page numbers)

Although Allen's focus in this paper was on a pre–Web 2.0 Internet (she notes that she is writing at a time when 'neither participants nor researchers have much experience in cyberspace' (ibid)), the negotiation and innovation of ethics suggested in this extract is still taking place today. The Internet continues to emerge as an arena of ethical destabilisation, an arena infused by competing ethical positions instantiated in illicit activities and tensions between 'open networks of collaboration' and 'closed structures of commercial competitive environments' (Humphreys et al. 2005).

In the absence of common ethical frameworks, rules of conduct are being negotiated and contested by users within online gaming and online worlds (such as *World of Warcraft* and *Second Life*), social networking sites (such as *Facebook*, *Myspace*, *YouTube*, and blogs), peer-to-peer file-sharing communities, and more traditional forums and websites. Within these diverse contexts, users are faced with ethical questions and dilemmas regarding the acceptability of particular forms of behaviour (seen in media coverage of virtual crime and bullying), the integrity of certain uses of content (seen in challenges to copyright legislation), and issues relating to the right to privacy in online domains. To date, understandings of appropriate and acceptable behaviour within these activities have been strongly contested, with individuals negotiating the contradictions of emerging forms of entertainment, sites of reception, and modes of consumption, production and distribution. Even within sites that have strict rules and regulations, users appear ready to test and push at the margins of what is acceptable, what is ethical, and what is not.

We can find evidence of this ongoing negotiation of ethics in different types of online activity. In a paper on the ethics of *eBay*, for example, Robert MacDougall describes how the highly constrained nature of the *eBay* website sustains interactions:

> Through a highly formalized feedback mechanism centered around the exchange of goods that is bound, almost gravitation-like, by the network effect of hundreds of millions of daily users. At first pass, these processes appear to be working symbiotically with and through eBay users who dutifully and often enthusiastically sustain a self-regulating social control system that explicitly models and patterns successful behaviour.
>
> (MacDougall 2010, 237)

Despite the presence of these formalised mechanisms, eBay users also appear to challenge the control imposed by the framing of interactions on the site. This testing of rules is evident in the activity of auction 'sniping', which involves buyers lying in wait for the final seconds of timed sales before pouncing, hoping to win the items by trumping other bidders at the very last moment. As MacDougall describes, such sniping has spawned an industry of 'books, products, and services' (including automated sniping software). He suggests that this activity demonstrates the testing of ethical behaviour in this environment:

> Loosed, then, from the ethical moorings most intrinsic to contexts of embedded, physical embodied interaction [...] a new communicative concept emerges, and with it a shadowy ethic that is captured succinctly in the snipe. [...] The whole enterprise betrays an underlying

> enmity among and between buyers. I have been sniped by humans and bots, and I managed to win a snowboard by manually sniping an item out from under another bidder. Sure, no one really gets hurt, but the activity is vicious pure and simple. [..] With all this comes increased difficulty in discriminating between ethical and unethical rule systems on the one hand, and practically advantageous or disadvantageous rule systems on the other.
>
> (MacDougall 2010, 242)

Online, confusion and disagreement is evident about the legitimacy of such actions. Coverage of the phenomena of *eBay* sniping on the Internet, for example, not only includes sites offering texts and guidance, and free and commercial sniping services, but also discussion of whether or not the activity is acceptable, against eBay's rules of use, or even illegal.

A similar negotiation and testing of ethical behaviour is evident in a different type of online enterprise: participation in online games and online worlds. Researchers have examined how the acceptability of different forms of cheating[1] is digested within game environments and related discussion boards. As Fields and Kafai (2010) suggest, the literature on online gaming has shown that 'among game players there is great variety on what counts as cheating, what the repercussions are, and how and when one should use cheats' (2010, 66). Their own work on cheating in player-run cheat sites surrounding the tween virtual world *Whyville* demonstrates this contestation. *Whyville* – a site aimed at young people – is part social environment, part learning environment, with members earning currency by completing science-related mini-games. Cheat sites created by these young people provide solutions and advice for successfully completing these games. Alongside these, Fields and Kafai note how some within the site also engage in more serious hacking and 'spoil-sport cheating' activity.[2] Examining the motivations of cheat site creators and the debate around cheating within *Whyville,* they argue that the activity provides a way into thinking about ethics more broadly:

> Cheating in *Whyville* brought up many contemporary ethical issues facing people in today's society: identity theft, intellectual property, sharing information, relationships, honesty, leadership, and even an implied critical look at the goals of the virtual world (is it for science learning or relationships?).
>
> (Fields and Kafai 2010, 84)

Here, as in the discussion of *eBay* sniping, we have an unsettling of behavioural expectations and a contestation of what it means to be 'ethical'. In each case, Internet users (whether adults or children) are trying out new possibilities for action and establishing different ground rules regarding the acceptability of different types of behaviour.

Each of these examples demonstrates the ethical implications of the move away from established understandings of ethics as situated within the physically embodied

---

[1] An activity which is central to videogame play (see Consalvo 2007).

[2] 'For instance, it is a frequent practice in *Whyville* to lie to *Whyvillians* [citizens of *Whyville*] to obtain their password so that one can log into another's account and send the money to oneself' (Fields and Kafai 2010, 70).

offline world. Such accounts remind us that Internet researchers are likely to enter into complex, ethically charged environments; environments in which Internet users, like Internet researchers, are confronting and working through ethical issues (although they may not be doing so quite so explicitly), where ethical codes and behaviours are being negotiated within the daily activity of online life, and where key questions, such as who owns the Internet, are being disputed. For both Internet researchers and users, there are no definitive answers to these questions.

Against this backdrop, this book explores the efforts of researchers to establish and maintain ethical stances in the practice of online research. The following chapters examine the resources that researchers can draw from when working through ethical issues in the planning and conduct of research. In doing so, the book considers the relationship between the ethical manoeuvring of researchers and the ethical manoeuvring of those they research. This idea of 'ethical manoeuvring' refers to the way that – in the face of the ethical instability described above – both Internet researchers and Internet users can be understood to be engaged in the ongoing production and performance of particular stances in respect of the ethics of their actions and behaviour (e.g. adopting specific positions in respect of the actions that are, or are not, acceptable or appropriate). In each case, these stances can be understood to be established and maintained but also challenged within and by the demands and expectations of the contexts in which they operate. As I will discuss in Chap. 2, the relationship between the researcher/researched has become increasingly significant in academic discussion of research ethics (both online and offline). The approach taken in this book pushes this interest further by examining the negotiation of ethics in academic and non-academic domains and the ways that these domains might (should?) inform each other.

In exploring the relationship between researcher and researched, this book outlines a framework for considering research ethics as constituted in relation to different domains: the empirical settings of research; the theoretical perspectives that inform the researcher's objectification of the research settings and practical methodological decision-making; the institutional contexts in which researchers work; and the ethical 'baggage' that each researcher brings to their project. These four domains are presented in more detail in the following chapter.

In its consideration of ethics in relation to the empirical as well as theoretical and methodological contexts of research, the book establishes a perspective from which ethics is constituted as lying at the heart of all social activity, whether or not ethics is constituted as a formal area of responsibility. As this suggests, my focus is on the practice of ethics, primarily in the context of research, but also more broadly. The book can therefore be contrasted with what Calvey has described as 'the standard discourse on ethics', a discourse that 'is abstracted from the actual doing, which is a mediated and contingent set of practices' (Calvey 2008, 905). It is the *achievement* and *performance* of these practices, our decisions and actions, that is my interest here. Before turning to the literature to trace some of the moves that might be used to inform this achievement/performance, I want to first consider why ethical issues have become an increasingly important focus of interest for social science researchers in recent years.

A Shifting Academic Terrain

Academic institutions have only relatively recently become concerned with regulating the ethics of social science research. Sieber has described how researchers in the USA:

> [...] always prided themselves on their methodological problem-solving skills, but particularly before the 1970s when federal regulations of human research were developed, gave little thought to ethics, assuming that good intentions would suffice. As the federal regulatory structure and institutional review board (IRB) oversight began to take hold on research activities, terms such as *informed consent* entered the lexicon of researchers.
>
> (Sieber 2004, 298)

Similar pressures have been seen in the UK context, where there has been increasing regulation of research ethics over the past decade (Wiles et al. 2010) as political developments have resulted in the bureaucratising and institutionalising of ethical review procedures within higher education.[3] Most significantly perhaps this has included the introduction of ethics committees within UK higher education institutions (in a similar way to the earlier introduction of institutional review boards (IRBs) in the USA), a move that has been informed by regulatory 'regimes' founded on the concerns of medical research (Murphy and Dingwall 2007), based on a central concern with potential harm to (human) subjects.

As Alderson and Marrow (2006) argue, this growing bureaucratisation has resulted in a change in the visibility of social science research ethics. What was, previously, primarily a personal endeavour (for the social science researcher to contend with) has been brought into a more public domain, documented, regulated and approved by those operating within institutional frameworks. For this reason, alongside the developments in new media technologies that have resulted in the growth of academic interest in the subject of online research ethics, the backdrop to this book also includes broader political developments within academia that have implications for the regulation and approval of social science research. These developments have been welcomed by those who recognise the need to ensure that research practice is scrutinised as a professional endeavour (e.g. Dowling and Brown 2010). Such changes have also been regarded more negatively, however, as 'placing unnecessary and unhelpful limitations on research practice' (Wiles et al. 2010, 2), whilst also challenging the traditional status and authority of the researcher-as-expert.

The move from the authority of the researcher to the researcher delivering predefined work suggests an 'ethical' model that can be delivered and also regulated and assessed by other professionals within the field. Researchers and students now need to be able to demonstrate and assert the legitimacy of their actions and ethical decision-making to a broader, more public audience than they would have in the past. This is particularly important where research involves controversial ethical decisions such as the use of covert observation, or deception of research subjects. These moves

[3] For discussion of these developments and their implications for social research within the UK context, see Dingwall (2006), Hammersley (2009), and Wiles et al. (2010).

can have particular implications for Internet researchers who may be faced with the added challenges of having to convey their research to those unfamiliar with the sort of empirical settings that they are interested in examining (Clark and Sharf 2007).

At the same time, Internet researchers are also faced with evidence of the harm that their research could result in. The literature on Internet research contains numerous cautionary tales which serve as reminders of the need for due consideration of ethical issues when carrying out research online. Alongside the negotiation and conceptualisation of rights and responsibilities in the ethical guidelines and personal narratives of Internet researchers lie numerous references to technologically mediated ethical misconduct and trespass. Thomas (1996, no page nos.), for example, describes the varied ethical violations of a 'cyber-project gone-awry', a now infamous study of pornographic material on Usenet (Rimm 1995). Thomas describes how this study gathered personal information, statistical data, and 'pornographic files' covertly, from non-public domains; how the reporting of the research suggested that those who blocked access to their files might be child molesters; and the suggestion in a resulting grant application that the research might assist in the prosecution of users in helping to 'identify and prosecute Rimm's research subjects' (Thomas 1996, no page nos.). This is clearly an extreme example of apparent ethical misconduct. Yet there are also suggestions of potential misconduct in research that is becoming increasingly common. Commentators have, for example, noted their disquiet regarding the growing number of research projects that appear to violate privacy and confidentiality by drawing material from emerging social networking environments such as *Facebook* (Zimmer 2009).

Scholarship on Internet research has also described the sometimes difficult relationship between Internet researchers and the online communities they study. Descriptions of these relationships include accounts of the feelings of betrayal expressed by communities and individuals having discovered the presence of researchers in their midst (see King 1996; Sharf 1999; Eysenbach and Till 2001); the attempts of Internet users to regulate and ban the activities of researchers (White 2002); and examples of the hostility of online communities towards 'drive-by researchers' (Cherny 1999). Such accounts provide stark evidence of the fact that the actions of researchers can destabilise (and in some cases lead to the destruction of) online communities. With their references to apparent ethical failings and irresponsibility – observation without notification or informed consent and the failure to then ensure anonymity, for example, and deception by researchers withholding their true identity/purpose[4] – these serve as cautionary tales. Like the famous and oft-cited cases of deception and mismanagement in earlier social science research projects (e.g. the 1950s study of 'Springdale' and Lloyd Humphrey's 1970 study *Tearoom Trade,* see Berry 2004), they serve to provoke conformity by establishing 'forbidden' (or, at the very least, frowned upon) acts.[5] As developments within the social sciences increasingly exert influence upon researchers' approaches to ethical

---

[4] Again, see Thomas (2004).

[5] See the *Wikipedia* entry on cautionary tales; www.wikipedia.org/wiki/Cautionary_tale.

decision-making, such tales draw attention to the challenges that Internet researchers face, raising the stakes for those entering the online field for the first time.

Faced with such warnings, new institutional pressures, researchers' responsibilities to their university ethics committees, their research subjects, and themselves, what might it mean to be an ethically 'good' Internet researcher?

The literature on qualitative Internet research provides some aspirations in respect of this aim. Much of this work – perhaps unsurprisingly as it is written by Internet researchers – emphasises the role of the researcher in developing existing understandings of ethical research practice rather than the institutional systems that oversee such work. In the context of the increasing bureaucratisation of ethics in academia, this emphasis can be seen to reattach expertise to the individual researcher who is often positioned as facing new challenges whilst endeavouring to establish the extent to which new problems relate to traditional concerns.

In this discourse we find an objectification of an ideal Internet researcher, a researcher who emerges in consistent ways in different writing and displays a number of key characteristics. Chief amongst these are the qualities of sensitivity and reflexivity, along with the ability to critically engage with the research process. These characteristics are suggested by Annette Markham's description of the 'ethical researcher':

> Online or off, an ethical researcher is one who is prepared, reflexive, flexible, adaptive and honest. Methods are not simply applied out of habit, but derived through constant, critical reflection on the goals of research and the research questions; sensitively adapted to the specificities of the context.
>
> (Markham 2006, 39)

It is not just Internet researchers who seek to pin down the attributes of 'ethical' researchers. In a recent book, for example, Bruce Macfarlane (2009) explores the 'virtues' of researchers. He identifies '*courage, respectfulness, resoluteness, sincerity, humility*, and *reflexivity*' as 'some (but not necessarily all) of the excellences of character needed to be a "good" researcher' (Macfarlane 2009, 5 – his emphasis).[6] Whether referring to online or offline research, such descriptions suggest an intimidating range of personal attributes to aspire to.[7]

Approaching Research Ethics – Two Emphases

As these descriptions suggest, the literature provides quite a clear sense of the personal qualities of the 'ethical researcher'. But how might researchers go about constructing such an identity? Recent work – both relating specifically to Internet research and

[6] I am not entering here into the debate as to whether good character necessarily leads to good ethical conduct – for discussion of this, see McNamee's description of character in virtue ethics, 2001.

[7] As I will explore in Chap. 5, written accounts of research demonstrate the challenges of trying to reach such aspirations.

more widely – has emphasised certain ways of thinking about the ethics of research that appear useful in this regard. In considering these, I want to trace two important conceptual moves that have informed my approach to ethics in this book.[8]

The first is an understanding of ethical decision-making as embedded in the local details of research rather than involving the application of general ethical principles. This emphasis suggests the inadequacy of universal ethical norms, focusing instead on contextually situated ethical practice where the actions of the researcher are informed by the specific nature of their research and research settings (rather than involving the application of a general principle such as 'informed consent should always be obtained', 'participants should always be anonymised', etc.). The second places an emphasis on the dynamic nature of research and, with it, suggests that we consider the contingent, fluctuating, and emergent nature of research ethics. Ethical decision-making is here configured as an activity that is engaged in throughout the research process and is therefore in motion rather than fixed: ethics as, and in, process. Whilst the first move provides a focus on the reference points the researcher draws from in establishing a particular ethical stance, the second suggests that research ethics can be regarded as involving an ongoing struggle to maintain and adapt this stance in the face of change.

Embedded Ethics

The emphasis in much recent writing on ethics within the broad body of work that can be gathered under the banner of 'Internet studies' has been on challenging 'monolithic' pronouncements of ethical conduct (Walther 2002) in favour of varying interpretations of contextualised ethical practice. This involves a conceptual shift away from the idea that researchers should comply with totalising ethical principles. Instead, we find a move towards the idea that, during research, researchers are involved in the development of ethical positions that are informed by the local details of their research, the nature of their observed settings, and – significantly for my interest in this book – the activities and perspectives of those they research. Such arguments suggest that our decisions should be informed by the cultures we study (see Cavanagh 1999), the audiences that have vested interests in the work (McKee and Porter 2008), and the technologies that we are engaging with (Roberts et al. 2003). They reflect the aim of being a researcher who is 'sensitively adapted to the specificities of the context' (Markham 2006, 39).

This work proposes a situated approach to ethical decision-making (Knobel 2002) that is embedded in the specific details of the research. The idea here is that the 'ethical' researcher does not stumble into the online field and apply general principles in respect of how he/she will collect data (e.g.) that may have been developed in the study of very different settings. Instead, researchers' decisions should be

[8] See also Whiteman (2010) for discussion of these moves.

based upon an understanding of their research settings and consideration of the specificities of their research interests (their research questions, theoretical underpinnings, methodological choices, etc.) that enables them to make decisions that are context specific. The production of such decisions is therefore presented as occurring at different levels of operationalisation, across different aspects of the research process, and in relation both to the object of research and to the activity and interests of the researcher.

Let us take one example of the ways that ethical decisions can be established in relation to different aspects of research design – a study that is particularly challenging for a number of reasons that become obvious quite quickly. In the book *Beyond Tolerance* (2001/2003), Philip Jenkins discusses his experience of carrying out covert observation of transactions within perhaps the most problematic of online environments: websites devoted to the exchange of child pornography. This in many senses is a limit case of the possibilities for carrying out ethical research online. Jenkins describes how different potential avenues of investigation into this criminal activity are closed to researchers and 'why, to date, no researcher has attempted to study this market' (19). A key obstacle to such work is the fact that accessing or viewing child pornography in any way is a criminal offence. Were the researcher to see such material, even momentarily, they would be liable to prosecution. At the same time, as Jenkins observes, other methods are also closed: 'it is inconceivable that an active child pornographer will allow himself to be interviewed or to permit an academic any kind of access to his traffic' (19). Yet the book reports the findings of Jenkins's 2 year–long study of this activity. How has Jenkins worked around the ethical challenges his research raises?

Jenkins presents the ethical decisions he made in relation to different issues and different points of reference. First, he describes how his work was based on observation of 'verbal, textual material collected from newsgroups and messageboards' (20). It is not illegal to observe such activity,[9] although Jenkins notes that his presence on the site had the potential to flag him up as a potential suspect participant to authorities (20). Secondly, in order to ensure that he was not party to any of the images that users might attach to their postings, Jenkins made use of the technical features of the Internet by 'deactivating the "autoload images" feature of my Netscape software' (20). Whilst this focus on written text meant that his understanding of the activity was limited to some extent, he argues that the nature of the content of the message boards he studied (which contained highly detailed descriptions of content and demonstrated a policing of the accuracy of such descriptions by users) enabled him to get a sense of the visual material that was shared on the sites 'without the necessity to view them directly' (21). Jenkins also explains a number of decisions he made regarding his handling and dissemination of data: his initial attempts to pass 'lists of URLs and related information' (22) onto the authorities (but how he stopped doing this after a while,

[9] '[...] though virtually any visual images involved in this trade are prohibited, words are subject to constitutional protections' (Jenkins 2001/2003, 19).

believing it to be futile), and how, when writing up the research, he decided not to provide the URLs or names of sites in order to prevent any person 'seeking such images' from gaining entry into the activity (rather than to protect the privacy of the sites).

Jenkins's ethical stance is here established in relation to different aspects of his research: the methods of his research project (observational but not participatory), the nature of the researched environments (dangerous and deviant, therefore 'unworthy' of privacy protection), the technological affordances of the Internet (which enable a certain filtering of content), his research questions (which did not require him to look at the visual content of the sites), and the legal issues that the study raised. Although there are a number of ethical issues that Jenkins does not discuss – not least the impact on his own well-being of reading such highly upsetting material over a prolonged period of time – he establishes a clear position in respect of his ethical decision-making that seeks to defend itself against potential challenges in relation to different resources. This example of localised ethical manoeuvring demonstrates the ways that potentially very significant ethical, legal, and methodological problems can be addressed via reference to the local features of research design, technology and environment.

Although the discussion of localised ethics has been prevalent in Internet research writing, the emphasis on the situated, contextual nature of research ethics is not new and extends beyond this field of research. As I will discuss in Chap. 5, it has been common in descriptions of qualitative fieldwork in offline environments and evident in different academic disciplines including sociology (Calvey 2008), geography (White and Bailey 2004), and education (Simons and Usher 2000). In their introduction to *Situated Ethics in Educational Research,* for instance, Simons and Usher (2000) describe an understanding of situated ethics in which our principles as researchers are 'mediated by the local and specific'. In their view:

> [...] the whole point about a situated ethics is precisely that it is *situated*, and this implies that it is immune to universalization. A situated ethics is local and specific to particular practices. It cannot be universalized, and therefore any attempt to formulate a theory of situated ethics, given that any theorization strives for universality, must be doomed to failure. This is not to say that in any particular practice universal statements or principles of a general nature are inappropriate and unhelpful. However, it is to say that any such statements or principles will be mediated by the local and specific – by, in other words, the situatedness which constitutes that practice.
>
> (Simons and Usher 2000, 2)

The 'situatedness' of the practice here suggests both the practice of the research – the specific questions and theoretical approaches that constitute and inform the researcher's activity – as well as the local details of the research settings and those participating within them.

The move towards embedded ethics therefore involves a shift in emphasis from the general to the local and from the universal to the contingent and specific. Such distinctions are at the heart of a number of critiques of refusals by university and research bodies such as IRBs in the USA to grant permission for Internet-based research projects. Central to the criticism of such decisions is the charge that these bodies fail to understand the particular nature of the settings within which researchers seek to operate, and instead draw on misplaced general preconceptions. Johns et al., for example, suggest that:

> Lack of understanding of the formal features of computer-mediated communication has left some IRB members confused when evaluating research proposals which seek to apply traditional research methods in the virtual realm.
>
> (Johns et al. 2004, 112)

These authors go on to argue that 'IRB regulations, and those who interpret them, are firmly grounded in the literate culture of paper and print' (119).

We can see similar positioning in Joseph Walther's (2002) engagement with the reporting by Frankel and Siang of a workshop on Internet research ethics held by the National Institute of Heath and the American Association for the Advancement of Science (Frankel and Siang 1999). Walther suggests that this report, which presents specific guidance to researchers and IRBs engaged in the conduct and review of Internet research projects, is problematic because it:

> [...] tends to characterize 'Internet research' in a more or less monolithic way, as though the issues it considers pertain to most kinds of research conducted online. Taking the report seriously may lead an IRB to require assurances from investigators that are impertinent, irrelevant, impossible, and unwieldy, depending on the nature and methodology of the specific study being proposed.
>
> (see Walther 2002, 207)

Walter describes how the recommendations presented appear to be underpinned by a narrow definition of Internet research as involving the deployment of qualitative methods at the exclusion of other methods such as surveys or experimental designs. He suggests that this restricted understanding of online research feeds into the voicing of particular concerns within the report, concerns that appear to influence the recommendations that the authors make regarding consent and the protection of subjects. This includes a central concern with protecting human subjects from the intrusion of privacy that might arise from the use of names or other identifying characteristics in the citing of verbatim data.

Walther also challenges the report for the way that it appears to discuss Internet research as if the challenges it presents are 'inherent' and 'unique' to the Internet (212). Regarding the report's concern with the verifiability of data (which are problematised by the possibilities for identity play online), he notes:

> The Report contends that because of the uncertainty of respondents' identity in Internet research, data may not be valid, and if not, research should not be conducted. It is well worth considering that historically there are other venues for research that offer very bid as much opportunity for deception: mail surveys, telephone interviews, questionnaires passed out in large classrooms, and other approaches. (212)

Going on to discuss the report's recommendations, he suggests that:

> While each specific observation has some merit in one specific context or another, the problem is that the admonitions are not confined by context. [...]
>
> (Walther 2002, 212)

Here, Walther consistently questions the way the report conceptualises both research and the challenges of the Internet in reference to specific, local cases that do not fit the general model implied by the guidance. We can understand the move from a preimposed ethical checklist and general principles to contextualised ethical decision-making in a similar way, as involving a tailored approach to the production of ethics based on 'concrete examples' (Allen 1996) rather than general rules or, in Walther's terms, approaches that are 'confined by context'. As I will discuss later in this book,[10] this does not involve a wholesale rejection of certain general aims – to do no harm, for example, (see McKee and Porter 2009) – but focuses attention on how these are interpreted in specific contexts.

What does this shift towards locally produced ethics do? Undoubtedly, it reduces the potency or 'descriptive power' (Dowling 2009) of our ethical conclusions, in that they are constituted in reference to specific cases rather than as rules that extend beyond particular reference points. Being context independent, general principles can unproblematically be applied elsewhere. In contrast, whilst they may draw from more general principles, the localised ethical stances that researchers develop are contingent on the specificities of the research context/questions/methods/theory, etc., and the outcome of a series of localising moves throughout the research process. It is therefore possible that we might amend our stance if we shifted our gaze onto another setting, for example. Whilst this limits the 'power' of our ethical statements, this delimiting also means that our decisions are more sensitive to the nature of the setting – or so the argument goes – and that the researcher is less likely (perhaps) to be destructive through a lack of consideration of the particular characteristics of the research and the research setting.

Ethical Instability

Whilst emphasising the local over the general, recent literature on social science research ethics (as well as Internet research ethics more specifically) has also focused attention on the dynamic nature of research and, with it, the researcher's need to respond to, and deal with, change and unexpected developments during the research process. This involves a focus on the 'contingent, dynamic, temporal, occasioned' nature of research ethics and the ongoing 'practical manoeuvres and tactics' involved in the 'management of situated ethics' (Calvey 2008, 912). Attention to the management of ethics in the face of uncertainty involves a move away from procedural approaches to research ethics that can suggest a clean progression through research stages with corresponding ethical issues (e.g. starting with issues of access and informed consent and moving towards closure with issues of dissemination). Instead, this emphasis forces an acknowledgement of the inherent messiness of research, and with it, the complexity of ethical decision-making.

[10] The relationship between general principles and local instantiations of ethics is explored in each of the chapters but discussed in most detail in Chap. 6.

The recognition of the dynamic and uncertain nature of research and the ethical manoeuvring within, reminds us that the researcher must be responsive to the unexpected and that the ethical stances we develop may change and may need to be stabilised. As I will explore later in this book,[11] the research accounts of those who have engaged in longitudinal fieldwork in natural settings have long discussed the challenges of working within shifting environments (as Mattingly (2005) notes, consideration of the emergent nature of research ethics and the dilemmas of fieldwork embedded in different cultures and contexts is well rehearsed within anthropology). Yet this point also extends more broadly and does not only apply to longitudinal studies, or indeed, to research involving qualitative methods. Within the event of a face-to-face interview, for instance, the researcher is engaged in the ongoing management of ethical issues within the interactions between interviewer and interviewee.[12] The collection of standardised data via the delivery of questionnaires in survey research might also present researchers with unanticipated developments that could provoke a reassessment of the ethics of the project (see the discussion of dealing with 'participant problems' in survey research in McKeown and Weed (2004)[13]). This can be the case whether the questionnaire is administered in person, or in a distanced manner online, via telephone, or by post.

Because they are grounded in the local details of research, ethical positions founded on contextual details rather than the application of universal principles are unstable. Rather than fixed, they are the product of moves and decisions made over time and in response to contingent events as well as being the result of more clearly defined design choices that researchers may make during the research process.[14] Established in relation to specific contexts which may undergo change, such moves/decisions will need to be reaffirmed, revised, and redefined in response to empirical events. The ethical stances researchers develop can therefore be seen to take shape as the research progresses. For that reason, they might be regarded as an outcome of the research process; like the theoretical perspectives researchers develop in the analysis of data, the researcher's ethics fully emerge only at the end of the research project. However this 'outcome' is always in production. Even when we

---

[11] See Chap. 5.

[12] As Oliver (2003) suggests, 'One has only to think of the complex interactions which take place during interview research, to imagine the apparently minor but still important ethical situations which arise. The respondent asks a question about the research process, and the researcher has to decide how to reply; the respondent asks to see a copy of the research data, or the respondent becomes slightly uncooperative – all these situations may have an element of ethical decision-making' (Oliver 2003, 45).

[13] As an example of the problems that researchers may face when administering surveys, McKeown and Weed describe how '[…] prior warnings in an informed consent of sensitive or private questions and reminders of the option to refuse to answer may not be enough. If we ask questions that can induce stress or anxiety, then we also have an obligation to assist those who are affected by those questions' (McKeown and Weed 2004, 67). The issue then is how these obligations are worked through by the researcher and how this informs their subsequent actions.

[14] See Whiteman (2010) for discussion of this tension between control and contingency in the design of research and maintenance of ethical stances.

have completed our research (or even years later), we may readdress our actions in our reflections on the decisions we made previously, and of course, our ethical stance will also be evaluated and interpreted by others. The researcher's ethical stance is therefore a product of stabilising moves in the face of change. It is developmental, a move towards coherence that can be unsettled by unexpected events, and is never fully achieved or completed.

Such ideas have been set in opposition to the more static models that underpin some approaches to the institutional regulation of research ethics. Mauthner et al., for example, suggest that there are:

> [...] inherent tensions in qualitative research that is characterized by fluidity and inductive uncertainty, and ethical guidelines that are static and increasingly formalised.
>
> (Mauther et al. 2002, 2)

According to these authors, researchers should pay closer attention to the ways that ethical 'theory and intention [are] lived in the research context' (Mauther et al. 2002, 2). In a similar way, Mattingly (2005) challenges two universalising assumptions that she suggests underpin institutional understandings (particularly in the context of clinical research) of how ethical behaviour might be monitored and governed by ethics review procedures: the idea that ethical rules are 'context-free' and the suggestion that research can involve the application of 'universal rules, norms and theories' to guarantee an ethical outcome (462). Through reference to the developmental nature of her 'ongoing relationship' (468) with one research participant during an ethnographic study of American hospitals, and related experience of 'how complex an ethic like "confidentiality" becomes in the context of real-life circumstances and research relationships' (457), Mattingly challenges these assumptions. She argues that her experience (like those of other researchers using ethnographic methods) 'illuminates the poverty of a research ethics that is supposed to be standardized, applied regardless of context' (458). This is not least because it denies the ongoing personal relationships that inform ethical manoeuvring in the field (462). Here, there is a recognition of both the embedded *and* contingent/developmental nature of research ethics.

The idea that the dynamic nature of research conflicts with the formal fixing of some ethical guidance also ties into Cannella and Lincoln's recent call for the need for 'ethical reflexivity' in research:

> By mandating ongoing attention to ethical concerns, ethical reflexivity reminds researchers that few research projects proceed as expected; many ethical issues are unforeseen in advance; participants have their own concerns regarding ethical behaviour which cannot be predicted by institutional review boards; ethic, as a general concern, reside in specific situations with the complex histories of individuals; and complexity theory is a better descriptor of human life than regularity and generalization.
>
> (Cannella and Lincoln 2007, 327)

As I will explore in Chap. 5, these moves remind us that, whilst it may be possible to identify key ethical issues pertaining to certain research projects from the outset, it is not possible to preempt and deal with all the issues the researcher may face at the beginning of the research process. Whilst the paperwork that researchers need to complete for ethical review tends to draw attention to ethical issues upfront, ethical quandaries can arise suddenly and unexpectedly during and post research (e.g. see Sikes (2008) on being caught up in a news panic). At the same time, the decisions we make also need to be made and reassessed in the face of less dramatic and more micro-level developments.

This is something that all researchers need to consider, whether or not they are engaged in online research. The question for the Internet researcher, then, is less about the specific challenges of Internet research practice as distinct from offline research, and more a consideration of what particular dimensions are added to the challenge of maintaining an ethical stance by the characteristics of online domains.

The Theoretical and Empirical Underpinnings of This Book

At the beginning of this chapter, I described the destabilisation of ethics in respect of the development of the Internet. My use of the word destabilisation here, and my concern with stabilising moves, is informed by a particular theoretical approach to the social: social activity method (Dowling 2009; formerly social activity theory, see Dowling 1998). This approach conceptualises social activity (whether it be an interaction between people, or an individual text or utterance) as involving the 'formation, maintenance and destabilising of alliances and oppositions' (Dowling 2009, 230). Focusing on the ongoing production of relations within social activity, Dowling's sociological language suggests particular methodological sensitivities: that the analyst focus on the emergent, relational patterning of the strategies involved in this formation/maintenance/destabilising and that they pay particular attention to the strategies by which authority is claimed or attributed within social activity (which Dowling refers to as 'authorising strategies') as these are key to the way that alliances/oppositions are established and unsettled (see Dowling 2009).

Dowling's work has informed the conceptualisation of the achievement of ethical stances that is presented in this book. Broadly, from this perspective, the production of ethics in research can be regarded as involving the production of a researcher identity in relation to different domains of social activity; an ongoing process of making and unmaking. The scholar of Internet research ethics might then focus on the strategies that are involved in the production of a coherent identity, in considering how a particular ethical stance is constructed and maintained during the research process (and beyond) and the alliances and oppositions that emerge within this construction/maintenance. Alliances might be established through the establishing of similar positions to those taken by other researchers or participants – or the recruitment of similar resources or rhetorical strategies, for example – whilst opposition would emerge in the marking out of difference from other stances/positions.[15]

[15] Dowling is also one of the co-authors of a research methods text (*Doing Research/Reading Research* (2010/1998), with Andrew Brown) that I recruit in Chap. 2. The approach to the production of research methods in this text can be seen to align with social activity method's focus on the ongoing and strategic patterning of social relations, in emphasising the relational and dialogic development of research methods over fixed or formulaic research procedures (see Chap. 2).

The issue of how authority is negotiated in social activity is not an explicit focus of this book, although the authorising moves involved in researchers' ethical action is clearly of relevance to the discussion presented in subsequent chapters. Dowling's focus on authorising strategies within social activity has, for example, informed my interest in the codification of ethical decision-making within the field of academic scholarship. This has shaped my approach to, and handling of, literature. In particular, it has influenced my interest in the ways that ethical stances are presented by researchers in their writing, the legitimising moves made in this work, and the ways that alternative stances/positions are rejected.

This book also arises from my own experience of researching online fan communities from 2004 to 2007[16] and my growing interest (some might call it obsession) during this time in both the challenges faced by those exploring other types of online environments and the formulation of ethics-related guidance and debate in the literature describing such research. This interest was provoked by the uncertainty and anxiety I felt about the ethical decisions that I needed to make during my study and by my struggles to get a confident sense of what the 'right' answers might be to the ethical questions I faced.

Because it is grounded in this personal experience of doing research ethics, on one level, this book can be understood as an exploration of the development of one researcher's situated ethical methodology – an exploration of the operationalisation of ethics in the process of research. It is rooted in the practical experience of carrying out research, the concerns that I grappled with during my study of online domains and my more recent interest in exploding some of the decisions I made and seeing what the pieces tell me. As I have suggested above, there is a connection between the personal aim of coming to terms with the decisions we make and the professional need to defend them. This is not always an easy connection to establish. Reflecting back on the work I did after I finished my research, I started to call into question some of the decisions I had made and the defensive position that I marked out in the writing up of my doctoral research. Reflecting on my decisions has led me to reconsider my actions and to think more broadly about what we might understand as constituting ethics in/of Internet research.

As my own research experience provides one key point of reference in the exploration of ethical issues presented in the chapters that follow, it is worth outlining the basic details of my study. My project examined activity within two online fan communities: City of Angel (COA) and Silent Hill Heaven (SHH). Although devoted to different media texts, these sites were similar in many ways – with COA focused on the television series *Angel* (a spin-off of *Buffy the Vampire Slayer*) and SHH devoted to the series of survival horror videogames *Silent Hill*. Each housed busy forums[17] as well as a range of information about their favourite media texts, and both were

---

[16] The study was funded by a 1+3 award from the Economic and Social Research Council (ESRC).

[17] At the point of its closure in December 2005, the forums on COA had 1,450 registered users, 495 threaded discussions (threads), and 19,183 posted messages (posts). At the point of writing up the research, the forums on SHH had 6,492 registered users, 7,830 threads, and 175,685 posts.

relatively well established.[18] On each site, the activities within the forums were managed and policed by a hierarchy of owners and staff.

My central interest during my study was in examining the ways that these two settings operated in respect of a number of key empirical questions. How did participants within these sites learn to become successful members and successful fans? How did members establish the legitimacy of their contributions to the sites and obtain status within these settings? What modes of authority were visible within the day-to-day interactions on the sites?[19] How were the objects of fan interest constituted and contested within these environments and what relationships did members establish with these objects?[20] I was also interested in exploring the relationship between the nature of these relationships/identities and the differences between the objects of fan interest (the presumed interactivity of videogames for example, in contrast to the idea of television viewing as a more 'passive' activity (see Whiteman 2007)). Like the attention to the dynamic nature of ethics described earlier, the approach that I took to analysing the activity on COA and SHH explored the de/stabilisation of social activity by paying close attention to the strategies that served to maintain and stabilise identities and relationships on these sites in the face of destabilising moves/events.

My study was based on observation and text analysis of posting activity on the publicly accessible bulletin boards of COA and SHH between 2004 and 2006. My visits to the sites involved a range of activities: reading posts; following discussions and developments within the forums and on other sites; archiving threads, initially by copying and pasting them into text files but then later by using software which enabled me to browse sections of the forums offline[21]; and keeping research journals regarding both methodological and substantive issues relating to COA and SHH. Although I visited the sites regularly (often daily), at no time during my study did I post a message onto the forums or speak to any of the members of these sites.[22] My involvement with the sites was therefore based solely on my engagement with the textually rendered interactions on the forums.[23]

A number of key decisions characterised my handling of ethics during my research project and raised key ethical issues and questions that I explore in the following chapters. The first was my decision to carry out unannounced observation of forum activity, to observe COA and SHH without their members' or owners' knowledge of my 'presence'. As I was reminded on a number of occasions when I spoke about my research in public (at conferences, and in teaching), the decision to carry out covert

[18] City of Angel had been online since December 1999 and Silent Hill Heaven since November 2002.

[19] See Whiteman (2008a).

[20] See Whiteman (2008b).

[21] See Whiteman (2007) for discussion of the development of my archiving strategy during the study.

[22] There were two exceptions to this statement, which I will discuss in Chap. 5.

[23] Regular visits to these sites generated a central sample of 7,338 posts from both sites; this constituted the primary focus of my analysis.

observation online can provoke strong criticisms, including suggestions that the unannounced observer is no more than a (evil) lurker or a spy. My decision to adopt this stance was based on consideration of a range of issues relating to how we define the status of our research settings in respect of the public/private distinction. This question – and the debate that surrounds it – is the focus of Chap. 3.

A second, related issue was the fact that I did not seek informed consent from the sites, their members, or their owners before using data from these settings in my analysis and subsequent writing. Informed consent is increasingly presented as a central tenant of 'good', ethical research, and so deviating from obtaining consent can be politically dangerous. However, as numerous Internet researchers have described, obtaining consent in online environments can be both difficult and disruptive, and there are no easy answers as to whether it is always right or appropriate to request it. In Internet research, this decision depends both on our understanding of the rights of the research participants and how we conceptualise these participants, whether we see online data, indeed, as constituting human subjects or whether we approach it as textual material. These considerations are explored in Chap. 4 where I examine the ways that researchers have defined the subjects of Internet research and the ethical implications of these definitions.

As a non-participant observer within COA and SHH, ethical issues also arose during the study regarding the points at which I should intervene in the settings. One example of this was after SHH was hacked and the archives deleted – an event that I discuss in Chap. 5. This raised broader considerations about my role and position in relation to the settings, and the responsibilities I had to them. These issues are explored in Chap. 5 where I examine the destabilisation of ethical stances through a consideration of the nature of participation in fieldwork. The chapter considers the ways that the position of Internet researchers (their relationship to, and involvement with, their research settings) may change over time. What events might trigger moves towards/away from greater involvement and identification with our research settings, for instance, and what are the implications of such change for the maintenance of the researcher's ethical stance?

A final key issue involved my decision to share my final research report (my Ph.D. thesis) with the members of SHH after the completion of the project. This event is discussed in the concluding chapter, Chap. 6, which also draws together the main themes of the book.

There is something of a contradiction in the structuring of these chapters and my earlier emphasis of the ongoing and dynamic nature of ethical concerns. The order of these chapters can be seen to focus on ethical issues that arise/are more prevalent at different 'stages' of the research process. The focus on how researchers might define their research sites and subjects in Chaps. 3 and 4 can be seen to relate to early decisions about informed consent, for example, whereas the discussion of the involvement/position of the researcher in the research settings in Chap. 5 and issues relating to dissemination in Chap. 6 focus on the later stages of research. However, as each chapter emphasises, whilst particular issues/decisions may be more pressing at different points of the research "journey", they continue to be of significance throughout the research process. In structuring the book in this way, I am not therefore suggesting that these represent distinct stages of research; instead, I am focusing on questions/concerns that may take on particular relevance at different times. Before exploring these issues, I present a general framework for thinking about ethics in research that underpins each of the chapters that follow. This framework is outlined in the next chapter.

Conclusion

In a review of the 2002 book *Ethics in Qualitative Research* (Mauthner et al. eds.), Jennifer Mason suggests that:

> [...] the case is convincingly made for a situational, contextual and relational understanding of research ethics but the difficult question that remains is how exactly that might be operationalized, and to put it baldly, can researchers be trusted to practice ethical research without more abstract or absolute principles?
>
> (Mason 2004, 1070)

To some extent, this quote suggests the aim of this book – to consider how situated, embedded ethics might be operationalised, to provide a framework for thinking about the diverse points of reference that researchers draw from in practicing 'ethical research', and to think about what we might make of general ethical principles in doing such work. I started this chapter by describing some of the challenges that researchers face when engaging in online research. This book does not provide answers to these ethical quandaries. Instead, I am arguing that answers to ethical questions must be produced relationally in specific contexts, texts, and practices. The book therefore seeks to provide the reader with resources to be used in their own production of ethical stances.

In this chapter, I have described the changing academic and political context in which social science and Internet researchers operate. I have argued that the emergence of the Internet and new media technologies has involved a destabilisation of established understandings of what it means to be ethical for both researchers and Internet users. I have also described two moves that have characterised much recent work on the ethics of research: the move from the search for general ethical principles to embedded, localised ethical decision-making and an emphasis on the dynamic and contingent nature of research ethics throughout the research process. Together, I suggest, these two moves can be seen to focus attention on the maintenance of localised ethical stances during research. These two themes – and the nature of this maintenance – run throughout the consideration of different ethical issues in the chapters that follow. They remind us that the ethical positions we establish at the outset of our research may be revealed as far more complicated and potentially more problematic than we might have anticipated in advance of our studies. Examined closely, particular instantiations of research are likely to reveal the complex and dynamic nature of research ethics.

This introduction has made reference to both the ethics of social science research and the ethics of Internet research. One issue is the extent to which the discussion that follows may be relevant to researchers who are carrying out research in offline domains. I would argue that it is, not just because I hope the framework presented might be of interest to researchers more broadly but also because of the way that consideration of Internet research ethics can help us to see offline research differently. The suggestion that one focuses on the ethics of Internet research suggests that such work might be demanding of special attention, that it has particular characteristics and challenges that set it apart from ‘regular’ offline social science research. Whilst this book explores these characteristics and their methodological and ethical implications, I hope to also demonstrate that one of the most interesting things about engaging with online research ethics is the way that it makes you look afresh at the doing of offline research.

Whilst this book is based on the particular case of the operationalisation of situated ethics in my own research, beyond this – as I have suggested in this introduction – it is also an exploration of the relationship between the configuration of ethics in different domains and a questioning of the interrelationship between the ethics of researcher and researched. For this reason, each of the chapters that follows draws from different points of reference including research literature, examples of empirical settings (online and offline), the research experiences of other researchers, and my own study. In examining the relationship between these, the book seeks to explore the continuities and discontinuities between research practice and online activity and between research activity in on- and offline environments.

References

Alderson, P., & Morrow, V. (2006). Multidisciplinary research ethics review: Is it feasible? *International Journal of Social Research Methodology, 9*(5), 405.

Allen, C. (1996). What's wrong with the ‘Golden Rule’? Conundrums of conducting ethical research in cyberspace. *The Information Society, 12*(2), 175–188. Available online: http://jthomasniu.org/Tis/go.christin.html

Baym, N., & Markham, A. (2009). Introduction: Making smart choices on shifting ground. In *Internet inquiry: Conversations about method.* Thousand Oaks: SAGE.

Berry, D. M. (2004). Internet research: Privacy, ethics and alienation: An open source approach. *Internet Research, 14*(4), 323–332.

Bryman, A. (2008). *Social research methods* (3rd ed.). Oxford/New York: Oxford University Press.

Calvey, D. (2008). The art and politics of covert research: Doing ‘Situated Ethics’ in the field. *Sociology, 42*(5), 905–918.

Cannella, G. S., & Lincoln, Y. S. (2007). Predatory vs. Dialogic ethics: Constructing an illusion or ethical practice as the core of research methods. *Qualitative Inquiry, 13*(3), 315–335.

Cavanagh, A. (1999). Behaviour in public? Ethics in online ethnography. *Cybersociology*, (6). Available online: http://www.socio.demon.co.uk/magazine/6/cavanagh.html

Cherny, L. (1999). *Conversation and community: Chat in a virtual world.* Stanford: CSLI Publications.

Clark, M. C., & Sharf, B. F. (2007). The dark side of truth(s). Ethical dilemmas in researching the personal. *Qualitative Inquiry, 13*(3), 319–416.

Consalvo, M. (2007). *Cheating: Gaining advantage in videogames*. Cambridge: MIT Press.

Dingwall, R. (2006). An exercise in fatuity: Research governance and the emasculation of HSR. *Journal of Health Services Research & Policy, 11*(4), 193–194.

Dowling, P. (1998). *The sociology of mathematics education: Mathematical myths/pedagogic texts*. London: Falmer Press.

Dowling, P. (2009). *Sociology as method: Departures from the forensics of culture, text and knowledge*. Rotterdam: Sense.

Dowling, P., & Brown, A. (2010). *Doing research/reading research: Re-interrogating education* (2nd ed.). London: Routledge.

Eysenbach, G., & Till, J. E. (2001). Ethical issues in qualitative research on internet communities. *British Medical Journal, 323*(10), 1103–1105.

Fields, D., & Kafai, Y. B. (2010). Contestations and effects of cheating in a tween virtual world: "Stealing from Grandma" or generating cultural knowledge? *Games and Culture, 5*(1), 64–87.

Frankel, M. S., & Siang, S. (1999). *Ethical and legal aspects of human subjects research on the internet: A report of a workshop June 10–11, 1999*. Washington, DC: American Association for the Advancement of Science. Available online: http://www.aaas.org/spp/sfrl/projects/intres/report.pdf.

Hammersley, M. (2009). Against the ethicists: On the evils of ethical regulation. *International Journal of Social Research Methodology, 12*(3), 211–225.

Humphreys, S., Fitzgerald, B., Banks, J., & Suzor, N. (2005). Fan-based production for computer games: User-led innovation, the 'Drift of Value' and intellectual property rights. *Media International Australia, Incorporating Culture & Policy, 114*, 16–29. Available online: http://search.informit.com.au/documentSummary;dn=010273434967423;res=IELHSS.

Jenkins, P. (2001/2003). *Beyond tolerance: Child pornography on the internet*. New York/London: New York University Press.

Johns, M. D., Hal, G. J., & Crowell, T. L. (2004). Surviving the IRB review: Institutional guidelines and research strategies. In M. D. Johns, S. Chen, & G. Jon Hall (Eds.), *Online social research: Methods, issues, & ethics* (pp. 105–124). New York: Peter Lang.

King, S. A. (1996). Researching internet communities: Proposed ethical guidelines for the reporting of results. *The Information Society, 12*(2), 119–128.

Knobel, M. (2002). *Rants, ratings and representation: Issues of ethics, validity and reliability in researching online social practices*. Draft paper presented at the annual meeting of The American Educational Research Association, New Orleans, 3 April, 2002. Available online: http://www.geocities.com/c.lankshear/ethics.html.

Law, J. (2004). *After method: Mess in social science research*. London: Routledge.

MacDougall, R. (2010). eBay ethics: Simulating civility today, for the 'Digital Democracies' of tomorrow. *Convergence: The International Journal of Research into New Media Technologies, 16*(2), 235–244.

Macfarlane, B. (2009). *Researching with integrity: The ethics of academic inquiry*. Oxon/New York: Routledge.

Markham, A. N. (2006). Ethic as method, method as ethic: A case for reflexivity in qualitative ICT research. *Journal of Information Ethics, 15*(2), 37–54.

Mason, J. (2004). Ethics in qualitative research (book review). *Sociology, 38*(5), 1070–1071.

Mattingly, C. (2005). Towards a vulnerable ethics of research practice. *Health: An interdisciplinary Journal of the Social Study of Health Illness and Medicine, 9*(4), 453–471.

Mauther, M., Birch, M., Jessop, J., & Miller, T. (Eds.). (2002). *Ethics in qualitative research*. London/Thousand Oaks: SAGE.

McKee, H. A., & Porter, J. E. (2008). The ethics of digital writing research: A rhetorical approach. *College Composition and Communication, 59*(4), 711–749. Available online: www.writing.ucsb.edu/wrconf08/Pdf_Articles/McKee_Article.pdf.

McKee, H. A., & Porter, J. E. (2009). *The ethics of Internet research: A rhetorical, case-based process*. New York: Peter Lang Publishing.

McKeown, R. E., & Weed, D. L. (2004). Ethical choices in survey research. *Social and Preventative Medicine, 49*(1), 67–68.

Murphy, E., & Dingwall, R. (2007). Informed consent, anticipatory regulation and ethnographic practice. *Social Science & Medicine, 23*, 2223–2234.

Oliver, P. (2003). *The student's guide to research ethics (open up study skills)*. Buckingham: Open University Press.

Rimm, M. (1995). Marketing pornography on the information highway: A survey of 917,410 images, descriptions, short stories, and animations downloaded 8.5 million times by consumers in over 2000 cities in and territories. *Georgetown Law Journal, 83*, 1849–1934.

Roberts, L., et al. (2003). Conducting ethical research online: Respect for individuals, identities and the ownership of worlds. In E. A. Buchanan (Ed.), *Readings in virtual research ethics: Issues and controversies* (pp. 62–78). Hershey/London: Idea Group Inc.

Sharf, B. F. (1999). Beyond netiquette: The ethics of doing naturalistic discourse research on the internet. In S. Jones (Ed.), *Doing internet research: Critical issues and methods for examining the net* (pp. 243–256). Thousand Oaks: SAGE.

Sieber, J. E. (2004). Using our best judgment in conducting human research. *Ethics & Behavior, 14*(4), 297–304.

Sikes, P. (2008). At the eye of the storm: An academic('s) experience of moral panic. *Qualitative Inquiry, 14*(2), 235–253.

Simons, H., & Usher, R. (Eds.). (2000). *Situated ethics in educational research*. London/New York: RoutledgeFalmer.

Thomas, J. (1996). When cyber-research goes wrong: The ethics of the Rimm 'Cyberporn' study. *The Information Society, 12*(2), 189–197. Available online: http://venus.soci.niu.edu/~jthomas/ethics/tis/go.jt2.

Thomas, J. (2004). Reexamining the ethics of internet research: Facing the challenge of overzealous oversight. In M. D. Johns, S. L. Chen, & G. J. Hall (Eds.), *Online social research: Methods, issues, & ethics* (pp. 187–202). New York: Peter Lang.

Walther, J. B. (2002). Research ethics in internet-enabled research: Human subjects issues and methodological myopia. *Ethics and Information Technology, 4*(2), 205–216.

White, M. (2002). Representations or people? *Ethics and Information Technology, 4*(2), 249–266.

White, C., & Bailey, C. (2004). Feminist knowledge and ethical concerns: Towards a geography of situated ethics. *Espace, Populations, Societes, 1*, 131–141.

Whiteman, N. (2007). *The establishment, maintenance and destabilisation of fandom: A study of two online communities and an exploration of issues pertaining to internet research*. Unpublished PhD thesis, Institute of Education, University of London. Available online: http://homepage.mac.com/paulcdowling/ioe/studentswork/whiteman(2007).pdf.

Whiteman, N. (2008a). Learning at the cutting edge? Help-seeking and status in online videogame fan sites. *Information Technology, Education and Society, 9*(1), 7–26.

Whiteman, N. (2008b). Homesick for Silent Hill: Modalities of nostalgia in fan responses to Silent Hill 4: The room. In L. Taylor & Z. Whalen (Eds.), *Playing the past: History and nostalgia in videogames* (pp. 32–49). Nashville: Vanderbilt University Press.

Whiteman, N. (2010). Control and contingency: Maintaining ethical stances in research. *International Journal of Internet Research Ethics, 3*(1), 6–22.

Wiles, R., Coffey, A., Robison, J., & Prosser, J. (2010). *Ethical regulation and visual methods: Making visual research impossible or developing good practice?* (ESRC National Centre for Research Methods, NCRM Working Paper Series), eprints.ncrm.ac.uk/812/2/ethical_regulation_and_visual_methods.pdf.

Zimmer, M. (2009). "But the data is already public!": On the ethics of research in facebook. *In Open conference systems, internet research 10.0*. Available online: http://ocs.sfu.ca/aoir/index.php/ir/10/paper/view/168. Last accessed 12 November 2009.

Chapter 2
The Achievement of Research Ethics

Abstract This chapter presents a conceptual framework for understanding the 'doing' of ethics in research. The chapter marks out four domains of ethics (the ethics of the academy, institution, researcher, and researched) that provide resources for, and can be seen to shape, the localised production of ethics in any research project. The chapter suggests the differing responsibilities that these domains may place upon the researcher and starts to question the relationship between them. To what extent, for example, should the researcher's actions be informed by those of the researched? This framework for thinking about the achievement of ethics in research is introduced through a critical engagement with two texts: an early paper on Internet research ethics by Susan Herring and an educational research methods text by Paul Dowling and Andrew Brown.

Introduction

The previous chapter introduced an understanding of research ethics as situated, localised, and unstable, the outcome of the researchers' moves to establish control and order in the face of contingency. Here, I outline an attempt to impose some conceptual order on this activity by introducing a way of thinking about the resources that can inform the construction of ethical stances in research. My focus is the *achievement* of ethics in research, the ways that a particular stance is established in respect of key ethical decisions, resources, and issues relating to the researcher's project. If, as described in Chap. 1, we understand research ethics to be embedded within the local details of research, this stance cannot simply be adopted but must be established and developed as the research progresses. This chapter develops a framework for understanding this ongoing achievement.

The chapter works towards the presentation of this framework via an analysis of a relatively early paper on the ethics of research into computer-mediated

N. Whiteman, *Undoing Ethics: Rethinking Practice in Online Research*,
DOI 10.1007/978-1-4614-1827-6_2,

communication by the linguist Susan Herring (1996). Writing at a time when ethical guidance for online research was just starting to be published, Herring's paper questions the need for specialised ethical frameworks and criticises recently published guidelines for excluding certain types of research and ignoring the diversity of online environments. Herring examines the ethics of doing research in text-based environments (such as the Listserv discussion groups that constituted the focus of her own research) and, in doing so, demonstrates a critical dismantling of totalising ethical principles. The analysis presented in this chapter focuses on the construction of Herring's argument. More specifically, I am interested in interrogating the moves that Herring makes between diverse points of reference in the configuration of her own ethical stance.

My analysis of these moves, and subsequent presentation of my own framework for conceptualising the production of ethical stances in research, is informed by a second text – a book on the practice of educational research by Paul Dowling and Andrew Brown (Dowling and Brown 2010; Brown and Dowling 1998). Dowling and Brown present a dialogic rather than process-based understanding of research, which regards research activity as being constituted by moves between different domains of academic interest. Following an initial description of Herring's paper, the chapter will describe how this methods text – with its attention to the distinct (but related) points of reference that inform the ongoing production and development of research – has informed the relational approach to research ethics that I develop in this book.

The chapter therefore moves between these two key texts. I begin with a brief summary of Herring's argument in the 1996 paper. This is followed by a consideration of Dowling and Brown's work and how it might inform the development of a framework for understanding the achievement of ethics in research. I then return to Herring's paper, drawing from Dowling and Brown to explore in more detail the ethical positioning within this work. I examine Herring's establishment of a stance in respect of key ethical issues (including the naming of research participants and need for informed consent in online research) and her dismantling of the generalised positions marked out by other researchers. In my own dismantling of Herring's paper, I extend Dowling and Brown's model of research to map four distinct, but interrelated, domains in which ethics are negotiated and articulated. I suggest that the ethical stances researchers develop can be understood as relationally established in reference to the ethical discourses of these domains. The chapter closes by identifying some of the tensions raised by this way of thinking about research ethics, tensions that will be explored in more detail in the chapters that follow in respect of specific ethical and methodological questions.

What's in a Name?

Let's start with a question.

Should the Internet researcher include identifying characteristics such as the names of websites, online groups, and users when using messages sourced from online environments?

In the paper 'Linguistic and Critical Analysis of Computer-Mediated Communication: Some Ethical and Scholarly Considerations' (1996), Susan Herring considers a number of different answers to this question. She begins by stating, and questioning, the stance she has taken in her own studies of the gendering of computer-mediated communication in academic discussion groups, one that avoids the use of real names in favour of pseudonyms, asking '[..] is this defensible on ethical grounds?'

Herring then goes on to examine two sources of guidance on this issue, two proposals that recommend opposing courses of action when handling online data. The first, promoted by those who consider online data to be 'published works and hence protected by copyright law' (Herring 1996, 154), argues that full credit should be attributed to sources and that researchers should consider the provision of identifying information such as the names of users and sites. The second, proposed by Storm King in his 1996 article 'Researching Internet Communities: Proposed Ethical Guidelines for the Reporting of Results', regards such messages as potentially private,[1] arguing that messages should therefore be 'carefully expunged of all group- and author-specific information' (Herring, 154) (including, where possible, being paraphrased). As Herring notes; 'the contradiction between these two views is obvious – one says to reveal one's sources, the other to hide them, regardless, in both cases, of the particular circumstances of the communication' (154).

Herring has a bone to pick with each of these conflicting stances. She criticises both for constituting an 'absolutionist position' based on a number of totalising assumptions that she sets out to undermine. The first assumption relates to the model of computer-mediated communication (CMC) that each position is founded upon. She argues that each source 'appears to assume one particular type of CMC' and then generalises 'recommendations based on that type to all of cyberspace' (154). She describes how the first position is based upon an idea of computer-mediated communication as involving the 'open debate of intellectual issues,' and the second emphases the more personal dimension of computer-mediated communication, being based on the idea of such communication as involving 'self-revelation of sensitive information in self-help groups' (154). The problem with these understandings of CMC, she suggests, is that '[…] cyberspace is a vast and varied domain, and rules that seek to generalize indiscriminately across all varieties of CMC do not "fit" the nature of the phenomenon' (154).

Herring identifies a number of other general assumptions that underpin these two positions, including the 'model of scholarship' each presents. She argues that these are based on contrasting ideas about the aims and activities of Internet researchers, and conflicting conceptualisations of the nature of the settings that constitute Internet researchers' sites of enquiry. In regards to the first, the copyright-focused position, she argues that:

> The idea that the source of all electronic messages should be credited assumes that (1) the messages are cited by the researcher for their content, rather than to illustrate some other feature of electronic messages that is largely out of the (conscious) control of the author

[1] I will return to this idea in Chap. 3.

(e.g., the configuration of mailer headings or the linguistic means of expression), and (2) the researcher is using the message in a way that its author would approve of and wish to be associated with. (155)

The approach to CMC as authored work whose origins should be attributed, Herring claims here, rests on an idealisation of the Internet researcher as an individual whose focus is on the content of online interactions and who is able to engage in an unproblematic recontextualisation and interpretation of online material. Herring suggests that King's position is based on a very different set of assumptions:

[…] the view that no identifying characteristics of participants should be revealed assumes (1) researchers are interested in general patterns of participant behaviour rather than specific patterns of, for example, language use (and thus that paraphrases are adequate for the purposes of the investigation), and (2) researchers would otherwise 'exploit' the self-revelations of participants for personal gain, although it is ethically wrong for them to do so. (155)

Here, rather than examining the micro-level nature of online interactions, the idealised Internet researcher is configured as being interested in the broad nature of online behaviour. This has implications for the sort of data they seek, data which is easier to anonymise because it can be reworded and summarised whilst still serving the researcher's purposes (in contrast to the challenges faced by those working with verbatim extracts of interactions which carry identifying marks). This perspective also characterises the online researcher as a potentially dangerous force, posing the threat of exploitation to participants within online environments. These participants, it is suggested, need to be protected, and one way of doing this is by guaranteeing their anonymity.

Despite the different characterisations of research they present, Herring argues that each position shares a common feature:

[..] neither proposal allows for the possibility of legitimate critical research; rather, both assume that there is (or should be) a consensus between investigator and investigated. More problematic yet, both assume a consensus model of interaction among participants, whose needs and interests are represented as essentially homogenous, albeit different in the two proposals.

(Herring 1996, 155)

In questioning these proposals, Herring suggests that we should examine the assumptions underpinning ethical rules and be critical of positions that involve homogenising conceptualisations of the nature of the Internet and/or the practices of Internet researchers. In Herring's assault on these assumptions, we find an unpicking of general principles and a criticising of such rules as unable to deal with the multiple sites/contexts of online research. This involves a focus on the local over the general, the substantive over the abstract.

As the paper continues, Herring reveals more about the construction of her own ethical stance. She outlines a number of key ethical decisions made in her work, including her decision to anonymise individual users (158) but to name the groups (159), her decision not to seek informed consent from the sites due to their public nature (163), and her efforts to disseminate the work as widely as possible in order to maximise its potential benefit (163). The paper demonstrates varied localising moves as Herring defines the position she takes through reference to the nature of her research and the settings she explores.

I will return to Herring's paper shortly to consider in more detail the ways that she dismantles and establishes ethical positions and how the ethical manoeuvring in this writing makes reference to a range of discursive contexts that might be seen to be recruited in the construction of a particular ethical stance. Before exploring these, however, it is worth thinking more broadly about how we might frame an understanding of the achievement of ethical stances in research.

Specialising and Localising Internet Research Ethics

I want to suggest that the development of an existing model of research can enable us to think about the diverse points of reference that might inform the ongoing production of an ethical stance. The framework that I am recruiting here was first presented in Brown and Dowling's *Doing Research/Reading Research* (1998) (subsequently developed in Dowling and Brown 2010). This conceptualisation of research draws attention to the different activities that researchers engage in during the research process (and the researcher's focus of attention in respect of these) and provides a key conceptual starting point for my approach to ethics in this book.

Dowling and Brown's model of research understands the practice of research to be based upon a 'fundamental dialogue' between two distinct but interrelated fields of interest; the theoretical and empirical (2010, 2). The theoretical field is presented as the 'broad area of academic and/or professional knowledge, research and debates which contains [the researcher's] general area of interest' (18). These are the antecedent ideas, concepts, and studies that inform research projects, understood by Dowling (2009, 239) as 'the field of principled discourse'. In contrast, the empirical field is the 'the general area of practice or activity or experience about which [the researcher intends] to make claims' (2010, 18). Here, we have the specific objects and settings of research that the researcher is concerned with or, as Dowling puts it, the 'field of [...] exemplary practices' (Dowling 2009, 239). This sets out a key distinction between the discursive productivity of the academy and the empirical world that the researcher turns their gaze onto.

Dowling and Brown present the process of research as involving the generation of an analytical 'language of description' from a series of engagements with these two domains; a conceptualisation of research activity that they term *constructive description*. The researcher is positioned in this model as manoeuvring between these two domains throughout the research process. This manoeuvring is presented as involving two methodological urges – *specialising* within the theoretical field (narrowing in on the core ideas, theoretical concepts, and arguments that will inform the work) and *localising* within the empirical field (moving from a general interest in a type of activity in a certain sort of setting towards the specificity of particular locations, individuals, and material, and ultimately towards the production of specific findings).

This describes distinct but related activities. Put in very simple terms, as researchers, we read around our specialist subject, examining studies that ask similar questions or look at similar settings. We also engage with concepts and ideas that might be useful in the development of particular questions or to our analysis. At the same time, we observe and gain experience of the sorts of sites we want to understand and explore, focusing on specific settings and individuals (as it is impossible to look everywhere). Just as reading may inform the sites that we choose to look at, so too things happen in our research settings that can lead us to engage with particular texts and particular ideas. Here then, we have a dialogic relationship between ideas and experience, between theoretical and empirical domains. To Dowling and Brown, this movement into and between theoretical/empirical domains and specialising/localising activity constitutes the trajectory of the research process.

This approach draws attention to the ways that researchers engage with, and move between, antecedent work and empirical material throughout the research process. Conceptualising research activity in this way is, I think, useful for a number of reasons. The emphasis on dialogue is valuable as it suggests the dynamism of the different efforts that the researcher is engaged with during research, whilst also implying the productivity of moving between settings and contexts.[2] As Dowling and Brown note, their conceptualisation of research begins ‘with an insistence that dialogue is more productive than monologue in generating new ideas’ (2010, 2). In emphasising moves between domains, this framework also moves beyond the linear model of research that is presented in some more procedural representations of the research process, where the literature review is a stage that is then followed by a distinct focus on data collection and so on. In doing so, it also suggests the dynamic and productive interrelationship between the theoretical ideas and empirical settings that researchers engage with.

Dowling and Brown (2010) also consider the specific localising and specialising moves that researchers make when assessing the ethics of individual research projects. This is presented as a product of the same movement between empirical and theoretical fields, as described above, and an outcome of the same specialising and localising moves as research activity.

Here, Dowling and Brown identify a number of ethical questions that might be asked of the theoretical and empirical fields of research. In respect of the ‘theoretical ethical field’ they suggest that the researcher is concerned with identifying the codes of practice and literature on ethics that are of particular relevance to the study (36). Their interest in the empirical settings – here presented as part of the ‘empirical ethical field’ – focuses primarily on ascertaining the ethical implications of the substantive details of the study: the what, who, and how questions that researchers ask of their settings in respect of the design of research. How will informed consent be obtained? Who will be contacted? How will access be negotiated? (see Dowling and Brown 2010, 37).

This extension of their earlier framework (1998) promotes the idea that, in reviewing the ethics of a research project, we engage in similar activities to those involved in the conduct of research. In each case, we draw from what we read (the experiences of other researchers, the textbooks on ethics and research, the ethics

[2] This emphasis on the productivity of dialogue is resonant with that raised by constant comparative methods within grounded theory approaches (see Glaser and Strauss 1967).

guidelines of research associations) and our understanding of the empirical objects (texts, sites, activities, etc.) we are interested in.[3] This approach to research ethics maintains Dowling and Brown's emphasis on the dynamic nature of the moves between theoretical and empirical domains, which includes the idea that engagement with one field affects the researcher's approach to the other.

The move between empirical and theoretical fields articulated in Dowling and Brown's work (and with it an understanding of research ethics as dynamic and the product of movement between different texts and contexts) is key to the approach to ethics that I present in this book. The emphasis on dialogue, responsiveness and development in this work has been especially influential in shaping my consideration of the ways that ethical stances are established and maintained in relation to change and contingency. However, I want to suggest that the model that Dowling and Brown present has a number of limitations that might be considered in the development of a framework for thinking about research ethics.

Firstly, the questions that Dowling and Brown put to the empirical field in respect of research ethics appear to focus primarily on the information that is required in order to define the internal mechanisms of the researcher's project (who do I need to speak to, how am I going to get consent from these people, etc.). This is somewhat limiting as it implies that the empirical contexts of research might inform the production of research ethics in a relatively narrow way. As the work on localisation in ethics described in Chap. 1 suggests, we can go further than this and consider the different questions that might be asked of the empirical field and how they might inform our work. This would involve a shift of attention from procedural ethical questions towards an interest in the ways that ethics are constituted in our empirical settings, and a consideration of the extent to which these (their) ethics might influence our own (and if they should at all).

This introduces a second, more significant, limitation of the model, by drawing attention to the position of the researcher and their own relationship to the empirical and theoretical fields. The research trajectory – the moves between theoretical and empirical fields – is presented by Dowling and Brown as being navigated by the researcher. It is presented as a strangely clean and mechanical journey, however, involving moves between the empirical and theoretical as if they – the ideas and settings – are sometimes speaking to each other. The researchers' influence on these moves is less clearly defined. Although they reference the varied professional responsibilities and

---

[3] Here then, we have an understanding of research ethics as involving similar processes to that of research. Brown and Dowling's position is thus in opposition to that of McKee and Porter who claim that:

> Ethical judgement requires a different kind of intellectual process than the kinds of intellectual process than the kinds of analytical procedures that are typically used in scientific, biomedical, or quantitative social science research. To put this another way, the methods that many science researchers use to conduct their studies are not well suited to addressing the ethical questions *related to* and *raised by* those studies – and we shouldn't expect them to be. As we have argued, ethical reasoning requires a different mode of analysis, one involving phronesis, or practical judgement. (McKee and Porter 2008, 16 – their emphasis)

obligations that researchers must consider, there is little sense of what the researcher brings to the process of research and how this might influence the nature of their moves between theoretical and empirical contexts. How does the researcher's own position inform the emerging sound of this dialogue? It is the researcher, after all, who is doing the localising/specialising and in doing so producing the objectified understanding of the 'empirical' and 'theoretical' that underpins their model. The issue here then is what the researcher brings to the table and how this informs the moves between, and recruitment of, the empirical and theoretical fields.

The following section marks out four distinct but interrelated domains in which ethical stances are articulated, embodied and enacted throughout the research process. These domains are based on an extension of Dowling and Brown's model. They are grounded upon a similar dynamic relationship between the theoretical and empirical, but involve an attempt to incorporate more explicitly a consideration of the position of the researcher, as well as an attempt to look to the empirical settings in a slightly different way. The framework I introduce also moves beyond Dowling and Brown's approach by drawing in a consideration of the ways that the researcher's institutional context can exert pressures on their research activity.

In marking out these domains, I am going to return to Susan Herring's paper, focusing now on how she presents her own ethical stance in the work. My consideration of this is intended to illustrate the moves between the theoretical/empirical fields that are central to Dowling and Brown's framework, whilst also suggesting how this might be extended.

Four Domains of Research Ethics

The consideration of Internet research ethics in Herring's paper involves two key actions. The first, as I noted earlier in this chapter, involves a critical dissection of ethical principles relating to specific questions and quandaries – a challenging of published guidance for what it excludes and how it conceives computer-mediated communication and research. Here, Herring focuses primarily on the acceptability of naming online settings/usernames, but also considers other issues such as the need for informed consent in Internet research. The second action involves Herring's construction of her own stance in respect of distinct ethical challenges – including the naming of participants and settings – and her decision to anonymise individual users but name public discussion groups. Below, I examine how this ethical de/construction can be seen to be established through reference to, and moves between, different domains in which ethics are embodied and articulated.

The Ethics of the Academy

As I have described, Herring's paper examines the legitimacy of published guidance relating to 'ethical' practice in Internet research. At the beginning of the paper, Herring announces that her work is informed by a:

> [...] theoretical background drawn from various disciplinary practices in the social sciences, especially the field of linguistics, and illustrations drawn from my own research into gendered language use in Listserv discussion groups on the Internet. (155)

Herring's primary focus at the start of her paper is on two texts (King 1996; Cavazos and Morin 1994) and the conflicting recommendations they present. This focus widens as the paper progresses, as Herring draws other guidance under her critical gaze (including Waskul and Douglass (1996) and Allen (no date) on MUDs). Alongside these works, throughout the paper Herring also recruits a range of literature relating to both online and offline research, distancing herself from certain perspectives and aligning herself with others.

Both the sources that Herring engages with, and Herring's paper itself, can be understood to be situated within what Dowling and Brown term 'the theoretical field'. They form part of the 'broad area of academic and/or professional knowledge, research and debate [...]' (Dowling and Brown 2010) that has taken as its focus the subject of ethics in research. This diverse area of knowledge, research and debate constitutes a domain of specialist discourse in which the ethics of academics are negotiated. It is here, for example, that we can trace the rhetorical moves towards the emphasising of localisation in ethical decision-making and consideration of ethics in/as process introduced in the previous chapter.

This domain serves as an important source of guidance for researchers as they move to establish positions in respect of key ethical issues. It is made up of a large and varied body of texts and publications that focus on the exploration and debating of ethical issues. This includes the public codification of ethics within a range of academic productivity: the negotiation and codification of ethical principles in scholarship and reports; institutional documents pertaining to the review and regulation of research; the codification of 'professional ethics' (Kimmel 1988) in the codes of different professional research associations; discussion of ethical debates/problems relating to particular methodological techniques;[4] and the growing body of literature on Internet research ethics.[5] The varied texts and documents that constitute the ethics of the academy demonstrate the diverse range of materials that researchers can engage with when working through their own handling of ethical issues.

Herring's use of material from this domain demonstrates that what we read not only provides a key source of guidance and inspiration but can also help the

[4] This has included writing on the researcher/researched relationship (e.g. Smyth and Williamson 2004); on issues relating to the reporting of sensitive and illegal activity (Stern 2003; Rowe 2007; Wiles et al 2008); the use of verbatim quotations (e.g. Corden and Sainsbury 2005, 2006); power dynamics and rapport within interviews (e.g. Wong 1998); and the use of covert participant observation (e.g. Bulmer 1982).

[5] Including books specifically focusing on Internet research ethics (Buchanan (ed.), 2003), collections on Internet methods which contain papers on ethical issues (for example Hine (ed.), 2005; Johns et al (eds.), 2004; Mann and Stewart 2000; Jones (ed.), 1999) and journals relating to ethics and internet (such as the *International Journal of Internet Research Ethics* (http://ijire.net/)). This work also includes papers on the methods of specific types of research design, such as the ethical challenges of naturalistic Phishing experiments (Finn and Jakobsson 2007).

researcher to relationally establish the legitimacy of their actions. In the first part of this chapter, I focused on Herring's rejection of certain positions; her critiquing of existing ethical guidance. As I will suggest, this criticism tends to be based on moves towards the empirical rather than theoretical. In presenting an alternative way of thinking about research and her own approach to handling data, however, Herring repeatedly draws from research and ideas from the academy. She makes reference to linguistics literature in her consideration of the status of CMC data as equivalent to text or spoken discourse, to critical research in her consideration of what might constitute an ethical research relationship (158), and to literature on spoken language research in discussion of conventions that researchers in this area have developed regarding the use of covert tape recording (suggesting that these conventions might inform the Internet researcher's approach (156)). In these moves, theoretical resources are recruited in the presentation of Herring's own ethical stance.

To take one instance from the paper, Herring states that her decision to anonymise usernames in her research was intended to protect participants from any damage to their reputations resulting from her potentially critical engagement with their words (158). However, she also relates this decision back to the conventions of linguistics research. She suggests that her decision was supported by reporting conventions within this discipline (particularly those developed in the reporting of spoken interactions that may be regarded by speakers as private, or at the least not for public consumption). Herring's moves between asserting the legitimacy of specific research actions and her references to disciplinary conventions are evident in the following two extracts:

> What renders such practices more or less acceptable in spoken language research is that there is a convention of representation (e.g., in writing up the research for publication in a journal), according to which the actual identities of the speakers are disguised. In linguistics research papers, speakers are almost never identified by name as being the source of data presented [..] Thus any given speaker could plausibly deny that she was the source of any examples used, and no one could prove otherwise. (157)

> My practice of not mentioning names also fits with a broader ideological preoccupation in linguistics research, namely, that what is important are patterns across groups of speakers, rather than individual linguistic variation. (159)

Here, both the conventions of disguising identities in spoken language research (extract 1) and the linguist's interest in the patterning of language rather than the specific speech of individuals (extract 2) are used to reinforce the legitimacy of Herring's decision not to name her research participants.[6] Recruiting the discipline of linguistics in two different ways, Herring draws from the theoretical field to help defend and market a specific position in respect of a particular ethical issue. In doing so, she positions her work firmly within a disciplinary tradition that is marked by

[6] Herring actually introduces an additional third point of reference – the fact that, because linguistic research focuses on form rather than content (content that 'is often banal, fragmented, or both'), speakers are afforded 'a certain protection as well' (157).

methodological and ethical conventions – established ways of approaching the empirical world/word.

The academy is not, however, the only domain in which ethics are negotiated that might inform the researcher's development of an ethical stance. Indeed, it is not the only context that Herring turns to in the articulation of her ethical position.

The Ethics of the Researched

Alongside her recruitment of what I term the ethics of the academy, Herring also makes a number of references to the nature of her research settings in presenting and defending the ethical decisions she has made in her work. This involves a shift in attention towards the empirical field; towards the activities and environments that constitute the focus of research. Our gaze here moves away from the codification of ethics within the discourse of academics, regulators, etc. to a consideration of the ethics of the researched, the way that ethics are institutionalised and embodied within the empirical phenomena that researchers study. Like the theoretical resources described in the previous section, our understanding of these settings can inform the ethical positions we establish and the presentation of our decisions to public audiences.

As Dowling and Brown suggest, when working through issues of access and consent, researchers need to make reference to the settings in which they hope to carry out research. We need to identify key gatekeepers and contextually appropriate ways of contacting and recruiting participants, for example. The work on situated ethics described in Chap. 1 has suggested that we can and should go beyond this to take into account the expectations and behaviours of those we research, and consider how these might inform our own research activity. The only way we can do this is by developing an understanding of the ethics of the research settings, some knowledge of what is and is not acceptable within these sites, and a sense of participants' expectations about what constitutes good (and bad) behaviour and the legitimacy of specific actions. This involves an analysis and objectification of the ways that ethics are negotiated within our research settings, as these expectations/understandings are not transparent or self-evident, and may be conflicting.

This sort of positioning in relation to the empirical is evident in Herring's paper. In a number of places, Herring makes reference to the nature of the computer-mediated communication that she studies. One of the reasons that she gives for naming public-access groups, for example, is the nature of the activity housed within them. She describes how the discourse within these environments has:

> [...] a flavour that is strongly public, even exhibitionistic at times – it is apparent that many individuals post with an audience in mind, aiming to persuade and impress others with their eloquence and reason. While we might not wish to claim that all messages posted to such groups are 'publications', that is, intended to endure through time, it seems entirely appropriate to compare them to public broadcasts, which are designed to reach a wide audience at a particular point in time. (This comparison holds even more strongly for Usenet, where the precise extent and nature of the audience for any given message is unknowable). (159)

Later, Herring again suggests the public status of these settings, linking this to her decision not to seek informed consent:

> I did not ask the group's permission to observe or analyze their interaction, as it seemed clearly to be public discourse; anyone could join the group and read the message posted to it by sending a 'subscribe' message to the Listserv, and the topics of discussion were generally impersonal and academic. (163)

These two extracts demonstrate how the characteristics of the empirical contexts of research can be used to explain and justify the development of a particular ethical stance in respect of the design of research. In each extract, Herring draws connections between the characteristics of the sites/material that she examines and the acceptability of specific research decisions. In respect of the naming of groups, her focus is on the nature of interactions. She aligns her approach with the public 'flavour' of interactions, the nature of the audience ('wide' and – in case of Usenet newsgroups – 'unknowable'), the posts (persuasive and 'exhibitionistic'), and the expectations of the posters (what individuals have 'in mind' and 'aim' for). In relation to the issue of informed consent, she builds on different evidence in categorising the sites as public settings, focusing on the ease of entry into these environments rather than their content. The definition of her research settings as public[7] – established in reference to different features of the researched activity – is then used to establish the legitimacy of two different decisions, to name the sites, and to not seek consent from participants.

Herring also makes reference to the local details of her research settings when criticising 'consensus' views of the researcher/researched relationship, a view proposed by those who call for the involvement of research subjects as collaborative partners in research (e.g. in moves to enable participants to 'correct or change what the researcher is writing about them before it goes to press' (160)). She argues that this idea of an 'ethical' research relationship:

> Flies in the face of the experience of many users that CMC is riddled with conflict. Groups conflict with groups (misogynists with feminists, white supremacists with liberals, expatriate Turks with expatriate Armenians, personal users with commercial advertisers libertarians with advocates of regulation, Chomskyan linguists with functional linguists, etc.), and individuals regularly enter into conflict with other individuals on Usenet newsgroups, chat channels, and academic Listserves alike. [..] the prevalence of conflict has as a consequence that users, even those subscribed to special-interest discussion groups, cannot reasonably be considered homogeneous populations with respect to their interests and social/political agendas. (160)

She goes on to suggest that:

> [...] the heterogeneity of CMC raises problems for many of the ethical recommendations proposed in this issue. For example, Waskul and Douglass in their article recommend that CMC researchers obtain informed consent and work only with key informants. But, informed consent from whom? (161)

---

[7] In the next chapter, I explore the tricky nature of such categorisation and other ways that the public or private status of a setting can be defined.

The disparate nature of CMC environments is here referenced in Herring's challenging of recommendations presented in the literature. Due to the conflict she has witnessed online, CMC cannot be thought of as a homogenous 'thing'. Because the 'researched' is not a stable or unified object, it is not possible to aim for consensus between the researcher and researched. A similar problem is faced, Herring argues, in respect of the issue of informed consent. If the researched body is made up of diverse populations, who should the researcher approach? The positions that Herring takes in respect of both the use of data and nature of the researcher/researched relationship involve strategic moves to challenge or support particular ethical positions via reference to the local features of the researched settings. In each case, the empirical is used to undermine theoretical positions proposed by other scholars.

Herring's references to the empirical draw from her experience and understanding of the nature of interactions on her research sites. She does not make reference to explicitly codified rules of behaviour on these sites (such as the 'Rules of Use' common on many websites today). However, it is worth noting that, as with the ethics of the academy, the constitution of ethical behaviour/understandings in different social settings may be more or less explicitly codified.[8] The ethics of a site may be articulated in organisational guidance similar to those of professional bodies. FAQs posted on websites may involve the stating of ethical principles regarding acceptable behaviours, fixing expectations about conduct, and performance of membership within a site (e.g. *Facebook's* 'Statement of Rights and Responsibilities'[9]). Texts and documents surrounding different activities may also seek to articulate standards – such as Linden Lab's Teen *Second Life* 'Commandments'[10] which, like professional codes of ethics, attempt to outline shared principles to aim towards and adhere to.

Alternatively, the researcher might also examine the ethical moves involved within the practices of their research contexts: the emergent and conflicting negotiation of ethics within online environments which appears to be Herring's focus in her paper. Such negotiation emerges within the day-to-day activity on websites, forums, and virtual worlds. Within the ongoing ethical work in such sites, we are likely to find contestation of appropriate/acceptable behaviour, understandings of privacy and audience, and expectations regarding gift and exchange. Attention to this tacit as well as explicit wrangling over ethics demonstrates that the negotiation of ethics is a focus of activity in very different contexts, whether or not it is constituted as a professional responsibility. The question then, is to what extent – and how – our understanding of these settings should inform the researcher's actions?

---

[8] I will return to this idea in my discussion of the public/private distinction in Chap. 3.

[9] http://www.facebook.com/terms.php.

[10] http://www.schome.ac.uk/wiki/Linden_Lab's_Teen_Second_Life_'Commandments'.

The Ethics of the Researcher

So far, I have suggested that the ethical stances researchers develop in respect of research can be understood as an outcome of an engagement with both the (theoretical) ethics of the academy and the (empirical) ethics of the researched. Here, I shift to a third domain, in thinking about what the researcher brings to this engagement. This focuses attention on the personal and professional commitments, affiliations, and interests of the individual researcher.

Any focus on the promotion of objective ethical principles negates both the relevance of the ethics of the researched but also the researcher as a preexisting entity by suggesting that the researcher can unproblematically take on and apply the ethics of the academy or institution. This ignores the complex ways that the subjectivity of the researcher might inform the ongoing production of research ethics. Here, then, we have a concern not with the ethics of research (e.g. as articulated within the academy) but with the ethics of *this* particular researcher, engaged in moving between theoretical and empirical domains. This suggests we might pay attention to the personal and professional baggage that the researcher draws on when defining their ethical stance.

Whilst it appears relatively easy to suggest the practices and texts that might constitute the discursive realisation of the ethics of the academy and ethics of the researched (even though these may be more/less explicitly stated), it is perhaps more difficult to define the subjective ethics of the researcher. This is due in part to the fact that the ethics of the researcher is often uncodified during the research process, tending to emerge in writing about research. It is articulated, for example, within the ethics of the academy in personal reflections and expressions of feelings relating to problematic research incidents/dilemmas (a subject to which I return in Chap. 5), within reflexive consideration of the role and position of the researcher, and in the way that researchers draw in autobiographical information in the reporting of research.

We can see examples of this codification of the researcher's ethics in Herring's paper. Alongside her references to the sites of her research and recruitment of literature, Herring makes reference to 'the subjectivity of my personal situation' (164) and – in a number of places – considers the implications of this for her research and ethical decision-making. At the beginning of the paper, Herring describes how she was one of the first researchers working in online environments. She suggests that this 'brought with it a sense of discovery and exhilaration, but also uncertainty at times on how best to proceed' (153), with this 'uncertainty' emerging partly from the absence of specialised guidance for online research ethics at that time. She goes on to state: 'thus it was with a vague sense of relief that I welcomed the first suggestions of how to cite e-mail messages […]' (153). Herring's critique of existing ethical guidance in the paper is therefore framed within the context of her own personal anxiety about her early research practice and her hopes that specialist guidance would prove useful. The fact that she is subsequently critical of the various guidelines she discusses – going on to reject specialist guidance in favour of localised applications of existing ethical codes of different disciplines – suggests a sense of disappointment with what had emerged in the field of Internet research up until that point.

Throughout the paper, Herring also appears to identify strongly with different types of research and, most notably, with the discipline of linguistics – a discipline that, as I have suggested, she draws on repeatedly in presenting her ethical stance. She makes reference to her 'own scholarly values' in her desire for critical rather than collaborative research and describes how the question of whether/when 'it is acceptable to use real names when citing electronic messages as data' is:

> [...] a matter of special concern to me as a linguist, since my research focuses on the language used in electronic interactions and involves quoting portions of actual messages verbatim. (154)

Such personal identification with this discipline can be seen to be established in relation to the theoretical field, involving a merging of personal and professional ethics, with Herring speaking as a linguist, bearing inherent ethical concerns relating to this disciplinary identity.

Herring also suggests that her 'personal stance', her investment in her research topic 'as a female academic', had implications for her research approach:

> Although I have made every effort to be rigorous in my methods and interpretations, I obviously can not claim a 'neutral' stance toward the topic of investigation. Inevitably, my results reflect the perspective of a female academic linguist computer network user. (163)

Herring's reporting of her personal involvement extends to a consideration of the dissemination of her work, which is framed in relation to a number of responsibilities that she feels as a researcher. She describes how she '[...] began to feel increasingly responsible to make the results to others who might benefit from them' (163) and goes on to describe:

> [...] the ethical responsibility I felt when my research results turned out to have social consequences. This responsibility can be characterized as a concern, not just to avoid harm, but to do good, for the researched population and for society as a whole. (164)

There is the suggestion of a moral impetus here, a personal sense of responsibility that, she says, led her to publish and disseminate her work in certain ways. This raises the question of how the researcher's personal commitments inform their research actions and ethical decision-making.

The move from a consideration of the researched to a consideration of what the researcher brings to the ethics of their practice raises a further question: how does the researcher position themselves in relation to the ethics of their research settings? A number of the ethical decisions presented in Herring's paper are based upon a distancing move away from her research subjects – specifically the male participants on the Listserv groups she studies. She is critical of their behaviour and treatment of female members of the groups, arguing that some of them 'were doing considerable harm, albeit probably unintentionally for the most part' (163) through their online actions. She describes how, because of this, she approached them from a critical rather than collaborative perspective: 'in the interests of raising the general consciousness about gender inequality on the Internet, I wanted to expose the behaviour of these men to public scrutiny' (163). The relationship between Herring and a section of her researched subjects is, in this regard, configured as being based on difference rather than commonality. Clearly, other possible relationships might be established (including those that might establish alliances with the ethics of research participants), and I will return to a consideration of the complex and sometimes problematic relationship between researcher and researched in Chap. 5.

The Ethics of the Institution

Although it does not emerge as a point of focus in Herring's chapter, there is another key context in which ethics are negotiated that may also inform the researcher's establishment of an ethical stance. Here, I refer to the institution within which the researcher or student operates. This represents a particular point of authority that is different to – and may be in conflict with – the expression and negotiation of ideas in the ethics of the academy, the negotiation of ethics in the research settings, and the ethics of the researcher. It also provides the researcher with specific guidance that may frame and delimit the researcher's actions (such as the ethical principles published by individual academic institutions and funding bodies).

Researchers' accounts of their engagements with ethics committees and IRBs demonstrate the potential impact of institutions' bureaucratic involvement in shaping the ethics of research. McKee and Porter (2008) make reference to two cases that provide contrasting examples of the ways that institutional review might influence the conduct of research, whilst also reminding us of the researchers' role in interpreting institutional guidance when establishing their ethical stance. The first example they cite is the experience of the Internet researcher Susannah Stern, whose research examined young people's personal websites (Stern 2004). McKee and Porter describe how the IRB that examined Stern's project advised her that the work did not involve human subjects and therefore was not eligible for review. As they note, 'this put Stern in a frame of mind that she was working with texts, not persons' (8). The result of this was that when Stern came across distressing material on the web pages that she was studying (expressions of the desire to commit suicide by one adolescent) she decided not to follow them up. She later found out that the author of these suicidal messages – utterances that she had observed but not acted upon – had committed suicide. McKee and Porter describe how:

> Stern was, understandably, shaken by the news. She realized that had she been thinking of her research as involving human participants she would have proceeded differently. By being shunted too quickly to NO ('The research is not research involving human subjects [...]'), her understandings of her ethical obligations as a researcher were curtailed. (8)

McKee and Porter's account of Stern's experience here suggests that the evaluation of the research by an authorising committee blinded this researcher to the potential dangers of her own inaction (whether or not Stern could have prevented this tragedy at all is a different issue). This example also implies the danger of uncritically engaging with the guidance of the ethics committee, and the need to regard this as one point of reference (or, in McKee and Porter's terms, 'audience') rather than the sole point of reference (McKee and Porter 2008).

A second example presented by McKee and Porter involves a researcher 'going beyond' IRB guidance (21). They describe how:

> David Clark, a technical communications researcher who studied the online and F2F communications of an organization, was told by the IRB that reviewed his research that the online communications he was studying were considered published texts and thus he did not need consent to observe or quote them but that he *would* need participants' consent to observe and quote the F2F [face-to-face] meetings. When comparing the differing expectations for online and F2F research, Clark decided to go beyond the IRB recommendations and seek (with IRB approval of his study modifications) the same permissions from both F2F and online participants because he felt online participants should be treated equally to F2F participants. (21)

Here, rather than accepting the guidance of the IRB, the researcher established a position that they felt comfortable with. These examples suggest that the institution does not fix the researcher's ethical stance. Instead, the institution should be regarded as one (key) point of authority whose influence may be felt in different ways.

Although the ethics of the institution is taken into account in the chapters that follow (particularly in Chap. 5, where I examine institutional discourses as potentially destabilising), my primary focus in this book is on the relationship between the ethics of the academy, the ethics of the researched and the ethics of the researcher. There are a number of reasons for this. Firstly, I would argue that the more the researcher has thought through their decisions in respect of these domains, the stronger the case that can be made when approaching those involved in the institutional review and surveillance of research.[11] From my own experience of reviewing research ethics applications and being a member of an academic ethics committee, submissions are more likely to be favourably received when they are thorough and well argued. Secondly, ethical issues also emerge in research that does not involve human subjects and thus often does not undergo institutional ethical review. These issues demand due consideration even though the institution may be less concerned with the regulation of such inquiry. Finally, despite the overriding authority of institutional review bodies to approve social research, as the cases described above suggest, it ultimately remains the researcher's responsibility to establish an ethical stance that they feel they can defend, both to themselves and to others.

---

[11] It is worth noting that in the case of my own research, the institutional context in which I worked did not exert pressures – other than the need to defend my work at my viva examination – because I started my research before the introduction of a research ethics committee at my university. I was therefore working in an academic context in which the responsibility for the ethics of my project was primarily my own and my supervisor's. This did not lessen my concern about the ethics of my project – indeed, in some ways it provoked greater reflection upon the decisions I was making as the project was not passing through an official review/interrogation. As I described in the previous chapter, other researchers have had very different experiences to my own.

	ETHICAL DISCOURSE	
ETHICAL DOMAIN	**I-**	**I+**
Researcher	***Personal Contingencies*** emergent commitments, affiliations	***Personal codes*** the researcher's political affiliations
Researched (empirical field)	***Setting contingencies*** the negotiation of ethics within the ongoing activity of the researched settings	***Setting codes*** agreements on rights/values – as expressed in rules of use for example
Academy (theoretical field)	***Academic contingencies*** discussion with colleagues, feedback, advice	***Academic codes*** Research ethics frameworks, guidance in journal articles
Institution	***Official contingencies*** announcements of university edicts, ethics committee advice	***Official codes*** University code of ethics etc.

Fig. 2.1 Four domains of ethics

Conclusion: The Achievement of Ethics in Research

This book conceptualises the achievement of an ethical stance as the outcome of the transaction between the four domains marked out in this chapter: the ethics of the academy, the ethics of the researched, the ethics of researcher, and the bureaucratic ethics of the institution. The achieved ethics – the specific ethical stance that is generated from the intersection of (1), (2), (3), and (4) – is understood as the outcome of the researchers' moves within/between these domains. I have proposed that these four domains can therefore be understood as constituting different resources for the construction and ongoing production/maintenance of ethical stances in research.

These domains are not homogenous and present the researcher with different types of resources. These are suggested in Fig. 2.1 (above), which introduces a distinction between the weakly (I–) and strongly (I+) institutionalised discourses of these contexts.

The distinction between weakly institutionalised contingencies and strongly institutionalised codes refers to the extent to which the ethical discourse of the domain 'exhibits an empirical regularity that marks [them] out as recognisably distinct from other practices (or from a specific other practice)' (Dowling 2009, 81). Strong institutionalisation can be recognised in the regularity of the discourse, the reinforcement of specific ethical perspectives through the repeated voicing of similar positions which suggest institutionalised alliances and oppositions. This distinction is evident in the consideration of the difference between the codes of conduct of online communities (e.g. where the specific ethical guidance of individual settings is reinforced in Rules of Use and FAQs), which are likely to be strongly institutionalised, and the more weakly institutionalised (and more unpredictable) ongoing negotiation of ethics in day-to-day activity in online environments (where alternative/unexpected positions might also be voiced). As I will discuss in Chap. 5, the distinction is important because it suggests discursive contingencies that cannot be anticipated in advance of the research and thus may unsettle the researcher's ethical stance (see Whiteman 2010). As I have suggested, these discourses may also be more/less explicitly codified.

The four domains I have outlined in this chapter introduce a consideration of the negotiation of ethics within and between academic and non-academic domains, and between the public negotiation of ethics within published documents/research and researchers' personal reflections upon ethical issues. These domains can be seen to feed into each other. Both the ethics of the researcher and the achieved ethics may be articulated in the writing up and dissemination of the research (through the researcher's reflections upon their personal stance, and the ethical decisions they have made), hence becoming part of the ethics of the academy. The ethics of the researcher may also feed back into the empirical settings, perhaps informing the ethics of the researched. As I have suggested, this way of thinking about research ethics introduces a range of questions. What, for example, is the relationship between the ethics of the academy and the ethics of the researched – or indeed between the researcher's ethics and the ethics of those they research?

As I will discuss in Chap. 5, the transaction between academic and non-academic ethical domains suggested in this chapter is significant because of the importance attributed to 'participation' within qualitative research (e.g. in the discussion of participatory research to counter the 'colonial' gaze of the researcher in anthropology) and within certain bodies of research (such as fan studies where researchers often present their insider perspective and shared ethical stances as a marker of authority). Existing work provides only a limited exploration of the relationship between the ethical practices of Internet researchers and the ethics of those participating within non-academic and, more specifically, online environments. The question is the position we take in respect of the different domains in achieving our own ethical stance. A key issue in respect of this is the extent to which the researcher should adopt the code of academic conventions and ignore the ethical practices of those involved in the researched activities (or vice versa). The Canadian *Tri-Council Policy Statement: Ethical Conduct for Research Involving Humans,* for example, argues that considering participant perspectives on research: 'enjoins researchers and research ethics boards to take a "subject-centred perspective"' when they consider ethical issues in their research: 'researchers and REBS must strive to understand the views of the potential or actual research subjects'.[12] How might this 'understanding' be gained, and how should it inform the researcher's decision-making?

There are also tensions here. Difficulties arise because researchers have multiple responsibilities that exert different pressures/requirements. The problem with focusing on the ethics of the academy, for example, is that the researcher also has a responsibility to the research setting/audience. The problem with focusing on the ethics of the researched is that researchers also have a professional, 'collegiate' (Dowling and Brown 2010) responsibility to other researchers (e.g. not polluting the field, ibid). Due to these different responsibilities, researchers need to establish a transactional approach between their own engagement with, and recruitment of, the ethics of the academy and the ethics of the researched.

We can look at the relational achievement of ethics then, in respect of the recruitment of these distinct but related discourses. As I have suggested above, this achievement is made available to other researchers through the publication of research reports that constitute a key part of the ethics of the academy. So it involves both pretextual activity – doing research – and the production of textual artefacts (e.g. Herring's paper and this book).

In looking at Herring's paper in this chapter, I have focused on the latter, the published performance of the achievement of an ethical stance. My selection of Herring's paper as the focus of this chapter was due to the way that it demonstrates both an interrogation of general, universalising principles and the establishment of an ethical stance in response, a stance based on a series of localising moves. Whilst the position that Herring establishes is rooted in general principles (for instance the idea that public broadcasts are of legitimate focus to researchers), the specificities of her ethical position is differentiated and defined in relation to a range of specific contextual and individualistic reference points, including the discipline she is working in, her research sites, and her personal aims for her own research practice. As I have described, the articulation of Herring's ethical stance in relation to the question of naming displays allegiance to disciplinary conventions/traditions (the field and concerns of linguistics) and affiliation to particular literature as well as to a particular stance on the nature of research inquiry. In each case, Herring uses these not just to explain but also to legitimise the decisions she has made.

Attention to the positioning involved in the rhetorical construction of ethical stances can not only help researchers to interrogate the ethics of other scholars, but also strengthen our presentation of our own research projects. This is important because every researcher's ethical decision-making can be criticised from some perspective. Researchers are now expected to be able to defend their stances and present their decisions to different audiences. In this context, the concern with marketing, defending and explaining this achievement becomes increasingly pressing. Awareness of this positioning can also inform the practice, as well as presentation,

[12] http://www.pre.ethics.gc.ca/eng/policy-politique/tcps-eptc/context-contexte/ See Kitchin (2003, 2007) for consideration of online research in the context of *Canada's Tri-Council Policy Statement.*

of research ethics, however, by provoking reflection upon the basis of our ethical manoeuvring and the different contexts that our decisions are rooted in. What do these tell us about the production of our own identities as researchers?

This chapter has presented an analysis of Herring's moves to build and dismantle different ethical positions. The chapters that follow seek to suggest how the moves between the ethics of the academy, researched, researcher, and institution outlined through my engagement with Herring's text might inform the ongoing production of an ethical stance during the practice of research. At the same time, they also involve a desire to question and unpick the achievement of ethics in my own research.

References

Brown, A., & Dowling, P. (1998). *Doing research/reading research*. London: RoutledgeFalmer.

Buchanan, E. A. (Ed.). (2003). *Readings in virtual research ethics: Issues and controversies*. Hershey: Idea Group.

Bulmer, M. (1982). *Social research ethics: An examination of the merits of covert participant observation*. London/Basingstoke: Macmillan Press.

Cavazos, E. A., & Morin, G. (1994). *Cyberspace and the law: Your rights and duties in the on-line world*. Cambridge: The MIT Press.

Corden, A., & Sainsbury, R. (2005). *The impact of verbatim quotations on research users: Qualitative exploration*. Social Policy Research Unit, University of York, York. Available online http://www.york.ac.uk/inst/spru/pubs/sstreps.html#2005.

Corden, A., & Sainsbury, R. (2006). *Using verbatim quotations in reporting qualitative social research: Researchers' views*. Social Policy Research Unit, University of York, York. Available online http://www.york.ac.uk/inst/spru/pubs/sstreps.html.

Dowling, P. (2009). *Sociology as method: Departures from the forensics of culture, text and knowledge*. Rotterdam: Sense.

Dowling, P., & Brown, A. (2010). *Doing research/reading research: Re-interrogating education* (2nd ed.). London: Routledge.

Finn, P., & Jakobsson, M. (2007). *Designing and conducting Phishing experiments*. IEEE Technology and Society Magazine, Special Issue on Usability and Security. Available online: http://citeseerx.ist.psu.edu/viewdoc/summary?doi=10.1.1.69.6779.

Glaser, B. G., & Strauss, A. L. (1967). *The discovery of grounded theory: Strategies for qualitative research*. New York: Aldine De Gruyter.

Herring, S. C. (1996). Linguistic and critical research on computer-mediated communication: Some ethical and scholarly considerations. *The Information Society, 12*(2), 153–168. Available online: http://ella.slis.indiana.edu/~herring/tis.1996.pdf.

Hine, C. (Ed.). (2005). *Virtual methods: Issues in social research on the internet*. Oxford: Berg.

Johns, M. D., Hal, G. J., & Crowell, T. L. (2004). Surviving the IRB review: Institutional guidelines and research strategies. In M. D. Johns, S. Chen, G. Jon Hall (Eds.), *Online social research: Methods, issues, & ethics* (pp. 105–124). New York: Peter Lang.

Jones, S. (1999). *Doing internet research: Critical issues and methods for examining the net*. Thousand Oaks/London/New Delhi: SAGE.

Kimmel, A. J. (1988). *Ethics and values in applied social research*. Newbury: SAGE.

King, S. A. (1996). Researching internet communities: Proposed ethical guidelines for the reporting of results. *The Information Society, 12*(2), 119–128.

Kitchin, H. (2003). The tri-council policy statement and research in cyberspace: Research ethics, the internet, and revising a 'Living Document'. *Journal of Academic Ethics, 1*, 397–418.

Kitchin, H. A. (2007). *Research ethics and the internet: Negotiating Canada's tri-council policy statement*. Halifax/Winnipeg: Fernwood Publishing.

Mann, C., & Stewart, F. (2000). *Internet communication and qualitative research: A handbook for researching online*. London: SAGE.

McKee, H. A., & Porter, J. E. (2008). The ethics of digital writing research: A rhetorical approach. *College Composition and Communication*, *59*, 711–749. Available online: http://www.writing.ucsb.edu/wrconf08/Pdf_Articles/McKee_Article.pdf.

Rowe, M. (2007). Tripping over molehills: Ethics and the ethnography of police research. *International Journal of Social Research Methodology, 10*(1), 37–48.

Smyth, M., & Williamson, E. (Eds.). (2004). *Researchers and their 'subjects': Ethics, power, knowledge and consent*. Bristol: Policy Press.

Stern, S. R. (2003). Encountering distressing information in online research: A consideration of legal and ethical responsibilities. *New Media & Society, 5*(2), 246–266.

Stern, S. (2004). Studying adolescents online: A consideration of ethical issues. In E. Buchanan (Ed.) *Readings in virtual research ethics*, (pp. 274–287). Hershey and London: Information Science Publishing.

Waskul, D., & Douglass, M. (1996). Considering the electronic participant: Some polemical observations on the ethics of on-line research. *The Information Society, 12*, 129–139.

Whiteman, N. (2010). Control and contingency: Maintaining ethical stances in research. *International Journal of Internet Research Ethics, 3*(1), 6–22.

Wiles, R., Crow, G., Heath, S., & Charles, V. (2008). The management of confidentiality and anonymity in social research. *International Journal of Social Research Methodology, 11*(5), 417–428.

Wong, L. M. (1998). The ethics of rapport: Institutional safeguards, resistance, and betrayal. *Qualitative Inquiry*, *4*, 178–199. http://qix.sagepub.com/cgi/content/abstract/4/2/178.

Chapter 3
Public or Private?

Abstract This chapter addresses the challenge of relating the public/private distinction to online environments and the implications of this for research. The chapter examines the significance of the distinction between the public and private for social science research and the varying strategies that researchers have developed for categorising online data in relation to this conceptual opposition. Tracing the distinction between perceived and technical approaches to the publicness/privateness of online environments and content, the chapter suggests that scholars pay attention to the expression of privacy in their research settings and marks out a distinction between explicit/implicit markers of privacy that can be recruited when approaching online environments.

When I first visited COA and SHH early in 2004, each site contained busy forums. Posts within these forums could be accessed without recourse to password entry points, and posters had no control over who read their messages once they had 'posted' to the boards. During my study, the status of these main forums was to change. In June 2005, COA introduced a log-on page for those wishing to view/access the boards and the posts within them. Whilst the forums still remained open to all (as anyone with an email address could register) and the registration terms did not mention copyright or a request for information from members as to their intentions in engaging with the site, the log-on page appeared to involve a restricting of the content of the forums. The repercussions of this change were complicated further in December 2005 when COA closed its forums. This meant that the interactions were now inaccessible, no longer visible, and lost to the gaze of any visitor to the site. In May 2006, SHH also restricted access to part of its forums in this way, closing off part of the site which contained general discussion and explicitly community-related forums from non-members. Registration on SHH to these areas

N. Whiteman, *Undoing Ethics: Rethinking Practice in Online Research*,
DOI 10.1007/978-1-4614-1827-6_3,

of the site remained – as on COA – 'open' (unlike sites that require the provision of an email address when seeking membership). However non-members now visiting SHH would initially be unaware of these forums as they were now only visible upon logging on.

Introduction

The description above outlines the development of COA and SHH during the two and a half years that I observed these settings. The changes described had significant implications for a key aspect of the ethical stance that I established in my research: my definition of the forum activity on these sites as being situated within the 'public domain' and hence – I argued – of legitimate focus without obtaining permission from participants to observe and cite their postings. Each development provoked a reconsideration of the status of the material that I was looking at and whether or not I felt I could legitimately include it in my study. Each led me to reassess and revise the stance I was taking in my approach to these settings.

Such (re)considerations are central to this chapter, which focuses on the implications of the public/private distinction for Internet research. The chapter considers the different types of evidence that researchers have recruited when asserting that specific online environments are, or are not, located within the public domain, and how this evidence might inform the use of material from such settings. The chapter argues that the construction of any distinction between the public and private can be understood in a similar way to the construction of an ethical stance in the context of research. Each can be understood to be relationally established rather than naturally defined, each is embedded in the local details of specific locations/activities as well as being informed by general principles, and each is dynamic and subject to change. Just as there is no fixed 'right' and 'wrong' in research, there is no self-evident 'public' or 'private'. Instead, in defining our research contexts or data as public and/or private, the researcher engages in an act of objectification, the production of a definition that may be based on different indicators of publicness/privateness, indicators that I am going to explore in this chapter.

Why is the public/private distinction significant? In everyday life, we establish understandings of our interactions and the appropriateness of behaviour in relation to expectations about the privacy or publicness of our actions. Our transactions in different environments are informed by our readings of material and environmental markers of context and access: the spaces we inhabit, the walls that surround us, the visibility of others in our vicinity, and the gatekeepers that grant us access to specific locations or deny us entry. Our readings of these markers are shaped by social and cultural expectations and understandings of the visibility/openness they signal, as well as related expectations about audience, confidentiality, and trust. These expectations are important because they are tied into concerns about surveillance, the relationship between self and others, and 'the conditions under which personal informational borders are seen to be legitimately and illegitimately crossed' (Marx 2001, 157).

Alongside this everyday relevance, the public/private distinction has specific implications for social science research. It plays a key role in academic discussion of the legitimacy of certain methods and, in particular, the contested acceptability of covert methods of data collection. This is because, despite a 'nearly universal' understanding of the need to protect the private sphere (Woo 2006, 951), there is a tradition of observational research in which 'it has been accepted that behaviour that is performed within the public domain may be observed and researched without consent' (see Sixsmith and Murray 2001). In raising questions of privacy, the public/private distinction therefore raises fundamental 'questions about the necessity of consent' (Hudson and Bruckman, 4). As Spicker has suggested, these questions have had a profound influence 'on the way we interpret the ethics of research', leading:

> [...] to the central precept that actions have to lie in the control of the research subject. Research subjects have the right to be informed about research, to consent, or to withdraw from it if they are not content.
>
> (Spicker 2007, 2)

The question of how we might define the status of research settings in respect of the public/private distinction is therefore of particular significance to those using unobtrusive observation – not least because charges of 'lurking' and 'spying' often surround such methods, as covert research becomes identified with deception (Spicker 2011, 119).[1] The relevance of this question is not limited to those employing covert methods however. Many decisions made in the handling of data and management of research relationships can be seen to be influenced by understandings of what is public and what is private. This includes the ways that researchers approach concerns over anonymity and confidentiality in the dissemination of research. For this reason, there is a need to define and fix (albeit temporarily) the status of the focus of our research (whether a setting or type of document etc.) in respect of this central distinction. This is the case whether research is carried out online or offline, focuses on one or more locations or individuals, or moves between numerous settings in the collection of data.

In the context of research, the right to privacy does not just raise procedural questions (Stern 2009) but is also implicated in broader arguments regarding how researchers should engage in 'showing respect' to research participants (e.g. by granting them a say in what is done with their data (Stern 2009, 95)). Whilst this chapter explores strategies that researchers have developed for defining online environments in relation to the public/private distinction when working through methodological questions, it also considers the implications of these strategies for the researcher/researched relationship and presents an initial consideration of the extent to which the expectations of Internet users should influence researchers' decisions (an issue that is discussed further in Chaps. 4 and 5 in respect of different ethical questions).

---

[1] As Spicker argues, non-disclosure in covert research does not equate with deception – 'where the nature of a researcher's action is misrepresented to the research subject' (Spicker 2011, 119).

The chapter begins with a consideration of the public/private distinction and the way that new media developments have problematised an already complex conceptual relationship. It then focuses in more detail on the literature on Internet research, tracing the objectifying moves that researchers have made when defining online locations as public or private, the ways that they have looked to their research settings to support these definitions, and the methodological issues that these moves raise. I then introduce a distinction between *tacit* and *explicit* markers of privacy, which I develop in the final part of the chapter where I return to my study of COA and SHH and explore how my ethical stance was established in reference to both the ethics of the academy and the ethics of the researched settings.

It is important to note at this point that there is no *natural* connection between the ongoing objectification of a research site as public/private and the selection of 'appropriate' data collection methods. Here, I am particularly interested in debates regarding the legitimacy of covert observation. Whether we define online material as public or private (or a mixture of both) does not instantly settle the question of whether it is acceptable to carry out covert observation within such settings (although as will be discussed, there are certain cases where the use of such methods would likely be regarded as more clearly problematic than others). A secondary strand in this chapter therefore involves tracing and challenging some of the arguments presented in Internet research writing regarding the legitimacy of different research approaches. Familiarity with these debates can be useful when the researcher is asked to defend their own research actions.

Problematising the Public/Private Distinction

I have suggested above the significance of the public/private distinction for researchers and the need to assert whether potential data is housed within a more or less public or private domain. This might perhaps seem like an easy question to resolve but is by no means straightforward. One way of starting to get a conceptual grip on the public/private relationship is to recognise the complexity of this distinction. As Marx suggests:

> Those making sweeping claims about either the death of privacy, or the public (and therefore presumably non-problematic) nature of [...] technology's emissions and receptions, use the former terms as if their meaning was self-evident. It is not. The public and the private involve multiple meanings over time and across cultures, kinds of persons and social categories.
>
> (Marx 2001, 160)

This complexity appears particularly evident online, where we find individuals broadcasting information to a potentially global audience within environments that – as will be explored later in the chapter – can present confusing, complex, and dynamic signifiers of privacy and publicness. This has led some commentators to argue that these 'altered patterns of social relationships and technological changes demand new understandings of public and private realms' (Rawlins 1998, 369), that conventional frameworks for understanding this distinction have become outdated and are unable to deal with the complex forms of communication and interaction of the Internet.

Counter to such arguments comes recognition of the fact that the public/private distinction has *always* been a tricky relationship, one that has been loaded with meaning in different ways. In *Public Goods, Private Goods* (2001), for example, Raymond Geuss argues that 'there is no such thing as *the* public/private distinction' (Geuss 2001). Geuss describes how:

> The public/private distinction does not mark out a single natural division in the world which could give us a straightforward way of orienting ourselves in action and in evaluating action; rather, it is a confused conglomeration of very distinct conceptual responses to *different* human problems and issues. (xix, his emphasis)

This rejection serves as a useful warning against the temptation of recruiting natural distinctions in the design and justification of research. Although these might be seen to provide a 'straightforward' approach to our research actions, or our evaluation of the actions of others, concepts such as the public and private are constructed rather than innate. Our methodological decisions are no less artificial.

Challenging the idea that the public and private constitute a 'single unitary distinction' (xviii), Geuss argues that the public/private has always been an 'ideological concretion' (Geuss, 10), one whose shape has shifted and been contested over time. Geuss's 'genealogical' approach traces this contestation, exploring the way that understandings of private and public spheres have been established,[2] and how these have shifted, with what was acceptable at one point in time in certain contexts becoming unacceptable at another. Describing the emergence of competing conceptualisations of what is public and private, he notes how:

> Disparate components – conceptual fragments, theories, folk reactions, crude distinctions that are useful in highly specific practical contexts, tacit value assumptions – from different sources and belonging to different spheres have come together historically in an unclear way and have accumulated around themselves a kind of capital of self-evidence, plausibility, and motivational force. The unreflective use of distinctions such as this one restricts our possibilities of perceiving and understanding our world.
>
> (Geuss 2001, 10)

As Geuss proposes here, uncritical use of the public and private distinction limits our analytical gaze; the meaning and significance of these terms need to be worked through in reference to specific locations/contexts rather than simply applied as if they were self-evident or natural. This is because, as his analysis suggests, these concepts are unstable and sites of struggle.

The challenging of easy distinctions between the public and private has been extended by scholars who have explored contemporary locations that defy easy categorisation into an either/or public/private typology. One example of this is work on the growth of "'privatized' public spaces", a term 'used commonly to describe the corporate plazas and open spaces, shopping malls, and other such spaces that are

[2] Why, for example, was the public behaviour of Diogenes of Sinope, inhabitant of fourth century B.C. Athens found to be offensive? – for the answer, see Guess 2001, 12–33.

increasingly popular destinations for the public' (Banerjee 2001, 21). Writing about such spaces, the urban planning scholar Tribid Banerjee describes how:

> There is a presumption of 'publicness' in these pseudo-public spaces. But in reality they are in the private realm. In many parts of downtown business districts, a thin brass line or a groove cut in the sidewalk, often accompanied by an imbedded sign, makes it clear that the seemingly unbounded public space is not boundaryless after all. The owner has all the legal prerogatives to exclude someone from the space circumscribed by sometimes subtle and often invisible property boundaries. The public is welcome as long as they are patrons of shops and restaurants, office workers, or clients of businesses located on the premises. But access to and use of the space is only a privilege, not a right. In San Francisco, the planning department requires owners to post a sign declaring that the space is 'provided and maintained from the Enjoyment of the Public [sic]' but any expectation that such spaces are open to all is fanciful at best. Many of these spaces are closely monitored by security guards and closed circuit television cameras, which has prompted critics such as Mike Davis (1990) to refer to them as 'fortress' environments.
>
> (Banerjee 2001, 12)

How is the publicness/privateness of these environments problematised here? The belief that these spaces are public is related to the idea that they are open to all. However, as Banerjee says, this idea is false, 'fanciful at best'. The spaces are policed and monitored. Entrants act under the panoptic gaze of surveillance systems and face exclusion should their actions (or very being) be in conflict with those intended or desired by the owners of the spaces. The 'subtle and often invisible property boundaries' that signal this ownership also establish the point that these are in fact private spaces. In this way the free space is revealed as 'fortress'.

Like Geuss and Marx, Banerjee questions the taken for granted use of the terms 'public' and 'private', reminding us that the destabilisation of this conceptual distinction extends beyond the Internet. Online environments are not unique in unsettling these concepts, but represent territories where an always complex relationship is emerging in new permutations. The challenges of defining settings in respect of this distinction therefore exists offline as well as online. Yet the environmental mutability of online domains does raise issues that are perhaps specific to the Internet. It is to these – and their implications for the public/private distinction – that I now turn.

The Internet and the Public/Private Distinction

Internet environments resemble the sorts of offline settings that – like the shopping centre – defy easy classification. Visitors to websites, social networks, and online worlds also face issues of access, surveillance, and potential exclusion, but do so without the conventional markers of privacy that may reassure us in offline environments. As boyd suggests:

> Offline, people are accustomed to having architecturally defined boundaries. Physical features like walls and limited audio range help people have a sense of just how public their actions are. The digital world has different properties and these can be easily altered through the development of new technologies, radically altering the assumptions that people have when they interact online.
>
> (boyd 2008, 14)

Whilst changing the nature of a physical environment can require great effort (walls must be knocked down, new boundaries built…), the architecture and affordances of online environments can be altered far more easily, dramatically changing the nature of participation within these settings and, with this, existing understandings of privacy.

boyd (2008) demonstrates the ways that structural developments can transform the public/private status of online settings by drawing parallels between the introduction of new features to two different environments. The first, the launching of *DejaNews*' Usenet search facility in the 1990s, introduced a search function to Usenet. For the first time, this enabled users to locate and view discussion without being members of individual Usenet lists. The second, the controversial addition of 'News Feed' on the social networking site *Facebook* in 2006, provided users with a summary of their friends' recent activities on their *Facebook* page. Announcing the introduction of News Feed, the product manager for this feature described how it would provide Facebook users with 'a personalized list of news stories throughout the day, so you'll know when Mark adds Britney Spears to his Favourites or when your crush is single again' (Sanghvi 2006, no page numbers).

Each of these developments involved a structural change that had implications for the visibility of users' utterances and how they were accessed, altering the nature of involvement within these settings. boyd describes how, whilst neither made 'anything public that was not already public',[3] each development 'disrupted the social dynamics' (14) of these sites. Users' discomfort resulting from these changes focused on two aspects – new exposure and a new sense of invasion (2008). Describing the impact of the *DejaNews* search facility, for example, boyd notes:

> When search was introduced, it became much easier to stumble on a newsgroup and even easier to read messages completely out of context. Tracking who participated in what group no longer required an individual to participate in all of the same groups. While the walls that separated newsgroups were always porous – anyone could come or go – they completely collapsed when search came along. DejaNews disrupted the delicate social dynamics in many Usenet groups; to regain some sense of control and 'privacy', many groups shifted to mailing lists. Little did they know that, a few years later, Yahoo! would purchase two of the most popular free mailing list services and make them searchable.
>
> (boyd 2008, 14)

As boyd describes here, the introduction of this search function provoked a radical transformation of the ways that users could enter into this activity; making it possible for individuals to parachute directly into the groups without establishing contextual understandings of the settings. Here, as with my example of COA and SHH at the beginning of this chapter, we see how structural, technological changes can shift the rules of the game for users of online environments. Such developments demonstrate the value of establishing a relational understanding of the public and private that is able to adapt to the changing nature of online settings. They also demonstrate the

[3] As Sanghvi goes on to reassure users that newsfeed does 'not give out any information that wasn't already visible. Your privacy settings remain the same – the people who couldn't see your info before still can't see it now' (Sanghvi 2006, no page numbers).

particular difficulties that researchers may confront when attempting to get a grip on the status of such environments.

Alongside such technical developments, researchers are also faced with uncertainty generated by the absence of shared understandings of generic indicators of privacy online. For those used to offline forms of interaction and publication, online environments can appear both strange and strangely familiar. As Bromseth puts it, they present:

> [...] features similar to both traditional public discourse like newspapers, being broadcasted to a large audience, and at the same time they consist of many activities and issues that traditionally have belonged to more private spheres and means of communication.
>
> (Bromseth 2002, 35)

In the context of dynamic and shifting online environments, diverse forms of publication and display, and often unknowable audiences, existing expectations and understandings of the markers of what is public and private have been unsettled. Responses to this unsettling have tended to fall back on understandings of the public and private that are regarded by some as ill equipped to deal with the challenges that technologically mediated environments present.

boyd (2007, 2008), for example, argues that in approaching the public/private distinction as an 'either/or, 0 or 1' issue, technologists have failed to take into account the complex nature of online environments and the dynamic signifiers of privacy and publicness that they may present to users and researchers. She argues that:

> More flexible definitions allow the two terms to sit at opposite ends of an axis, giving us the ability to judge just how private a particular event or place is. Unfortunately, even this scale is ill equipped to handle the disruption of mediating technology. What it means to be public or private is quickly changing before our eyes and we lack the language, social norms, and structures to handle it.
>
> (boyd 2007, no page nos.)

boyd's claim that the features of online communication make mediated environments unapproachable from traditional understandings of the public and private challenges the stability of distinctions between these concepts. Like Banerjee, boyd does not move away from the metaphor of the boundary or the idea that distinctions can be made between public and private contexts. Instead, she suggests that the public is multiplied and made increasingly complex online, that the 'persistence and search-ability' of the Internet leads to 'multiple degrees of public-ness' (boyd 2005, no page numbers), and that we find a 'layering' of notions of publicness in environments where 'people can negotiate multiple social contexts simultaneously' and need to learn to 'manage invisible and potential audiences' (ibid).

It is perhaps unsurprising that in such settings, as Eysenbach and Till note, 'researchers may have difficulty separating spaces regarded as private from spaces regarded as public' (2001, 1105). It is not just researchers who are struggling to grasp online forms of privacy and publicness however. Researchers have described consumers' mixture of confusion and overconfidence in their understanding of the status and ownership of online data and the meaning of privacy policies (LaRose and Rifon 2006). Growing evidence also suggests that Internet users display conflicting responses to their privacy online: they are increasingly concerned about their privacy, but are lax in seeking to protect themselves and willing to sacrifice privacy for 'material benefits' (Woo 2006, 950; see also LaRose and Rifon 2006).

Other users – and those involved in the production of weblogs (or blogs) are an obvious example – appear to have become extremely comfortable seeking and handling public exposure, using the Internet more directly as a broadcast medium to connect with their own public audiences.[4] Here too, however, research has suggested that there are inherent tensions within these users' expectations of their publicness and intended/imagined audiences:

> Many bloggers want to find others who have something in common. They want serendipitous interactions. They perform as digital flaneurs, to see and be seen. They want to be public. *But only so public.*
>
> (boyd 2005, no page numbers – my emphasis)

Against this backdrop of confusion and contradiction, an additional problem emerges. As well as facing the challenge of formally defining the status of online settings, Internet researchers also need to consider the responsibility they have to those participating within these environments, individuals who may have conflicting understandings of the visibility of their online actions.

Research Ethics and the Public/Private Distinction

The complexity of the public/private relationship is also evident in the professional codes of ethics that researchers can turn to for guidance when attempting to think through the challenges of online research. In these codes, references to the public and private become tied into the official sanctioning and legitimising of certain research activities. Here too, however, the public/private distinction and its implications for research emerge as a site of negotiation and contestation.

How is the public/private distinction configured in this guidance? Despite the significance of the public/private relationship for research, Spicker has suggested that ethical codes 'tend to be vague about the distinction between the public and private' (2007, 2). As he notes however, a number of codes do mention this relationship specifically. Spicker cites the Social Research Association who suggest that:

> There can be no reasonable guarantee of privacy in 'public' settings since anyone from journalists to ordinary members of the public may constitute 'observers' of such human behaviour and any data collected thereby would remain, in any case, beyond the control of the subjects observed.
>
> (SRA 2003, p33, cited in Spicker 2007, 2)

[4] McCullagh suggests that such activities can be regarded as a 'provocative challenge since the act of publication implies some waiver of privacy' (McCullagh 2007, no page numbers).

The extent to which the observed subject is able to control the audience that is party to their behaviour is central to the definition of public domain settings presented here. There are different aspects to this control however: firstly in respect of delineating the *who* of the watching audience (in private domains, the guidelines suggest, the observing audience can be contained; in public ones, this is impossible) and secondly in respect of controlling *how* this audience makes use of their observations (in public spaces this too is out of the individual's control, whereas in private settings, it is implied, there would be shared expectations of how the audience will act).

Other guidelines make similar references to research in public settings. The British Sociological Association guidelines suggest that research in public environments is potentially exempt from the ethical imperative to maintain confidentiality and privacy. These guidelines state that:

> There may be fewer compelling grounds for extending guarantees of privacy or confidentiality to public organisations, collectivises [Sic], governments, officials or agencies than to individuals or small groups.
>
> (BSA 2002)

The notion of 'publicness' is recruited in different ways in this extract. The guidelines suggest that the privacy of individuals need not be maintained if they are strongly affiliated with public bodies (i.e. if they are officials rather than regular citizens). At the same time, there is also the suggestion here that size matters; that smaller groups might be considered differently from larger bodies. The notion of what it means to be 'public' therefore emerges as relational, rather than fixed or innate.

Specialising to the Internet, the preliminary report of the Association of Internet Researchers Ethics Committee is more specific in presenting a number of examples of ethically acceptable covert research, one of which is research in:

> [...] contexts such as chatrooms which are always open to anyone and thus are 'public' in a strong sense, and in which:
>
> 1. user names are already pseudonymous
> 2. in light of their option to always 'go private' if they wish
>
> users thus <u>choose</u> to participate in the public areas of the chatroom and may thereby be understood to implicitly give consent to observation.
>
> (Ess 2001, no page nos., his emphasis)

Like the Social Research Association guidelines, this extract suggests that 'public' settings/contexts may be legitimate sites in which to carry out covert research. The use of inverted commas suggests the slipperiness of this term however, an inflection that is reinforced by the suggestion that a context can be public in a 'strong sense' (which introduces the possibility of a site being public in a 'weak sense'). Whilst this guidance suggests that it may be acceptable to carry out covert forms of research within public spaces, beneath this example is the caveat: 'it should be noted that not all committee members agree'. With this comment, the openness of the guidance is established and the onus placed back on the researcher to establish a position in respect of whether the contexts of their research are more or less 'public' or 'private'.

Internet researchers' responses to this challenge have been founded on localised moves which – like the approach to ethics described in Chap. 1 – have involved the rejection of general principles and steps towards more complex, relational definitions of the status of online sites/material. This move emphasises a similar challenge to the idea of there being a unitary, natural distinction between the public and private that can unproblematically be recognised, as that expressed by Raymond Geuss. This production of localised definitions of public/private can be seen in the rejection of conceptualisations of the public/private distinction as 'uni-dimensional, rigidly dichotomous and absolute, fixed and universal' (Marx 2001, 160), in favour of the configuring of this relationship as:

> [...] multi-dimensional (with dimensions sometimes overlapping or blurred and at other times cross cutting or oppositional), continuous and relative, fluid and situational or contextual, whose meaning lies in how they are interpreted and framed.
>
> (Marx 2001, 160)

Those promoting such positions have suggested that, in defining the status of online research settings, researchers should take into account the complex and dynamic nature of technologies and the activities they support. However, in doing so, scholars have looked to the Internet in very different ways. In thinking about how we might go about approaching the definition of online settings in the context of our own research, it is worth examining the contrasting moves made in this literature.

Approaching the Public/Private Distinction: Technical/Perceived Privacy

Researchers' varying responses to the challenges of assessing the status of online phenomena have suggested contrasting perspectives from which readings of online data as public and/or private can be produced. Two approaches have been particularly influential. These propose that data is public 'either (1) if publicly accessible or (2) if perceived as public by participants' (Rosenberg 2010, 24). These perspectives – and the 'technical' and 'perceived' approaches to privacy that underpin them – provide a key starting point for the consideration of the strategies by which Internet researchers have fixed their research data in relation to the public/private distinction.

'Technical' Approaches to Online Environments

In approaching the task of defining online material as private or public, we might begin by considering the nature of the environment that houses the activity that we are interested in. From outside of the setting, we could focus on the organisation of the setting and ways that access to the environment is granted and regulated.

How does one arrive here? How does one enter? Who is allowed in? Who is excluded? The answers to these questions will not provide us with a rich understanding of what goes on in the setting, focusing instead on the specifications of the context. Here, definitions of what is public and what is private would be based on the site's visibility and openness.

This emphasis is suggested in Storm A. King's 1996 paper 'Researching Internet Communities: Proposed Ethical Guidelines for the Reporting of Results' (one of the works that Susan Herring took as her focus in the paper discussed in Chap. 2). Writing at a time when consideration of the ethics of online research was relatively new – regarded by some as a new frontier separate from conventional concerns about the protection of human subjects – King is critical of those who disrupt online communities through their research activities. He is particularly critical of those engaged in the covert observation of online environments and any subsequent naming of sites in the reporting of research. In seeking to develop ethical guidelines for such work, King presents a distinction between two 'dimensions' 'by which individual Internet communities may be evaluated in order to assure the ethical reporting of research findings' (King 1996, no page nos.), suggesting that each dimension can display different degrees of publicness/privateness.

The first of these is the technical level of publicness/privateness of the environment. King refers to this as 'group accessibility', 'the degree with which the existence of and access to a particular Internet forum or community is publicly available information' (ibid). A focus on 'group accessibility' suggests that the prospective Internet researcher can approach an online environment by looking for certain markers of openness that might be regarded as signalling the publicness of the setting. Just as we might ascertain the publicness of an offline setting in reference to closed doors and invitations to enter, the researcher can check for access-related markers of privacy online. Is a password required to access the content held within the environment? Are gatekeepers involved? How is the site advertised to an external audience? Such an approach can be used to contrast sites with different levels of publicness/privateness. King suggests that an unmoderated bulletin board community has a high level of group accessibility, whereas a 'private, closed email group where the subscription address is not published and there are enforced requirements to join' has a far lower level of group accessibility (King 1996, no page numbers).

By focusing on the accessibility of online environments, the researcher can argue that if a site is open to the gaze of an uncontrollable audience, it should be deemed public. In Christina Allen's paper, 'What's wrong with the "golden rule"? Conundrums of Conducting Ethical Research in Cyberspace' (1996), for example, Allen distinguishes public from private spaces within MOOs, arguing that the former are open for study without the need for informed consent due to the openness of access (Allen 1996, see also Roberts et al. 2003).

This position is rooted in the idea that 'the community which declares "All are welcome" thereby foregoes its privacy' (Homan 1980, 57), an equating of visibility and access with publicness that supports the idea that 'Public actions [are those that] can be publicly observed' (Spicker 2007, 2). This conceptualisation of the constitution of public spaces is suggested by Erving Goffman's description of the public/private distinction in *Behaviour in Public Places*:

> Traditionally, 'public places' refer to any regions in a community *freely accessible* to members of that community; 'private places' refer to *soundproof regions* where only members or invitees gather.
>
> (Goffman 1963, 9 – my emphasis)

Here, we have what Frankel and Siang (1999) term the 'technological point of view', the suggestion that technical accessibility equates with publicness (Bakardjieva and Feenberg 2001, 232).

If our research involves clearly demarcated regions that have clear borders and entry points, it might be relatively easy to take such an approach. But assessing the openness of access to a site can be tricky. Whilst the sorts of environments that King is talking about involve the bounded communities of early forums (King gives the example of discussion groups, support groups, Usenet, and MUDs) – all of which are easily recognisable as distinct contexts and are presented as having quite stable technical markers of access – not all online environments share these features. Many raise questions about what we might mean by open access (access to what?, openness in respect of what?).

A site like *Facebook*, for example, is problematic because it could be regarded as technically open or technically closed. It is public, in that anyone with an email account can gain access to it, but also private, as a membership account and password is required to enter. Yet, as anyone with access to a computer can request a password, despite this entry point, the site is 'freely accessible'. Such sites have been termed 'semi-public' as they involve membership and require registration but are open to all (Sveningsson Elm 2009, 74).[5] Within *Facebook*, there is further regulation of access: access to content is constrained by personalised privacy settings which enable users to set their own levels of visibility and openness. The status of the content within the site can therefore be differentiated between understanding of *Facebook* as a whole (what it presents to the friendless visitor who enters and searches for contacts) and the status of individual profiles.[6] At the same time, despite

[5] Sveningsson makes a distinction between four degrees of privacy – public sites such as open websites; semi-public settings such as social networks; semi-private sites, which require registration and place certain restrictions on memberships; and completely private sites, which are hidden and invitation-only (Sveningsson Elm 2009, 75). These distinctions enable a move away from either/or public/private distinctions.

[6] During the writing of this book, the media has been reporting an ongoing saga relating to changes to *Facebook's* privacy settings; specifically the introduction of an 'everyone' setting which would have made public posts visible to Facebook's entire userbase. Despite Facebook's promoters encouraging users to select this status in respect of their posting activity (but not personal information such as phone numbers (Kirkpatrick 2009a)) – the introduction of this setting raised concerns about users' awareness of the visibility of their actions. Although it was introduced with the ability to segment the visibility of certain types of messages to certain audiences – demonstrating the tailored way that users of the site can control access to their information – this development made 'public messages' visible to the entire community for the first time. This encouragement of public visibility was seen by many as problematic, not least because there were concerns that individuals do not understand privacy settings – and also because, if users have not made changes to their privacy settings in the past, they would automatically be set to 'everyone' (Kirkpatrick 2009a, b; Oreskovic 2009).

the appearance of control that *Facebook's* privacy settings imply, as the small print suggests, all content is owned by *Facebook*:

> Any Facebooker who bothered to read the fine print when signing up should already know they've granted the social networking giant 'an irrevocable, perpetual, non-exclusive, transferable, fully paid, worldwide license to use' their personal information at leisure. (http://news.ninemsn.com.au/article.aspx?id=323524)

The resulting fortress nature of the environment has been reflected in concerns over third-party access to personal information on the site (Oreskovic 2009), as even if users deploy the strongest privacy settings, they cannot control the ultimate destination of their contributions to the site.

Facebook demonstrates some of the challenges of applying technical criteria to online environments. Although assessing the openness of access to an online environment can be difficult, this approach does suggest distinct points of focus that can be used to establish a working definition of the public/private status of a setting. Whilst these questions can only be answered by looking at the specificity of the context, they come from outside of the setting and are based on markers of privacy and openness that are external to it (e.g. absence of registration = openness). The focus here then is on the regulative organisation of the environment, a consideration of its specifications, and how it is framed in relation to other types of settings.

From Technical to Perceived Privacy

By focusing on technical, organisational features of access, researchers can define the status of an environment in relation to external criteria that are relatively stable (if not always easy to apply). Yet the argument that the technical openness of a site is a marker of its publicness and that the setting, once so defined, can be studied without the need to acquire permission from its inhabitants has been condemned as tactical, convenient, and ethically flawed. A central concern in critiques of technical approaches is that although posting a message online 'may have parallels to publishing a letter in a newspaper or saying something in a public meeting', researchers cannot assume that those participating online are always 'seeking public visibility' (Eysenbach and Till 2001, 1104). A contrasting approach has developed in this work, one that focuses on these participants and 'emphasises paying attention to the users' own experience of the context with they interact within [sic]' (Bromseth 2002, 37). This approach challenges the conceptual foundations of technical approaches to the public/private distinction by focusing on the expectations of privacy held by the subjects of online research. Specifically, how do participants within online environments understand their surroundings?

Dennis Waskul and Mark Douglass, for example, suggest that a focus on technical access has led to the 'oversimplified public versus private dichotomy of "domains" of cyberspace' (Waskul and Douglass 1996, 131). Challenging such easy distinctions, they make reference to the expectations of Internet users, asserting that:

> A participant that posts a message to a sexual abuse survivors group intends the message to be read by participants of that sexual abuse survivors group – not by persons accessing alt.sex.erotica, members of an Alcoholics Anonymous support group, a social researcher, or anyone else, in spite of the fact that such messages may be accessible to these persons. [...] Because the medium is generally 'publicly' accessible, some persons seem inclined to define the activities that comprise it as equally 'public.' This is an ethically dangerous misconception. [..] It is misleading to conclude that on-line environments labelled or otherwise described as public are necessarily representative of participants' social definition of that environment. The declaration of some domains of cyberspace as 'public' can encourage researchers to perceive such interactions as 'fair game.'
>
> (Waskul and Douglass 1996, 131–132)

Such arguments suggest that the researcher should defer to, or at least take into account, the ways that inhabitants understand these environments and remember that even though they may be participating in technically 'public' environments, some community members 'do not expect to be research subjects' (Eysenbach and Till 2001).

Here, we have the second dimension that King suggests, the level of 'perceived privacy'. In contrast to the focus on access, this dimension of privacy is understood through consideration of 'the degree to which group members perceive their messages to be private to that group' (King 1996, no page numbers). King suggests that 'approaching a community from the perspective of a participant' can enable Internet researchers to evaluate the status of the group 'on several dimensions in order to determine if non-reactive[7] methods are necessary or justified' (King 1996, no page numbers).

How might one gain an understanding of users' perceptions of the privacy of their actions? The extract from Waskul and Douglass's paper presented above is perhaps problematic as it suggests that the expectations of a particular type of Internet user (the imagined member of the 'sexual abuse survivors group') can be presumed from the nature of the site they are participating in. Although it is easy to imagine that an individual involved in such a setting might expect or hope for a certain type of membership/audience, this description seems to be underpinned by an idea that particular domains of cyberspace house particular expectations regarding privacy. This would appear to be guilty of the same ontologising move that Waskul and Douglass challenge in their criticism of attempts to define domains of cyberspace in relation to the public/private distinction, it is just that the reference point has shifted from 'public or private' to 'expectations of public or private'.

The work of other Internet researchers suggests that privacy expectations might be gauged in alternative ways. The researcher might survey Internet users' understanding of the privacy of their actions, for instance (e.g. Viegas 2005). Or they could set up an experimental design and intentionally disrupt online settings in order to gauge reactions to the presence of researchers (as James Hudson and Amy Bruckman did in their study of users' expectations of privacy in chat rooms (2004, 2005)). 'Covert' researchers, who have decided not to make contact with their participants, might make reference to their postings or online actions, looking to the setting to ascertain participants' stated understandings of the environment and its

[7] By which King appears to be referring to unannounced observation.

audience. This approach has been proposed by Alison Cavanagh (1999), who suggests that the researcher should examine how participants respond to two main issues: firstly how they react to lurkers[8] and secondly how they express their understanding of the degree of openness of the space they are inhabiting (Cavanagh 1999, no page nos.). It is also possible to ascertain understandings of privacy expectations from the responses of participants within online environments to external interventions that do not involve the actions of researchers. Bromseth has described the expressions of surprise that members of the online group she studied voiced when 'people outside the group responded to what they had written' (Bromseth 2002, 46), and the hostile response of the administrators of a feminist list to the recontextualisation of postings from the list onto another site by a male member of the group (46). Such responses suggest a sense of outrage that might appear to signify a breach of a personal border (Marx 2001, 158).

As well as exploring the articulation of expectations of *privacy* online, researchers have also made reference to perceptions of *publicness* in delineating their approach to online environments. The fan studies scholar Matt Hills, for example, has explored fans' awareness of the (public) audience in the 'self-representation and self-performance of audience-as-text' (Hills 2002, 177) within fan communities. Hills emphasises the authored, published, and attention-seeking nature of interactions on such sites, suggesting they:

> [...] are thoroughly rather than contingently textual insofar as they are composed with an imagined audience in mind and are thus always already claims for attention prior to any academic scrutiny.
>
> (Hills 2002, 176)

Here then, we can see how a researcher might examine activity within a site to ascertain users' perceptions of publicness/privateness. Eysenbach and Till (2001) take a slightly different approach. They propose that researchers might assess the 'perceived level of privacy' within a site by moving from a focus on the opinions/expressions of individuals to a consideration of the characteristics of the site that might be understood to inform participants' expectations of privacy. This introduces a half-way position between technical and perceived privacy approaches, involving localising moves in respect of different aspects of the site. This includes whether or not registration is required (they suggest that if it is, 'most of the subscribers are likely to regard the group as a "private place"' (1104)), and the number of members of the site (they argue that 'a posting to a mailing list with 10 subscribers is different from a posting to a mailing list with 100 or 1000 subscribers' (1104)); 'perhaps most importantly', they state, the researcher should examine the 'individual group's norms and codes, target audience, and aim, often laid down in the "frequently asked questions" or information files of an Internet community' (1104). This involves a call to draw in a consideration of the ethics of the setting into researchers' emerging understanding of the relative publicness/privateness of online environments.

[8] Those who visit sites without ever posting.

From Environment to Content

Alongside consideration of the features of the environments in which researchers operate, scholars have also emphasised the significance of the subject matter and substantive *content* of online settings when considering the public/private status of online data (e.g. Sveningsson Elm 2009). This focus emphasises the notion that 'information is defined as public by its character, not by its location' (Spicker 2007, 2). Variability emerges here in terms of the varying sensitivity of material, vulnerability of users, and disclosure of personal information online. Like the technical/perceived privacy approaches to the status of online environments described above, attention to the status of online content requires local understanding of our research contexts, but shifts attention away from the nature/understanding of environments, towards consideration of the status of the material held within them.[9]

It is possible to start from an external understanding of what content, population, or subject matter might be regarded as sensitive or vulnerable. Topics that have been flagged as sensitive (e.g. 'safe sex practices, domestic violence, alcoholism' (Dickson-Swift et al. 2008, 4)), for example, have tended to be categorised as such from outside the activity. We would be aware that a setting likely to be populated by children would be regarded as containing sensitive content, and, even before entering into such sites, we might imagine that a support group would be more vulnerable than the sort of fan communities that I have studied (which, as Hills suggests above, are often confident in their presentation of self to public audiences). These are the sorts of external reference points that get flagged in ethical checklists ('Does your research involve children, or sensitive groups?'); checklists that are imbedded in the ways that research ethics are themselves regulated.

These questions can be asked because they reflect general concerns that extend across different contexts of research, and are based on external assessments of what groups/topics/activities require heightened ethical protections. They also reflect external attitudes about the status of different types of empirical activity. Reference to other interest groups provides illustrations of the ways that external assessments of subject matter may lead researchers to differentiate between settings. Whilst it might be easier (indeed necessary) to support covert research in the study of a hate group, it might be more difficult to defend the covert study of health-related discussion boards such as the autism discussion groups studied by Charlotte Brownlow and Nancy O'Dell. These authors suggest that such groups are 'the most vulnerable populations' on the Internet (Brownlow and O'Dell 2002).

---

[9] Interestingly, there seems to be some merging of content and context in King's (1996) presentation of degrees of perceived privacy. Rather than looking to actual examples of how participants understand the settings, he defines this through a focus on content. King presents an academic discussion group (where visibility is an aim) as an example of low perceived privacy, and support groups as an example of sites with high perceived privacy (King 1996, no page nos.). This appears to involve a presumption based on the content of the sites (the subject that is the focus of the group's interest) rather than the perceptions of participants.

Sites where users share personal information – such as social networking sites – also appear to present particular challenges to researchers because they draw in participants' offline identities, involving the display of the personal within public arenas (Snee 2008). As described earlier, a site like *Facebook* can be defined as private or as public (or as Sveningsson Elm (2009) has suggested, semi-public). One reason that this is so problematic is that the site contains personal information. Discourse surrounding *Facebook* contains anxiety about the status of information on the site and the vulnerability of users in respect of identity theft, and the ways that 'private' online information can impact the offline self (as demonstrated by the growing use of *Facebook* in the USA by law enforcement officers (Hodge 2006)). It is for this reason that such work is regarded as problematic by some (e.g. Zimmer 2009).

Focusing on content as an indicator of privacy, we might, therefore, be wary of subjects that are 'taboo' (Faberow 1963), that have the potential to generate harm to the researcher/researched, or that deal with personal or sensitive issues (Lee 1993; Renzetti and Lee 1993). This external classification of what material is, and is not, sensitive can be seen to be based on a similar external stance to the technical approach to defining the publicness of a particular environment. In each case, the focus is on external criteria, generally identifiable topics/interests/populations that are flagged as particularly sensitive, private, or vulnerable.[10] There is also an attention here to the institutionalisation of differences between discourses, distinctions that would regard health, or education, or discussion of personal information as serious and demanding of increased ethical attention (in order to protect against harm), whereas the discussion of television programmes, for example, might not. Such judgements would also be external to the activity itself.

The sensitivity or vulnerability of researched activity cannot just be defined from an external perspective however. Scholars have also recognised the fact that 'the topics and activities defined as sensitive vary widely across cultures and situations' (Dickson-Swift et al. 2008, 3) and that the 'definition of a "sensitive" research topic is dependent on both context and cultural norms and values' (McCosker et al. 2001, no page nos.).[11] The methodological literature on sensitive research suggests that it is a mistake to define 'sensitive' studies without taking into account the local contexts in which researchers operate. For this reason, like those promoting attention to Internet users' perceptions of their online privacy, researchers have also focused on insider perceptions of the sensitivity of specific activities.

The limitations of what might be termed 'technical' approaches to the sensitivity or privacy of content become evident when we look at how Internet users react to the presence of researchers. As I described in Chap. 1, Internet users have, on occasion, responded angrily to researchers' observation of their online activity, even when this activity would not be regarded as 'sensitive' from an external perspective. As Herring has argued (1996), it would be a mistake to regard computer-mediated communication as homogenous.

[10] Lee has referred to such themes as topics of 'perceived sensitivity' (1993) – here, however, the perception of sensitivity comes from the outside observer, rather than participants involved in the activity.

[11] At the same time, there is need for cautious attention throughout the research process as 'the sensitive nature of the research may not be apparent at the beginning of the research project, alternatively a subject that was presumed to be of a sensitive nature may not be' (McCosker et al. 2001, no page nos.).

At the same time, our expectations about specific types of activity may be misplaced. Empirical material may surprise us, as Lee and Renzetti (1993) suggest in their consideration of what is meant by 'sensitive topics' in social science research. They note how:

> The sensitive nature of a particular topic is emergent. In other words, the sensitive character of a piece of research seemingly inheres less in the topic itself and more in the relationship between the topic and the social context within which the research is conducted. It is not uncommon, for example, for a researcher to approach a topic with caution on the assumption that it is a sensitive one, only to find that those initial fears had been misplaced. Neither is it unusual for the sensitive nature of an apparently innocuous topic to become manifest once research is underway.
>
> (Lee and Renzetti 1993, 5)

Sveningsson Elm presents a different inflection on the uncertain status of sensitive topics, describing how in online contexts; 'what may seem private/sensitive to an observer is not necessarily apprehended so by the individual who exposed the content' (Sveningsson Elm 2009, 82). She goes on to describe how:

> In my study of a Swedish web community [...], the users' practices suggest that they do not consider their personal pages, including personal profile, diary, and photo album, as specifically private. For example, they often put out 'ads' in the more publicly visited spots of the web community, where they urge people to come visit their personal pages, to watch and comment on their photos and diaries, and to sign their guest books. Not only do they seem to be aware of the risk of having their material observed by others but also the attention from others is often what they seek.
>
> (Sveningsson Elm 2009, 82)

Such accounts remind us both that 'topics and activities defined as sensitive vary widely across cultures and situations' (Dickson-Swift et al. 2008, 3) and that we cannot assume that people wish to be protected online.

Rather than deciding which content is sensitive from an external perspective, it is, then, also possible to take an approach that focuses on how the sensitivity of content is interpreted within our research settings. This involves taking an insider perspective, using local understandings of activity to inform our handling of data in a similar way to the perceived privacy approach to defining the status of online contexts. It also implies a more complex assessment of the sensitivity of the content of online environments than that offered by external checklists. Different sites might indeed need to be handled differently. Just as discussion of an apparently trivial topic could be taken seriously by participants, however – with high stakes investment regarding online identity, for example – so too an apparently vulnerable or sensitive site could contain playful discussion that might not be deemed 'sensitive' by its inhabitants.

Unsettling Distinctions

The contrast between technical/perceived privacy approaches to environment (and content) draws attention to the varying evidence that may fuel the production of a definition of a site or activity as public/private. It also suggests that researchers should consider, and be explicit about, their objectification of their research settings. Those who fail to do so may open themselves up to criticism. Langer and Beckman (2005), for example, defend their use of covert methods in sensitive research by stating that the sites that constituted their research settings – Internet message boards devoted to the discussion of cosmetic surgery – were 'regarded as a public communication media' (197) and contained 'intentionally public postings by the authors' (197). Yet the grounds for this definition are not clearly specified. In this case, the explanation and defence of research actions would be strengthened were the reader to know more about the empirical basis of these statements. As I have described, there are different indicators of privacy that researchers might signal in marking out their approach to their research settings. These can be used in combination to reinforce or challenge a particular reading of the status of a site or type of data; as Sveningsson Elm (2009) stresses, although they have often been set in opposition, technical and perceived approaches to the status of online environments/content are not mutually exclusive.

The contrast between technical and perceived approaches to privacy does however introduce an important distinction between 'objective' and 'subjective' markers of privacy. Because they focus on external, generalisable markers of privacy, technical indicators of access- like categories of 'sensitive' research- appear to suggest objective recognition principles: if the door is closed, the setting is private; if the door is open, it is public; if a site is dedicated to the discussion of certain types of activity/subject matter, it is sensitive, etc. In contrast, approaches that focus on users' interpretations of online environments/content – in suggesting that the public/private distinction be understood 'as a perception, not a fact' (Sveningsson Elm 2009, 72) – emphasise more subjective negotiations of what constitutes privacy.

These contrasting perspectives have methodological implications, suggesting different observational stances. A focus on more 'objective' markers of privacy, for instance, configures the researcher as standing outside the researched activity, recruiting criteria that are external to it. In contrast, a focus on more subjective markers implies an understanding of the activity that is informed by an insider perspective. The former (being based on external criteria) requires less direct, or prolonged, involvement with the setting. The latter demands that the researcher 'goes in' to the site in order to gain a sense of the way that participants understand it. (This does not mean, however, that the researcher needs to make themselves visible within an activity, e.g. by posting, or make direct contact with participants.) The more embedded stance, with the researcher looking to local instantiations of the researched activity to explore users' 'perceptions', also suggests something of the ethnomethodological in developing a sense of the expectations and interpretive strategies that are brought to bear on behaviour in social settings (see Bromseth 2002 for a discussion of the insider/outsider distinction in relation to access/perception approaches to privacy).

There are, then, different ways of distinguishing between public and private contexts. Within qualitative Internet research however, approaches based on perceptions of privacy have increasingly been presented as being more virtuous than those that focus on technical features of access. Both Rosenberg (2010) and Sveningsson

Elm (2009) describe this development: Internet researchers' move away from an initial reliance on technical openness as providing an open door to research, towards perspectives informed by the idea of perceived privacy. A narrative emerges here, implying that researchers have advanced in their thinking, moving away from earlier, less sophisticated, and more limited interpretations of online contexts. According to Rosenberg, for example, this shift is:

> [...] a move in the right direction [as] viewing the people we study as experts, rather than subjects, is likely to produce more comprehensive and nuanced accounts of online environments. Letting our research be guided increasingly by those we wish to study may also lead our own conceptions to be expanded or even challenged in the process.
>
> (Rosenberg 2010, 24)

The growing emphasis on users' experiences is perhaps unsurprising due to the interpretive nature of qualitative research and the increasing recognition of the complexity of the public/private distinction as manifest in online environments. Yet as moral value has been attributed to more subjective approaches to privacy, this work has occasionally slipped into a reification of perceptions as presenting 'true' or authentic markers of privacy.

Such positioning is visible in discussion of the extent to which, in establishing their methodological approach, the researcher should defer to the expectations of the researched. Take, for example, the propriety of researching situations that persons might mistakenly believe to be private to themselves but are open to the gaze of outsiders – seen online in the actions of Internet users who may 'seem to consider themselves hidden even while their writing is completely public' (Busse 2009, no page nos.).[12] In a 1959 paper on covert observation, Edward Shils argued that:

> Although there might be some uncertainty regarding the propriety of entering, by permission, into the private sphere, there seems to me to be no doubt at all about the impropriety of unauthorised entry when the persons are observed in situations *which they legitimately regard as private to themselves*, as persons or as a corporate body.
>
> (Shils 1982 [1959], 133 – my emphasis)

What if these expectations of privacy are not 'legitimate'? As I described earlier in this chapter, understandings of the publicness of online contexts are complex and diverse. What if our research subjects' expectations appear misguided? Should we respect them? How should researchers approach activity where, in Goffman's terms, 'open, unwalled public places' may be (mis)regarded by members of Internet communities as 'soundproof regions' (Goffman 1963, 10)?

Waskul and Douglas (1996) take a strong position on this issue, prioritising the experience and expectations of the researched, even if this expectation might not appear 'legitimate'. They complain that:

[12] Busse suggests that this may be related to assumptions that 'information overload will hide them in semi-anonymity'.

> Apparently, it is easy for some researchers to legitimize the exploitation of a 'public domain' by simply declaring participants as having a 'false' sense of privacy, or in 'denial' of the public nature of their communications. Or worse yet, through legitimizing a 'fair game' mentality solely in appeals to law and/or ethical theory, such a viewpoint can promote a researcher to completely fail to acknowledge participants altogether. Such a perspective is intellectually barbaric and clearly unethical. Simply stated, researchers do not have the right to redefine the context of the research situation (the experience of the participants) to meet their own vested interests and aims.
>
> (Waskul and Douglas, 132)

Bakardjieva and Feenberg (2001) establish a similar position somewhat more gently, arguing that:

> [...] the very fact that many members of online communities are only vaguely aware of the public nature of their exchanges suggests the need for caution. Their trust may be misplaced, but nevertheless it is not good for researchers to violate it without a compelling rationale.
>
> (Bakardjieva and Feeberg 2001, 239)

These arguments are founded upon the notion that even if the expectations of participants are misplaced, they should, on the whole, be respected. The problem with this is that it suggests that adhering to the ethics of the researched is the best thing we can do for our research participants. As I described in Chaps. 1 and 2, it is important that we attend to the ethics of our research contexts in developing our ethical stances. This may involve greater or lesser interaction and reciprocity in the formulation of research between researcher and researched, depending on the nature of the study. What is questionable here, however, is the idea that the expectations of our participants – the way they define the research contexts – should impose decisions on research (unless 'compelling' alternatives can be found). This ignores the fact that listening to our participants might not prevent us from doing them harm. It also implies a certain type of relationship to the setting – one that is based on similarity, rather than potential differences between researcher/researched (as I will describe in Chap. 5 not all research relationships are the same...).

Such perspectives can be contrasted with positions that suggest that, rather than adhering to the expectations of the researched, researchers should attempt to shape Internet users' expectations by taking a more pedagogic stance. This educative drive has been suggested by a number of scholars (e.g. Herring 1996; Walther 2002). For Walther:

> More fruitful efforts might be made in educating the public about the vulnerability of Internet postings to scrutiny – an inherent aspect of many Internet venues – than by debating whether or not such scrutiny should be sanctioned in research.
>
> (Walther 2002, 207)

As Nancy Baym has suggested,[13] posters to Internet sites are potentially under the gaze of other agents such as marketing companies, whose interests are perhaps more problematic than those of researchers. In such contexts, is it not the researcher's responsibility to educate rather than respecting users' potentially misguided

[13] Association of Internet Researchers conference in 2004.

perceptions of the settings they inhabit? Such calls configure a different sort of relationship between the researcher/researched to that presented by those who argue that researchers should broadly adhere to the expectations of Internet users, and represent a very different view of the idea of researchers' responsibilities to their research settings.

These debates might appear to be more relevant to online than offline research. However, researchers working in offline environments can experience similar dilemmas. We might observe private activity in public settings (Homan 1991), and, as Marx suggests:

> Even in the clearest of locations as with a bench in a public park, expectations regarding private behavior (apart from the right to enter) are manifest. Allen (1988) for example notes that when venturing into a public area we hardly give up *all* expectations of privacy.
>
> (Marx 72001, 163 – his emphasis)

Wakeford's (2003) account of observational research in Internet cafes provides an example of the way that Internet users can fail to comprehend the visibility of their actions in offline settings. She describes computers that had not been logged out of after users had finished their previous sessions, and CVs left on desktops offering up private information to the next unknown user (Wakeford 2003, 397). In these offline environments, private content was technically made public. Here too there was an apparent need to educate.

The focus on users' perceptions of the privacy of their environments/actions can also be unsettled by a consideration of *whose* perspectives we should privilege when studying online domains. In their description of the website Gaygirls.com, for example, Bassett and O'Riordan's (2002) focus on language use as an indicator of participants' expectations of privacy. Their analysis of the setting suggests a tension between the expectations of the members and owners of the site:

> The language used [by members] was personal, informal and intimate in content. There was an illusory sense of partial privacy because the participants constructed utterances that they stated they would not convey to certain audiences such as their family. This facilitated the participant's illusion that Gaygirls.com was a space over which they exercised some control, and in which they could expect quite high levels of confidentiality, safety and freedom. In contrast to the participant's expectations, there was, in actual fact no control over who viewed the material on the web site: forums on Gaygirls.com are in no way 'private'. The language used by the producers of Gaygirls.com indicated that the forum was open and public and they likened it, through simile, to a way of amplifying voices in public debate.
>
> (Bassett and O'Riordan 2002, 241)

The disjunction identified here between the perspectives of the owners and members of this site demonstrates that the membership of an online environment is unlikely to form a unified group with shared expectations. In light of this, we might consider which expectations the researcher should heed attention to if taking a perceived privacy approach: whether, for example, the opinions of owners carry more weight than those of individual members. Such questions are not unique to Internet research of course. Similar dilemmas are evident within debates over the authority of gatekeepers when obtaining access to offline domains. Discussion of these issues is common, for example, in relation to school-based research, which presents different levels of potential gatekeepers (heads of school, teachers, parents) and raises questions about the extent to which researchers protect the autonomy of children to decide whether they wish to participate in, or withdraw from, research (see Wiles et al. 2004).

Although they appear to be more objective/subjective, technical and perceived privacy approaches to privacy are always the outcome of the researchers' analysis. The description of Facebook's complex technical nature suggested the challenges of applying technical criteria to online sites but also signals the more general uncertainty that can exist regarding the interpretation of apparently 'objective' technical markers of privacy. The presence or absence of a password, for example, provokes an interpretation, rather than having a fixed meaning. We can also question the status of the more 'subjective' perceptions of Internet users. Like our readings of technical markers of privacy, 'perceived privacy' is the outcome of an engagement with empirical phenomena. The development of understandings of users' 'perception' is therefore an outcome of the researchers' analysis of the evidence available to them – whether this is responses to lurkers, postings on forums, or answers to our questions. It therefore involves an empirically based objectification, rather than channelling, of the setting and its membership. The authority we invest in these perceptions therefore needs to be assessed in relation to our own interpretive efforts in bringing them into being.

Finally, it is important to note that a working definition of a site/activity as public or private does not naturally lead to the identification of a 'right' course of action in the design of research or generation of data. The local gazes to the empirical involved in the presentation of technical/privacy approaches have, however, become linked to generalised arguments about the acceptability of different methods, presenting different attitudes towards covert research and the need for informed consent. Those promoting technical approaches, and focusing on access, have often argued for the use of data without informed consent (Rosenberg 2010), whilst those emphasising the perspectives of users have tended to be more critical of covert research methods, calling for the use of informed consent in Internet research.

At the same time, just as defining a site as 'public' should not lead us to unquestioningly use the data without consent, deciding that a setting's content is sensitive or vulnerable should not *automatically* lead to taking a protectionist stance.[14] Yet

[14] Other researchers have been more defensive in their presentation of work that examines - without informed consent - material that would be deemed sensitive from a regulative perspective – justifying their decisions in relation to different domains of ethics. In their study of online communication relating to breast and prostate cancer and sexual health, for example, Seale et al. (2010) justify their use of data from the sites in relation to the open access nature of the material and the authority of academics. They note that two of the authors – moderators of one of the sites involved – 'have given their permission for the material to be used for research purposes for this study' (598) and note how, in deciding to use material from the site, 'we have found support from editors and reviewers of academic journals who have thus far published our reports on these data' (598). Here, the researchers' stance is not just based on the technical features of the (open access) contexts, or the insider position of the authors, but also via an appeal to the authority of other academics who have approved the work (whether or not one is persuaded by their position is another matter of course).

this too is sometimes forgotten. Sveningsson Elm (2009), for example, suggests that in closed spaces such as private chat rooms, covert research would be 'clearly unsuitable, or even illegal' (76), noting that it is 'unnecessary' to state that the researcher should obtain consent in such places (80). Such judgements appear to fit into wider criticisms of covert research, and the way that (as Spicker has described) 'covert research is often seen as intrinsically illegitimate' (2011, 119). Although (as Sveningsson Elm notes) working in closed environments may raise practical difficulties (especially if the researcher seeks to enter into invitation-only sites), it is possible to imagine studies of online phenomena that could argue for the legitimacy of using covert methods to study private spaces. There is, after all, an established history of such work in offline research (e.g. in the fields of sociology and criminology), where covert methods have been used to explore dangerous, illicit, or illegal activities. The idea that it would 'clearly' be inappropriate to carry out covert research in private online settings therefore negates the possibility of researchers adopting approaches similar to those used in the 'real world'. This criticism of covert research therefore sets up an artificial, and perhaps unhelpful, distinction between online and offline research.

Beyond Technical/Perceived Privacy: Tacit and Explicit Markers of Privacy on COA and SHH

Two ideas can be taken from the unsettling of the technical/perceived privacy distinction presented above. Firstly, that the researcher should aim to be explicit about the empirical data that informs their definition of online data as public/private. Secondly, that they should consider their research actions in relation to, but not as prescribed by, these definitions. This again moves us away from the suggestion of 'natural' ethical methods or general principles (e.g. covert research in private contexts is bad, whereas use of data from public contexts is acceptable). Instead, what feeds our objectification should be separated from our ongoing concern that our research actions do not cause harm, so that we can consider the specific characteristics of our research when establishing our ethical stances, without slipping into moralising.

Because they have become closely tied into the articulation of value judgements about the legitimacy of methods, it is also perhaps worth stepping away from the distinction between technical and perceived (or objective/subjective) approaches to privacy. One way of doing this, I would argue, is to focus on the codification of privacy in the sites and activities we are interested in, the ways that publicness/privateness is articulated in our research settings.

Keeping hold of the separation of environment and content, I want to suggest that a useful distinction can be made between *tacit* and *explicit* markers of privacy. This involves a contrast between explicit statements regarding the public/private status of a setting or type of content, and tacit, generic, markers of privacy or sensitivity. We might, for instance, consider two different types of private documents: a bank statement and a love letter. Each may present the reader with explicit statements

	Explicit	Tacit
Environment	explicit statements/rules regarding regulation and access	generic expressions of privacy/openness
Content	explicit statements/rules regarding the nature of content	generic expressions regarding the nature of content

Fig. 3.1 Markers of privacy

regarding the nature of their content – 'private and confidential' or 'personal' written on the envelopes, for example. Yet each will also present a tacit and generic codification of privacy that needs to be interpreted as private, or personal, by the reader, the expression of romantic sentiments, for example, or presentation of financial information. Whether or not the reader recognises these documents as private will, of course, depend on the extent to which they understand the varied codification of privacy that they present. In this way, explicit statements can be seen to presume a general audience. In contrast, tacit markers of privacy assume a more informed audience.

The dimensions environment/content and explicit/tacit produce the schema (Fig. 3.1) presented above.

The varied types of evidence presented by scholars as examples of technical and perceived privacy include both tacit and explicit expressions of privacy. A site may have stated rules about access to the setting. In a note for visitors, the *Doctor Who* Forum at the fansite Outpost Gallifrey, for example, used to state the following explicit statement: 'The Outpost Gallifrey forum requires you to *register an account* before you read or post; this is a *private community* open only to registered users (to protect our users' privacy by preventing messages being archived in web searches such as Google.)'. As described earlier, a site may also present tacit markers of privacy by displaying/failing to display regulating entry points (passwords, gated areas) that implicitly signal privacy or openness. Participants too may make explicit statements about their perceptions of a site or its content as sensitive or open. Or they may share personal information, or make reference to shared histories (etc.), in ways that imply that they do not anticipate a public audience. For the researcher, uncertainty arises in respect of the meaning of tacit markers of privacy, due to the lack of shared understandings of generic privacy online. Yet explicit statements also need to be interpreted. The tacit/explicit distinction therefore reminds us of the constructed nature of any definition of a site as public or private.

The distinction between tacit and explicit markers of privacy can be used to consider my objectification of COA and SHH as being situated within the public domain. This definition was established in relation to both the ethics of the academy (the literature discussed in this chapter and the experience of other fan studies researchers as articulated within fan studies research) but also through my engagement with the local empirical details of the sites that constituted my research settings and a reading of different markers of privacy presented within these environments.

My initial engagement with COA and SHH included a search for explicit statements regarding the privacy expectations of the sites and their users. Upon reflection, this search involved a somewhat naive desire for external confirmation that my observation of the sites would be legitimate – that they were 'in fact' public – placing the responsibility to establish a position on the settings, rather than on myself. I was to be disappointed however, as neither setting contained guidance as explicit as that on Outpost Gallifrey. COA's Registration Agreement Terms outlined rules of behaviour for new members (i.e. outsiders) ('You agree not to post any abusive, obscene, vulgar, slanderous, hateful, threatening, sexually-oriented or any other material that may violate any applicable laws') and stated that anyone registering on the site should be '*over* or *exactly* 13 years of age' (therefore suggesting that access was restricted rather than open to all), but did not state how data from the site could (or should) be used, or how the privacy of the site was assessed by its owners. Later (as I will discuss in Chap. 6), I gained some understanding of the response of the participants of SHH to my approach to their activity as being in public domain when I shared my research with them. This provoked explicit reflection about how they understood the privacy of the setting and its content. This was, however, a side effect of disseminating my work to the site. Prior to this direct engagement with SHH, I relied more upon other evidence from the forums in approaching the settings. This led me to focus my attention onto the tacit markers of privacy presented on the sites.

A key (tacit) marker of the public status of these sites was their openness – their publicly accessible nature embodied in the lack of any need to register membership in order to view the posting activity on the forums. This openness had been significant in my selection of these sites, as I started by seeking locations that were technically open. Even within these two forums however, this 'publicness' was not all encompassing. The sites also contained closed-off areas that I excluded from my analysis, gated areas that were marked off with explicit statements stating them to be 'private' areas, unavailable to the gaze of visitors. These spaces (*The Underground Area* on COA, and the *Faculty Room* and *Library Reserve Room* on SHH) required registration or a particular level of status/membership for access and thus could not be regarded as 'public' in the same way as the rest of the forums. Access to these areas could be further differentiated. On COA, for example, the 'citizenship' necessary in order to access the restricted areas of the site could be achieved by simply registering; these areas thus remained relatively 'open' (when I registered as a member of the site, my account was activated by one of the site's administrators – yet this did not involve any interaction between us, or any request for me to provide information about my interest in the setting). In contrast, members of SHH needed a degree of status within the site (such as being a moderator or administrator) in order to enter the restricted SHH rooms. This served to complicate the public/private distinction in relation to this environment.

Like those promoting perceived privacy approaches, in approaching these sites, I also attempted to gain an understanding of how the publicness/privateness of the settings and the sensitivity of their content was understood by participants. This involved a process of education: learning about the nature of interactions on the site, and the types of exchanges common within day-to-day activity. I became particularly interested in the tacit awareness of audience articulated within forum activity, the ways that posts on COA and SHH appeared linguistically to make an appeal to a presumed but uncertain readership. This suggested an awareness of a public audience, indeed one that was necessary to the maintenance of activity within the sites. This expectation of audience is evident in the following post from the forums of SHH:

Posted: Wed 23 Jun, 2004 1:56 am Post subject: Help?
Um... Its not help with the game that I need... I need help finding pictures from the Silent Hill series. Maria ones would be nice. I'm having a hard time finding anything for Maria at ALL. Its always the same pictures and the quality is never that good. *frowns* I want to make a batch of Silent Hill icons, ya see. I'd really appreciate it if you guys could gimme a hand here. *puppy dog eyes*

The difficulty here is that the appeal to 'you guys' might appear to suggest a presumed inclusion (and hence, exclusion). The imagined audience might not, for example, include researchers (although as I noted earlier in this chapter, researchers such as Matt Hills have argued differently). The suggestion that 'there is a tendency to assume that participants are similar to oneself' (Smith 2004, 228) is evident in discourse on these sites, which often appeared to involve an imagined 'like-minded people' assumption.

Yet the forums also contained posts that emphasised the unknown status of this audience and the impossibility of members 'seeing' to whom they were speaking:

Anyone else still here?
Author: Date: 01-23-05 20:23 i hope i am not alone.

(*City of Angel* post)

Here, the audience is marked as unknowable and therefore out of the control of the poster.

In developing my understanding of the privacy expectations of the sites' members, I also looked at 'unlurkings' within these environments (see Baym 2000, 132) – moments when members come out to the group as having been observing the activity without positing up until this point (a practice that is referenced in other fancentric texts (Macdonald 1998; Gatson and Zweerink 2004)). Similar unlurkings were visible in my chosen research contexts where members introduced themselves to the sites:

> Greetings and salutations. I've been *lurking* around as one known as a guest for *quite some time* and I finally decided to join up seeing as the other forum I frequent crashed.
>
> Just wanted to say hi. I've been *lurking* on this board *for awhile* so thought I'd finally join ya.
>
> Hi everyone I'm new here. I've been a SH fan ever since the 1 was released and have been *lurking* on these forums *for some time* and decided to sign up My fave SH is 2 and I plan on getting 4 when its released over here in the UK! *(my emphasis)*

In these posts from SHH, we see an emphasis on lurking as an acceptable stage of initial involvement, but it can also be a preference (Wohlblatt 1996); there is no requirement that you have to post. Katherine Smith makes reference to the acceptability of lurking in her research setting to support her decision not to inform the site of her research (Smith 2004). Initially, I made a similar argument in defending my observational position on the forums. As I will describe in Chap. 5, this idea – that the acceptability of lurking on the sites meant that it was legitimate for me to also lurk – was later challenged.

My objectification of COA and SHH as being situated within the public domain can therefore be regarded as the outcome of a prolonged reading of both tacit and explicit markers of privacy. This definition of the settings as 'public' informed a number of key methodological decisions that I made during my study, including my decision to name the sites.[15] Whilst I would not reproduce a message sent in private email correspondence without the consent of the author – as the medium seems to attribute a firm (if perhaps illusory) sense of privacy – I decided that I would quote from these forums without asking for the consent of the participants. In doing so, I was careful to ensure that sensitive or personal material was not disseminated. Although the subject matter of these sites did not appear sensitive from an external, 'technical' perspective, as they focused on discussion of forms of popular entertainment, the forums did contain potentially sensitive material (including personal information such as email addresses that I did not present in my thesis). If I had been studying communities devoted to the discussion of sensitive topics, my own decisions would likely have been very different.[16] My research design, and the arguments that underpinned it, was accepted by those overseeing the project from an institutional perspective (although as I noted in Chap. 1, this did not involve full ethical review by an ethics committee as one had not yet been introduced in my university at that time).

My decisions were therefore based upon the 'public domain' status of the phenomena that constituted the empirical focus of my research. Yet, as I described at the beginning of this chapter, the status of the COA/SHH forums shifted during my study as restrictions were placed on access to previously open areas of the settings. As a member of the sites, I continued to observe the activity housed within these areas, but as a researcher, I decided to exclude these newly privatised areas from my

[15] To some Internet researchers, the identification of these sites in this way is a cardinal sin. Storm King (1996), for example, privileges the need to anonymise research settings as *the* key ethical move in Internet research. The decision to name research settings is a stance that has been taken by other researchers working in similar fan environments (including Jenkins 1995; Baym 2000; Gatson and Zweerink 2004; Bailey 2005; Black 2005; Gray 2005). However other researchers, such as Lori Kendall (2002) in her study of the MUD 'Bluesky', have chosen to anonymise their research settings. The repercussions of such an approach might be considered further. In the context of my own research, for example, the decision to anonymise the sites would have meant that I would potentially have had to also anonymise the TV series and videogame that the sites are devoted to. This would have had serious implications for any analysis of fans' discussion of these texts. In contrast, Kendall's research setting was an online 'pub'; the discussion was therefore not tied to anything as specific and identifiable as the *Silent Hill* and *Angel* texts.

[16] In such a situation, I think I would have been more likely to have contacted the owners to notify them of my interest, perhaps even requesting the opportunity to set up a forum or thread relating to the research project so that anyone taking part within the discussion within that part of the site would have been granting permission to use the data (an approach taken by Ito et al. in their study of SeniorNet 2001).

study, focusing my data collection on the main 'public' boards. The instability of these sites suggested the developmental, as well as contextual, nature of such definitions and the need to reestablish ethical stances during research (an issue to which I will return in Chap. 5).

The Public/Private Distinction and the Conduct of Research

In the early part of this chapter, I cited Geuss's statement that 'there is no such thing as *the* public/private distinction' (Geuss 2001), a rejection of the idea that there exist stable, natural, or common understandings of what is 'public' or 'private'. This chapter has explored the methodological implications of this statement, considering how researchers might operate in relation to the complex meshing of expectations and signifiers that signal notions of publicness/privateness in the empirical world. Doing away with the idea of there being a natural distinction between the public/private focuses attention on how such distinctions are constituted within research activity, and within the activities of those we research. My aim has been to identify different strategies for establishing working definitions of our research settings in respect of this intricate and tricky distinction. As my description of COA and SHH attests, defining the status of a site in relation to the public/private distinction can be a difficult endeavour. Websites are not homogeneous, and the activities of Internet users often suggest confusion and conflicting understandings of the privacy or openness of their actions. Both offline and online, the expectations of those we observe may be in conflict with more 'objective' definitions of the status of the environment. It is therefore important to emphasise the significance of paying attention to the local detail of our research contexts.

The chapter has explored different ways that researchers have approached the task of defining online contexts in relation to the public/private distinction. It has considered the difference between technical and perceived approaches to privacy and has introduced a distinction between tacit and explicit indicators of privacy. These different frameworks suggest that the ethical stances that researchers establish in respect of this distinction can be the outcome of different localising moves. They also emphasise particular points of emphasis and bias: as Herring (1996) suggests, the distinction between technical and perceived privacy is based on an understanding of computer-mediated communication as involving a 'personal dimension', looking to the human subjects involved in the settings. As I will discuss in the next chapter, there are other ways of approaching such material which informed my own focus on the codification of privacy. The consideration of tacit and explicit markers of privacy seeks to provide a way of moving beyond the moralising inherent within the perceived/technical privacy debate by focusing attention on the expression of privacy online, and the audiences that this expression assumes.

The chapter has also signalled a conceptual break between the production of a definition of a site as public or private and the legitimacy of the researcher's subsequent methodological actions. The researcher might feel that as long as they can establish that they are operating within a 'completely public' environment, it is safe to do so covertly and use data from the site. However, even if a site is defined as public, the decisions to carry out covert research will likely be challenged. Bakardjieva and Feenberg – who acknowledge the complex nature of the public/private distinction but also the public nature of certain environments – are firm in their criticism of covert observation:

> Methodologically, the best way to collect data on group discussions would probably be not to reveal one's presence and task to group members in order not to affect their behaviour and thus to be able to capture their naturally occurring discourse. This is technically feasible in the case of all online forums that are open to anyone to join. From an ethical perspective, however, if we had performed this kind of 'naturalistic' observation on unsuspecting subjects, we would have been little better than spies.
>
> (Bakardjieva and Feenberg 2001, 234)

Even those who discuss the public nature of particular settings provide mixed messages. Susan Barnes, for example, argues that certain settings are indeed public, but also that 'when researching any Internet group, it is a good idea to contact the group in advance and ask for permission to observe them' (Barnes 2004, 219). For this reason, the researcher needs to be confident that they are able to explain and defend the position they have taken.

I want to finish this chapter with a reference to my research journal from 2005, which suggests the complex way that the public/private distinction can be experienced. Working late one night, I was listening to Capital Radio's[17] 'Late Night Confessions' and a young-sounding girl (who said that she was 21) called up and said that (and I am paraphrasing here) 'her boyfriend wanted her to do something that she did not want to do, but that he had said that if she did not do it, it meant she did not love him'. The host of the phone-in was reacting as many would ('he's an idiot, get away from him' etc.) when suddenly the girl gasped, said that there was a call coming through on call waiting, and that she thought it might be him. The line then went dead.

In this incident, an individual mistook a broadcast for a private interaction. This broadcasting placed her words into the public domain and denied her control of their destination. We see similar moves everyday when people give out personal information whilst travelling on public transport (e.g. reading out telephone numbers or bank details into mobile telephones on the bus). The question then arises as to what the researcher should do when faced with material that has been presented within an apparently public setting due to a lack of awareness or forethought by the individual.

I have suggested that the public domain status of COA and SHH was of particular significance to the methodological choices I made. This is particularly the case in relation to my decision to carry out covert observation in these settings. In making an utterance in these contexts, members are unable to control their audience. This lack of control is implied in these settings in addresses to an unseen audience and in references to lurking. Like the girl phoning into Capital Radio, any assumption that the audience can be determined would be misguided, misreading a public setting as a private one. The final destination of an utterance posted in such contexts cannot be constrained, and neither can its audience. As this example suggests, when dealing with the complex nature of the public/private distinction (both offline and online), our responsibility as researchers might indeed be to educate rather than to protect.

---

[17] A local radio station in London.

References

Allen, A. (1988). Uneasy access: Privacy for women in a free society, Totowa, N.J.: Rowman and Littlefield.

Allen, C. (1996). What's wrong with the 'golden rule'? Conundrums of conducting ethical research in cyberspace. *The Information Society, 12*(2), 175–188.

Bailey, S. (2005). *Media audiences and identity: Self-construction in the fan experience.* New York: Palgrave Macmillan.

Bakardjieva, M., & Feenberg, A. (2001). Involving the virtual subject: Conceptual, methodological and ethical dimension. *Journal of Ethics and Information Technology, 2*(4), 233–248.

Banerjee, T. (2001). The future of public space: Beyond invented streets and reinvented places. *APA Journal, 67*(1), 9–24.

Barnes, S. B. (2004). Issues of attribution and identification in online social research. In M. D Johns, S. Chen, G. Jon Hall (Eds.), *Online social research: Methods, issues, & ethics* (pp. 203–222). New York: Peter Lang.

Bassett, E. H., & O'Riordan, K. (2002). Ethics of Internet research: Contesting the human subjects research model. *Ethics and Information Technology, 4*(3), 233–247.

Baym, N. (2000). *Tune in, log on: Soaps, fandom, and online community.* London: Sage.

Black, R. (2005). Access and affiliation: The literacy and composition practices of English languages learners in an online fanfiction community. *Journal of Adolescent & Adult Literacy, 49*(2), 118–128.

boyd, d. (2005). *Blogging outloud: Shifts in public voice.* Paper presented at LITA conference, October 1, 2005. Available online: http://www.danah.org/papers/LITA.html.

boyd, d. (2007). *Social network sites: Public, private, or what?* Available online: http://kt.flexible-learning.net.au/tkt2007/wp-content/uploads/2007/04/boyd.pdf.

boyd, d. (2008). Facebook's privacy trainwreck. *Convergence: The International Journal of Research into New Media Technologies, 14*(1), 13–20.

British Sociological Association. (2002). Statement of Ethical Practice for the British Sociological Association, available online: http://www.britsoc.co.uk/equality/Statement+Ethical+Practice.htm.

Bromseth, J. C. H. (2002). *Public places – public activities?* Paper presented at InterMedia, University of Oslo, April 8, 2002. Published in *Researching ICTs in Context*, A. Morrison (Ed.). Available online: http://www.intermedia.uio.no/konferanser/skikt-02/docs/Researching_ICTs_in_context-Ch3-Bromseth.pdf.

Brownlow, C., & O'Dell, L. (2002). Ethical issues for qualitative research in on-line communities. *Disability & Society, 17*(6), 685–694.

Busse, K. (2009). Attention economy, layered publics, and research ethics. *FlowTV, 9*(14). Available online: http://flowtv.org/2009/05/attention-economy-layered-publics-and-research-ethics-kristina-busse-university-of-south-alabama/.

Cavanagh, A. (1999). Behaviour in public?: Ethics in online ethnography. *Cybersociology*, Issue 6, Available online: http://www.socio.demon.co.uk/magazine/6/cavanagh.html.

Davis, M. (1990). *City of quartz: Excavating the future in Los Angeles.* New York: Verso.

Dickson-Swift, V., James, E. L., & Liamputtong, P. (2008). *Undertaking sensitive research in the health and social sciences: Managing boundaries, emotions and risks.* New York: Cambridge University Press.

Ess, C. (2001). AoIR ethics working committee – a preliminary report. Available online: aoir.org/reports/ethics.html.

Eysenbach, G., & Till, J. E. (2001). Ethical issues in qualitative research on Internet communities. *British Medical Journal, 323*(10), 1103–1105.

Faberow, N. (1963). *Taboo topics.* New York: Atherton Press.

Frankel, M. S., & Siang S. (1999). Ethical and legal aspects of human subjects research on the Internet: A report of a workshop June 10–11, 1999, Washington, DC: American Association for the Advancement of Science. Available online: http://www.aaas.org/spp/sfrl/projects/intres/report.pdf.

Gatson, S. N., & Zweerink, A. (2004). Ethnography online: 'Natives' practising and inscribing community. *Qualitative Research, 4*(2), 179–200.

Goffman, E. (1963). *Behavior in public places: Notes on the social organization of gatherings*. New York: Free Press.

Gray, Jonathan (2005). Antifandom and the Moral Text: Television Without Pity and Textual Dislike. *American Behavioral Scientist, 48*(7), 840–858.

Guess, R. (2001). *Public goods, private goods*. Princeton: Princeton University Press.

Herring, S. C. (1996). Linguistic and critical research on computer-mediated communication: Some ethical and scholarly considerations. *The Information Society, 12*(2), 153–168.

Hills, M. (2002). *Fan cultures*. London: Routledge.

Hodge, M. J. (2006) . Comment: The Fourth Amendment and Privacy Issues on the 'New' Internet. Facebook.com and Myspace.com. *Southern Illinois University Law School Journal*, 2006, 31, 95–12

Homan, R. (1980). The ethics of covert methods. *The British Journal of Sociology, 31*(1), 46–59.

Homan, R. (1991). *The ethics of social research*. London/New York: Longman.

Hudson, J. M., & Bruckman, A. (2004). 'Go away': Participant objections to being studied and the ethics of chatroom research. *The Information Society, 20*(2), 127–139.

Hudson, J. M., & Bruckman A. (2005). Using empirical data to reason about Internet research ethics. *Proceedings of the European Conference on Computer-Supported Cooperative Work (ECSCW)*, Paris, France, 287–306.

Ito, M., O'Day, V. L., Adler, A., Linde, C., & Mynatt, E. D. (2001). Making a place for seniors on the net: SeniorNet, senior identity, and the digital divide. Available online: http://citeseerx.ist.psu.edu/viewdoc/download?doi=10.1.1.85.1404&rep=rep1&type=pdf.

Jenkins, H. (1995). Do you enjoy making the rest of us feel stupid?: alt.tv.twinpeaks, the trickster author, and viewer mastery. In D. Lavery (Ed.), *Full of secrets: Critical approaches to Twin Peaks*. Detroit: Wayne University Press.

Kendall, L. (2002). *Hanging out in the virtual pub: Masculinities and relationships online*. Berkeley/California: California University Press.

King, S. A. (1996). Researching Internet communities: Proposed ethical guidelines for the reporting of results. *The Information Society, 12*(2), 119–128.

Kirkpatrick, M. (2009a). The day has come: Facebook pushes people to go public. *ReadWriteWeb*, December 9, 2009, http://www.readwriteweb.com/archives/facebook_pushes_people_to_go_public.php.

Kirkpatrick, M. (2009b). Why facebook changed its privacy setting. *ReadWriteWeb*, December 10, 2009, http://www.readwriteweb.com/archives/why_facebook_chenged_privacy_policies.php.

LaRose, R., & Rifon, N. (2006). Your privacy is assured – of being disturbed: Websites with and without privacy seals. *New Media & Society, 8*(6), 1009–1029.

Langer, R., & Beckman S. C. (2005). Sensitive research topics: Netnography revisited, *Qualitative Market Research: An International Journal, 8*(2), 189–203.

Lee, R. M. (1993). *Doing research on sensitive topics*. London: Sage.

Lee, R. M., & Renzetti, C. M. (1993). The problems of researching sensitive topics: An overview and introduction. In C. M. Renzetti & R. M. Lee (Eds.), *Researching sensitive topics* (pp. 3–13). Newbury Park: SAGE.

Macdonald, A. (1998). Uncertain Utopia: Science fiction media fandom & computer mediated communication. In C. Harris & A. Alexander (Eds.), *Theorizing fandom: Fans, subculture and identity* (pp. 131–152). Cresshill/New Jersey: Hampton Press Inc.

Marx, G. T. (2001). Murky conceptual waters: The public and private. *Ethics and Information Technology, 3*, 157–169.

McCosker, H., Barnard A., & Gerber R. (2001). Undertaking sensitive research: Issues and strategies for meeting the safety needs of all participants. *Forum Qualitative Social Research*, *2*(1), Article 22.

McCullagh, K. (2007). Blogs: A privacy perspective. Edinburgh: e-Science Institute. Presentation available online: http://works.bepress.com/cgi/viewcontent.cgi?article=1010&context=karen_mccullagh. Last accessed January 4, 2009.

Oreskovic, A. (2009). Facebook privacy revamp draws fire. *Reuters*, http://www.reuters.com/article/idUSTRE5B82F320091210?type=technologyNews.

Renzetti, C. M., & Lee R. M. (Eds.). (1993). *Researching sensitive topics*, Newbury Park, CA: SAGE.
Rawlins, W. K. (1998). Theorizing public and private domains and practices of communication: Introductory concerns. *Communication Theory, 8*(4), 369–380.
Roberts, L., et al. (2003). Conducting ethical research online: Respect for individuals, identities and the ownership of words. In E. A. Buchanan (Ed.), *Readings in virtual research ethics: Issues and controversies* (pp. 62–78). Hershey/London: Idea Group Inc.
Rosenberg, Å. (2010). Virtual world research ethics and the private/public distinction. *International Journal of Internet Research Ethics, 3*(1), http://ijire.net/issue_3.1/3_rosenberg.pdf
Sanghvi, R. (2006). Facebook gets a facelift. Tuesday, September 5, 2006, http://blog.facebook.com/blog.php?post=2207967130.
Seale, C., Charteris-Black, J., MacFarlane, A., & McPherson, A. (2010). Interviews and Internet forums: A comparison of two sources of qualitative data. *Qualitative Health Research, 20*(5), 595–606.
Shils, E. (1982 [1959]). Social inquiry and the autonomy of the individual. In M. Bulmer (Ed.), *Social research ethics: An examination of the merits of covert participant observation* (pp. 125–141). London: Macmillan.
Sixsmith, J., & Murray, C. D. (2001). Ethical issues in the documentary data analysis of Internet posts and archives. *Qualitative Health Research, 11*(3), 423–432.
Smith, K. M. C. (2004). 'Electronic eavesdropping': The ethical issues involved in conducting a virtual ethnography. In M. D Johns, S. Chen, G. Jon Hall (Eds.), *Online social research: Methods, issues, & ethics* (pp. 223–238). New York: Peter Lang.
Snee, H. (2008). "Web 2.0 as a Social Science Research Tool," Presented at The British Library, 4 November 2008. Paper available online http://www.bl.uk/reshelp/bldept/socsci/socint/web2/web2.pdf.
Social Research Association (SRA) (2003). Ethical Guidelines. Available online http://www.the-sra.org.uk/documents/pdfs/ethics03.pdf.
Spicker, P. (2007). Research without consent. *Social Research Update*, Issue 51, Winter 2007, 1–4. Available online: http://sru.soc.surrey.ac.uk/SRU51.pdf. Last accessed April 21, 2008.
Spicker, P. (2011). Ethical covert research. *Sociology, 45*(1), 118–133.
Stern, S. R. (2009). A response to Malin Sveningsson. In A. N. Markham & N. K. Baym (Eds.), *Internet inquiry: Conversations about method* (pp. 94–98). Thousand Oaks/London: Sage.
Sveningsson Elm, M. (2009). How do various notions of privacy influence decisions in qualitative internet research? In A. N. Markham, & N. K. Baym (Eds.), *Internet inquiry: Conversations about method* (pp. 69–87). Los Angeles: Sage.
Viegas, F. B. (2005). Bloggers' expectations of privacy and accountability: An initial survey. *Journal of Computer-Mediated Communication, 10*(3), Article 12, http://jcmc.indiana.edu/vol10/issue3/viegas.html.
Wakeford, N. (2003). The embedding of local culture in global communication: Independent internet cafes in London. *New Media & Society, 5*(3), 379–399.
Walther, J. B. (2002). Research ethics in Internet-enabled research: Human subjects issues and methodological myopia. *Ethics and Information Technology, 4*(2), 205–216.
Waskul, D., & Douglass, M. (1996). Considering the electronic participant: Some polemical observations on the ethics of on-line research. *The Information Society, 12*, 129–139.
Wiles, R., et al. (2004). Informed consent in social research: A literature review. ESRC National Centre for Research Methods, *NCRM Methods Paper Series Methods Paper* No. 10, http://www.sociology.soton.ac.uk/Proj/Informed_Consent/litreview.rtf.
Wohlblatt, K. (1996). The sweetness of lurking. In A. Sondheim (Ed.), *Being on line: Net subjectivity* (pp. 36–38). New York: Lusitania Press.
Woo, J. (2006). The right not to be identified: Privacy and anonymity in the interactive media environment. *New Media & Society, 8*(6), 949–967.
Zimmer, M. (2009). "But the data is already public!": On the ethics of research in facebook. *Open Conference Systems, Internet Research 10.0*. Available online: http://ocs.sfu.ca/aoir/index.php/ir/10/paper/view/168. Last accessed November 12, 2009.

Chapter 4
Text or Subjects?

Abstract What constitutes 'human data'? How do we recognise the 'living persons' in mediated environments? What are the implications of the separation of author and utterance in online settings for research ethics? Making reference to the diverse nature of identity formation in online environments, the chapter explores the significance of the 'human subject' for research and how the 'subjects' of online and offline research are brought into being in research methods texts. The chapter examines both text and human subject approaches to Internet research and explores the ways that maintaining these approaches can be unsettled by the actual experience of research. The chapter also considers the challenge of verifying online data and the difficulties that can arise when researchers encounter distressing material during the conduct of research.

During my study, I became increasingly interested in The Adversary and Miss Krissy, two of the moderators on the forums of SHH. Each was occasionally criticised on the forums: Miss Krissy was denounced for using aggressive and/or explicit language and The Adversary's expression of their expert knowledge of the Silent Hill games was described by some posters as a domineering influence on the site. Yet each maintained a secure position of influence and authority during the time frame of my study. Each featured heavily in my analysis of modes of authority on the site, in which I explored their very different ways of managing interactions, policing deviance and demonstrating expertise. Yet everything I 'knew' about these posters came solely from their interactions on the site – a collection of utterances unified by shared usernames. And even these usernames proved unstable. After a while, The Adversary disappeared, and St Thomas, a moderator with a remarkably similar tone and manner, appeared. By the end of my study, Miss Krissy appeared to have become Krist.

N. Whiteman, *Undoing Ethics: Rethinking Practice in Online Research*,
DOI 10.1007/978-1-4614-1827-6_4,

Introduction

This chapter examines two ways of conceptualising online data: as textual material or as the properties of human subjects. As in Chap. 3, this involves a consideration of the objectifying gaze of the researcher on the researched activity. Here, however, my focus shifts from examining moves to define this activity in respect of the public/private distinction to an exploration of how we conceptualise our data. Specifically, does our research involve human subjects or not? The key issue here is whether textual material sourced from online environments is regarded as bearing the subjectivity of a real author, whether it is approached 'as text or embodiment' (Markham 2003a, 53). Like the public/private distinction, this question has significant implications for the establishment of an ethical stance – specifically in regard to whether we decide to seek informed consent, a central tenet of human subjects research. It also has institutional implications, in that typically only research involving human subjects is required to undergo ethical review.

I start the chapter by looking at the concept of the research subject, the way it is positioned in research ethics guidance, and its tricky recontextualisation into Internet research. I then trace a move that is key to any stance that accepts, or denies, the relevance of the human subject model to a particular study, a move that either separates or draws together the subjects and their utterances. I then introduce two broad and contrasting approaches to the conceptualisation of online material as either text or subject and examine ethical guidance that is based upon these approaches. First, human subjects perspectives that pull the subject into the frame of the research by seeking to reattach author to utterance (e.g. in terms of the need to ask permission to quote). Second, perspectives that understand any material placed in public spaces as published work, jettisoned from authoring subjects and hence up for grabs (so to speak). Each position can, I suggest, be difficult to sustain, and I explore different ways that such stances can be undermined by the empirical material that the Internet presents. This is followed by a brief consideration of the difficulty of verifying online material in respect of a human subjects framework and the challenges that can arise in respect of this when the researcher encounters distressing material during the conduct of research. The chapter closes with a consideration of the approach taken in my work, one that began by conceptualising the material on COA and SHH as textual rather than as interactions between persons, but was ultimately torn between these perspectives, haunted by the subjects that I was denying.

Defining 'Human Subjects'

> Fichter and Kolb have observed that the obligations of the modern scientist are to search for truth, be objective, discern the relevant, check data meticulously, and, in some cases, accept responsibility for the effects of publication. Such a view may be based upon the conceptualization of phenomena as *objects*. The ethical issues specific to the conduct of

> the social sciences, however, arise from the conceptualisation of phenomena as *subjects*: and subjects – that is, people and their behaviour – have rights which must be respected.
>
> (Homan 1980, 56)

As I described in Chap. 1, recent developments in ethical regulation in the UK have been informed by a medical model of research ethics based upon the concept of the human subject. Guidance has drawn around a central concern with preventing potential harm to these subjects, who provide a unifying point of reference for both definitions of the responsibilities of researchers and the rights of the researched.

This human subject is, for example, a central point of reference for the six key ethical principles in the framework for social science research of the Economic and Social Research Council (ESRC).[1] Four of the ESRC principles make reference to the rights of research subjects:

- Research staff and subjects must be informed fully about the purpose, methods and intended possible uses of the research, what their participation in the research entails and what risks, if any, are involved. Some variation is allowed in very specific and exceptional research contexts for which detailed guidance is provided in the policy Guidelines.
- The confidentiality of information supplied by research subjects and the anonymity of respondents must be respected.
- Research participants must participate in a voluntary way, free from any coercion.
- Harm to research participants must be avoided (ESRC 2005, 1).

These principles establish a specific relationship between researcher and researched, a relationship in which the ethical researcher is configured as a practitioner who ensures that their subjects have certain rights (consent, confidentiality, protection from harm). In this way, the idea of the human subject is used to bring the idea of the ethical researcher into being.

The ESRC define this subject in the following way:

> 'Human participants' (or subjects) are defined as including living human beings, human beings who have recently died (cadavers, human remains and body parts), embryos and foetuses, human tissue and bodily fluids, and human data and records (such as, but not restricted to medical, genetic, financial, personnel, criminal or administrative records and test results including scholastic achievements).
>
> (ESRC 2005, 7)

There is a key distinction here, in the shift from living/deceased 'human beings' to 'human data and records', between the idea of the human subject as a site for the (medical) exploration of physical, bodily properties (bodies, tissues, cadavers, etc.), and the human subject as source of personal data. Although the latter is more commonly the focus of social science research, each subject is attributed the same rights. For those interested in studying online forms of life, the question might then be what constitutes 'human data and records'? One way of answering this involves looking at what work is excluded from the principles outlined above.

---

[1] The ESRC is a major funder of economic and social research in the UK and funded my study of COA and SHH.

The ESRC notes that 'within the definition of research given above, all data collection involving human participants normally requires prior ethical approval' (ESRC 2005, 10). They go on to state that some research is excluded from this requirement. This includes projects, which, under the terms of the ESRC framework:

> [...] are not considered 'research': routine audit, performance reviews, quality assurance studies, testing within normal education requirements, service evaluations, polling on current public policy issues, and literary or artistic criticism. While data collected and stored as a record at an individual level is considered 'human data', material already in the public domain is not. For example, published biographies, newspaper accounts of an individual's activities and published minutes of a meeting would not be considered 'personal data' requiring ethical review. Nor would interviews broadcast on radio or television or online, and diaries or letters in the public domain.
>
> (ESRC 2005, 10)

This conceptualisation of human subjects research can be aligned with the definition of 'research' in the US Health & Human Services Protection of Human Subjects policy, as involving data collected from 'living persons' either 'through intervention or interaction with the person, or identifiable private information' (http://www.niaid.nih.gov/ncn/clinical/humansubjects/hs01.htm). So whilst some research designs (such as the use of interviews in face-to-face environments or laboratory experiments) clearly involve human subjects, data obtained from public settings, where the researcher does not need to directly engage with the living people who may have produced it, might be regarded as exempt.

As I described in the previous chapter, the idea of 'data obtained from public settings' is not straightforward. Even when working in offline environments, researchers may be faced with the issue of whether or not their research should be understood as involving human subjects if 'private' interactions are evident. When we shift to a focus on online settings, the researcher is faced with additional challenges, a destabilisation of the definition of the 'human subject' and also questions relating to how we understand the broadcast nature of online environments. How do we recognise the 'living persons' in mediated environments? Should interactions between online avatars be regarded as equivalent to 'interviews broadcast on radio or television or online, and diaries or letters in the public domain' (ESRC 2005, 10)?

Online Subjects?

The consideration of the public/private distinction in the previous chapter introduced the question of whether the privacy expectations of Internet users should be respected, even if they could feasibly be regarded as misplaced. There are many researchers who argue that they should. It is common to find in such arguments reference to the subjects of research, the individuals whose assumptions and understanding of their settings should be respected (or at least considered). In the 1996 paper in which Storm King introduced the distinction between 'group accessibility' and 'perceived privacy', for example, King presents a moral stance that is very vehement about the responsibility of the researcher not to disturb 'interpersonal processes' displayed online (King 1996). King argues that a 'subject does not have to be deliberately deceived in order to suffer consequences' (ibid) and makes reference to 'the depth of emotional feelings' that can develop between members of technologically mediated communities. He is critical of any attempt to 'objectify the participants' within public forums 'due to the seemingly impersonal nature of text based exchanges' and urges researchers 'to consider the personal implications to cyberspace participants who may discover, after the fact, that they were subjects' (King 1996, no page numbers).

The subject appears here in two ways: in the suggestion of individuals who might, unwillingly or unknowingly, be drawn into becoming the focus of research and – in King's emphasis on the interpersonal nature of CMC (identified by Herring 1996) – a broader expectation that those participating within online environments should be regarded as (real?) individuals who deserve the protection afforded to (human) subjects. A key move in King's favouring of perceived privacy therefore involves a focus on the person, a bringing into being of the subject-hood of online identities.

There are, of course, other ways that we might approach the activity housed within publicly accessible online environments. Researchers working in different fields to King (a scholar in the field of psychology) have approached such interactions as published artefacts rather than constituting human subjects. This involves a quite different conceptualisation of the material and activity sourced within such settings, one that is based on the idea of online material as published text.

On one level, the relevance of the human subjects model to an online research project depends on the researcher's questions and aspirations. The researcher may intend to use online methods to draw connections between reported/observed data and specific groups of people. In such cases, they will need to establish reliable links between online data and offline subjects – between on- and offline identities – in order to establish the validity of findings (e.g. when differentiated in terms of gender or age). The case of 'Subject Naught', described by Konstan et al. (2005) provides a memorable example of the difficulty of verifying online material in relation to offline individuals in Internet-based surveys. Their account describes the challenges of 'assuring participant eligibility and unique participation' (Konstan et al. 2005, no page nos.) when using online questionnaires and suggests the need for different techniques for validating responses. In their study (an exploration of the sexual risk behaviours of Latino men), they 'developed an extensive validation protocol to manually review data' (ibid). This included reviewing any duplication in responses (looking for duplicate names, IP, and email addresses but also flagging up surveys that had short completion times). They describe how 'of 1,150 completed surveys, we rejected 123 (11%), including 119 (10%) that were repeat surveys, 65 (6%) of which came from the same individual participant – the person we call Subject Naught',[2] and suggest that these findings demonstrate the 'vulnerability' of survey research 'to sabotage by one subject' (ibid). Clearly, their account warns, researchers cannot take online data at face value. Whilst this example involves an attempt to link offline identities to online utterances, the connection they establish

[2] They state that the other 54 repeat surveys were submitted by 17 repeaters.

between these online/offline personas is not definitive. They do not know who their respondents 'really' are. Instead, this work involves an imagining of individual subjects that they have not met, whose 'true' identities cannot be confirmed via their validation protocol. The mysterious 'Subject Naught', for example, might in fact be multiple subjects.

Ethnographic studies have also drawn the 'real' subjects of research under the gaze of the researcher by moving between domains to explore the relationship between activities and identities as constituted online and off. Such moves are evident in TL Taylor's study of online gaming *EverQuest* (2006), Lori Kendall's study of the MUD 'Bluesky' (2002), and Miller and Slater's study of Trinidadian's use of the Net (2001). In each case, the research design involves passing between online and offline domains and meeting research participants face to face. Here, the concern is not with validating findings, or checking 'to see the extent to which the [textual and physical] images match' (Markham 2003b, 59), rather with exploring the experiences of individuals in respect of their use of the Internet and/or participation in online environments. Such appeals to, and moves towards, the referential 'persons' involved in these activities draw the subjects of the research into the focus of the study.

As I will discuss later in the chapter, I did not share the imperative to validate my findings via reference to the 'real' or seek to explore relationships between online and offline domains by attempting to identify the people involved in COA and SHH. This was because I was interested in the patterning of interactions within these sites, rather than the correspondence between these interactions and their offline sources. The relevance of the human subject model to my work therefore appeared less obvious, more open, than it would have if my research interests had straddled the online/offline divide. In projects such as this – where the researcher's focus is on the nature of online activity – there appears no right or wrong answer as to whether human subjects' guidance should be followed. Instead, a case must be made and decisions justified. In making their case, the researcher can look to contrasting ethical frameworks for guidance, specifically, perspectives that emphasise the textual nature of online material.

From Subject to Text

The argument that we might regard postings as separate from human subjects involves contemplating a rending apart of the individual and the online material that can be attributed to them (this might be postings or actions in online worlds, blog or wiki entries, etc.). I want to suggest that we might begin to think about this separating move by looking at recent discussion of a very different activity to social science research: olfactory surveillance.

Olfactory surveillance involves the 'monitoring of personal odour' (Marks 2008, 6) for the purposes of crime detection through the use of various surveillance techniques including sniffer dogs. Although they appear very different, there are similarities between the context of surveillance and the challenges of online research. Like the Internet, the increasing use of surveillance activity has introduced a range of privacy issues, as well as concerns about consent, and raised ethical and legal quandaries that institutions have had difficulty resolving. These developments have resulted in a confused state of affairs in which ‘common law jurisdictions across the world are struggling to come to terms with [the] sensory mutation of police searches and interrogations’ (Marks 2008, 8). Here we have a destabilisation of established understandings of the legal status of particular actions, one that is similar to that seen in respect of the Internet. As with debates about Internet research ethics, responses to this destabilisation are contradictory, establishing a site of contestation around the acceptability of certain surveillance actions.

Particular attention has been paid to the contested issue of whether the use of sniffer dogs and other such ‘technologies’ constitutes a search of the person. The UK’s response to the uncertainty surrounding this question has seen The Association of Chief Police Officers (ACPO) establishing a slippery position that constitutes a sundering of the human subject (which by law requires protection from illegal searches) and their smell, which is configured as a property of the subject, but one that can be considered in isolation and as distinct from the originating subject. Describing the ACPO position, Marks notes how:

> [...] it is possible to define a dog ‘sniff’ as a ‘search’ in which case reasonable grounds of suspicion would need to exist before a dog could sniff a person. The ACPO training manual states that except for where a person is ‘funnelled’ in order to facilitate the deployment of the dogs ‘...the use of Passive Alert dogs does not constitute a search’. Their explanation for this assertion is that ‘The dog is deployed to *scent the air surrounding* an individual person and indicate the presence of the smell of category A and B narcotics *in the close vicinity* of an individual...’ ACPO is asserting that because the dog does not physically touch the subject, the action does not constitute a search. There is an internal inconsistency in ACPO’s reasoning: it seeks to distance the subject from the source of the odour in order to deny that the surveillance amounts to a search of the subject, and simultaneously, to link the subject to the information obtained from that odour in order to provide a legal basis for any subsequent physical search.
>
> (Marks 2007, 267, her emphasis)

The ‘internal inconsistency’ that Marks identifies in this extract involves a strategic separation of the authoring subject of the smell and the smell as utterance, which is then reattached to the subject when the utterance suggests guilt. This smell is thus marked as distinct from the person (or subject of surveillance) but attributable to them if it provides evidence of wrongdoing. These moves also relate to the public/private positioning described in Chap. 3. As with the defence of covert research, it is significant to this line of argument that the odours of the person are defined as a legitimate focus of surveillance activity *because they are deemed to be situated within the public domain*. To the ACPO, the lack of invasion by a police officer – due to the smell being accessible within a public context – means that this surveillance activity is not constituted as involving a search (although, as Marks argues, the use of the sniffer dog as an instrument for the detection of odours ‘which are not exposed to the plain perception of the public at large’ (Marks 2007, 269) can be seen to undermine this position).

Clearly, smells are different to posts to online forums or exchanges in online worlds. Whilst we are relatively unable to control the odours we give off, acting or posting material online involves an act of performance, an act of publication.[3] At the same time, it is quite difficult to link the online utterance back to its author. For the sniffer dog, this task is less difficult. Despite these differences, it is worth thinking about the strategic move that is being made here by the ACPO and, shifting settings, how it relates to the moves that researchers might make in respect of their handling of online material.

Take, for example, this post from the forums of COA:

> I was watching 'Graduation part 2' and it came to the part when Angel had to drink Buffy's blood to cure the poison from Faith. It seemed like he was just havin at it when he was drinking her, but in season one the Master drank Buffy for like 2 seconds and she was supposedly dead. I'm not gonna go through all the examples and time differences from each vampire attack through out the shows, but is it all just out of convienence or what's the deal with how long it takes avampire [sic] to drain someone?

Here, Moment of Happiness (a member of COA) poses a question about an apparent discrepancy between two episodes of the television series *Buffy the Vampire Slayer:* the episode 'Graduation part 2', where the central protagonist Buffy is bitten by her vampire boyfriend Angel, and an earlier episode in which Buffy was bitten by another vampire ('the Master') and 'supposedly' died. The question that is introduced here – 'how long it takes avampire to drain someone?' – refers to an inconsistency in the series. How can Buffy be 'killed' after being bitten by the Master 'for like 2 seconds' when Angel drank from her for a longer amount of time and she survived?

We can go so far as to assume that the purpose of this post is to get an answer to this question, to resolve or obtain a reasonable explanation for this discrepancy. But, beyond this, what is this post an instance of?

We could regard this data as involving a human subject, the username 'Moment of Happiness' reflecting an offline self and (his? her?) authoring 'I' being the expression of a unified author. We can perhaps start to imagine Moment of Happiness's offline identity, an individual who has watched these episodes and is confused, asking for advice from other fans, but also apparently knowledgeable (they are aware that there are other examples of such discrepancies/time differences within the series). The style of Moment of Happiness's posting activity would shape our imagining of this individual (with, as Markham has suggested, the form of messages and 'predilections' of the researcher informing the way that we visualise this virtual subject (Markham 2004)). Taking such a position might then lead us to include Moment of Happiness as subject in our research by contacting this offline identity and seeking consent (or, in the terms of the sniffer dog case, a warrant), attempting to protect them from harm, and granting them control to some extent of their participation in the study. If we did not, would our research activity be legitimate?

Alternatively, we could approach this post as distinct from an authoring subject, as published textual material located in the public domain and therefore the object of legitimate focus without consent. From such a position, a warrant to use this material would not be necessary. Rather than human subject, 'Moment of Happiness'

---

[3] Although the selection and use of a perfume (etc) might perhaps be thought of as a type of publication.

would instead be regarded as the sum of textual utterances, distinct from their originating source.

In the rest of this section, I want to look at the negotiation of these issues within the ethics of the academy. I will first look at proponents of the subject position who draw together the utterance and the authoring human subject. I will then consider the moves made by those who suggest a textual approach which, in contrast, is based on a separation of subject and utterance. Like the public/private distinction, these do not provide natural categories for the classification of research. As Heidi McKee has noted; 'what constitutes "person-based" research in cyberspace is much disputed – one person's "text-based" study is another's person-based study' (McKee 2008, 106). In demarcating these perspectives, I also want to suggest that our engagement with the empirical details of online environments can disturb and make it difficult to sustain each of these positions.

Human Subject Approaches

Michele White has described how human subjects' perspectives have influenced guidelines for Internet research:

> Most of the ethical guidelines and concerns start with the presumption that Internet research involves human subjects and needs to follow current governmental guidelines.
>
> (White 2002, 251)

This conflation of utterance and human subject is seen in recommendations for ethical practice found within Internet research writing. It is evident in Bruckman's argument that the 'real author' of 'creative work' on the Internet needs to be verified (see White 2002, 254) and Bakardjieva and Feenberg's claim that a '"non-alienation principle" should be the basis of emergent social conventions in cyberspace' (2001, 233), a principle by which participants should be granted the 'right to control their own product' (2001, 236; see also Berry 2004). Each involves the move to (re)establish the connection between online avatars and (authoring) subjects (see Jordan 1999).

Eysenbach and Till (2001) – making reference to the fact that posts to online communities can sometimes be retrieved via the use of search engines – assume a unified human subject in their advice that consent should always be sought:

> Participants should therefore always be approached to give their explicit consent to be quoted verbatim and should be made aware that their email address might be identifiable. Another reason why researchers should contact individuals before quoting them is that the author of the posting may not be seeking privacy but publicity, so that extensive quotes without attribution may be considered a misuse of another person's intellectual property. (1105)

Eysenbach and Till here establish the subject's continued ownership of their utterances even when they are posted online, both in terms of protection of privacy *and* publicity. Utterances are positioned as a property of, and *the* property of, these subjects. Their empirical focus (self-help groups and medical communities, which from an external perspective would be regarded as vulnerable groups) perhaps has implications for the stance they are taking. Significantly, they also acknowledge the difficulty of gaining consent online; the way that contacting such groups to obtain prospective consent via email is potentially invasive (1104), the difficulty of gaining retrospective consent, and the challenge involved in giving those participating the opportunity to opt-out of the study (1104).

The equating of text and subject is also visible in arguments over the citing of data generated from such settings. Annette Markham, for example, calls for researchers to protect the unity of the subject. She suggests that the ways that researchers select, edit, and disseminate material sourced from online environments (specifically posts) in their work can potentially reconfigure the 'person's very being', placing its utterances 'into a context of a research account rather than left in the context of experience' (Markham 2004). The recontextualisation of utterances is here presented as being potentially damaging to the (real) subject. Markham notes that this is not unique to CMC research but argues that:

> [...] computer-mediated environments seem to highlight this dilemma of research reporting because it's so clear that text can be the primary, if not sole means of producing and negotiating self, other, body, and culture. (ibid)

The idea that the researcher can damage the 'very being' of online participants appears to equate the online 'body of work' with the identity of an authoring subject. This perspective is supported by Sharon Boehlefeld's advice to researchers to ask permission of posters before reproducing long extracts of quotes (Boehlefeld 1996).

A different, but connected, issue relates to the need to obtain validation from the offline self – to move beyond the screen to confirm research conclusions. In these moves, authenticity, as Markham has described, is established in reference to the physical embodiment of the offline subject:

> [...] social scientists persist in seeking the authentic by privileging the concept of the body. The desire to add validity to findings often results in research design that holds up the textual representation of the participants next to their physical persona. Often, the goal is to see the extent to which the images match.
>
> (Markham 2003a, 59)

Here, the human subject is established 'as the "location of 'true' knowledge"' (Markham 2003a, 59). The issue of verifiability in the context of online environments therefore relates to the absence of contact with 'real' physical subjects in cyberspace, with the offline subjects positioned as providing an authenticating point of reference in relation to identity markers such as age, gender, and ethnicity.

Avatar In/Stability and Attachment

The conceptualisation of online material as the property of offline subjects is supported by the formal characteristics of many online environments. It is common to find material differentiated by unifiable reference points – such as online 'handles', usernames, or graphical avatars. On many discussion boards, and sites like *Delicious,*

YouTube, Facebook, and *Twitter,* names serve as unifying signifiers. Like physical bodies in offline domains, these house a multiplicity of utterances and actions under one banner. Because of this, it is quite easy to slip into equating such points of reference with a unified offline subject/author.

As a number of researchers have suggested, the activity on many Internet sites also displays a drive towards unitary and consistent identities. Studies of CMC have examined the fixing of identities in online communities, documenting the role this consistency plays in the establishment of social relationships. In a paper on identity management in Usenet newsgroups, for example, Jason Rutter and Greg Smith (1999) argue that the members of their research setting demonstrated a heavy reliance on the 'poster's ability to know with whom they are interacting' and that:

> [...] a practised familiarity with others allows members to understand the nature of their online relationships, assess the validity of information offered to them by others, and place in context comments and actions of other posters. Unlike the often-fantastical environments of some synchronous online interaction, the identities enacted in the newsgroup are taken to be 'real' in a serious sense. When messages are posted to the group or address individuals a level of trust is offered and expected between those involved in the group. (no page nos.)

In her study of the newsgroup 'Bluesky', Lori Kendall similarly suggests that members 'do not role-play, expecting that others will represent themselves more or less as they appear off-line' (Kendall 1999, 68). She argues that this stance:

> [...] emphasizes identity continuity and interpersonal responsibility and contrasts with representations by participants and researchers who emphasize the flexibility of identity in on-line interaction (ibid)

Such descriptions, perhaps surprisingly, align with work on more 'fantastical' environments, the 'preoccupation in MUDs with getting a "fix" on people through fixing their gender' (Turkle 1995, 211) and Susan Crawford's description of how in online virtual worlds, 'Identity and reputation go hand in hand, as individuals gain reputations that are connected to particular contexts and groups' (2004, 213). The suggestion is that for this to work, identities need to be stable, whether or not they are 'truthful' in respect of an offline self.

Alongside this focus on the stability of identity in online environments, researchers have also explored the attachment that Internet users express towards their online avatars. In a study of player's relationships to their graphical avatars in three-dimensional worlds (such as *Lineage* and *World of Warcraft*), Jessica Wolfendale (2007) examines how players feel bound to their avatars and how the avatar operates as 'a form of self-expression and online identity' (116) which is 'linked to personal narratives, identity and self-conception' (118). Drawing from TL Taylor's (2002) earlier work on presence and embodiment in 3-D worlds, she describes how online avatars serve as:

> The embodied conception of the participant's self through which she communicates with others in the community. Of course, players often choose avatars with physical, emotional and personality traits that are very different from their actual traits, but avatars are still experienced as being expressive of the participant's personal identity.
>
> (Wolfendale 2007, 114)

Wolfendale provides different forms of evidence for this 'experience'. She identifies continuities between the movements of online avatars and offline gamers in virtual and face-to-face contexts (such as maintaining body distance when interacting with strangers or moving closer when being threatening, for example (Taylor 2002)). She also looks at the ways that players talk about their online selves, arguing that a 'strong connection between the self and avatar is evident in the language participants use to describe interactions in virtual worlds' (114). *EverQuest* players, for example, 'make no distinction between harm caused to their avatar and harm caused by them: "*I* was ignored"; "*I* never let anyone talk to *me* like that again"' (Wolfendale 2007, 114 – her emphasis). As Wolfendale suggests, the alliance between avatar and user (with harm done to avatars being felt by players) leads to misbehaviour being taken very seriously in online worlds. This is evident in the production of ethical codes and development of safe spaces in such environments.

The association between user and online avatar has also influenced the way that academic work in this area has been published and disseminated. The researcher Cecilia Pearce, for example, has published an ethnographic study of online gaming and virtual worlds under both her 'real' name and that of her online avatar Artemesia. She describes how:

> Many presentations, most notably the thesis defense, as well as public talks, have been given partially or entirely in situ, in-game, and in-character [...] In addition, a number of publications are credited as coauthored by Cecilia Pearce and Artemesia, prompting one publisher to request that Artemesia sign an author permission form, even though she was well aware that Artemesia was a fictional character.
>
> (Pearce and Artemesia 2009, 199)

Describing her research experience, she argues that 'as players in the study often pointed out, the avatar is an extension of the player's real-life persona, even if it instantiates in ways that digress significantly from her real-world personality or life roles' (198).

These studies, and the empirical phenomena they describe, highlight the continuity of online identities and Internet users' identification/allegiance to their online selves. Emphasising the maintenance of, and investment in, individual avatar identities over time (rather than swapping between alternative identities), they also suggest the importance on these sites of there being some link between the identities articulated online and 'an' identity of an offline author. This supports the imagining of subjects and, indeed, the idea that there is a subject that can be contacted.

We can see in these different examples a drawing together of the online avatar and offline self similar to that proposed by those who take a human subjects position. If we were to follow the 'perceptions of privacy' argument outlined in the previous chapter, such evidence of apparent attachment to online material might lead us to agree that these feelings should be protected, that if people feel attached to their online persona and harmed when their online self is attacked – as if it is a part of them – the researcher should respect this and seek consent before drawing the avatar into the focus of research. Yet, as I want to now consider, such connections can be unsettled, as well as supported, by the nature of online embodiment.

Who Is Anonymous?

> It is not fully clear how Internet researchers are studying human subjects or what provides them with verifiable information about people since the bodies and direct actions of individuals are not visible.
>
> (White 2002, 261)

As White's quote above suggests, the coherence of online identities is undermined by the disconnection between flesh and data that makes identity play possible in online environments. As Lori Kendall has described, accounts of the stability of online identity provide a very different perspective to that found in the reporting of more open online identity play. Many of the hopes and fears relating to the Internet relate to this openness and possibility for experimentation. Just as technological mediation makes it difficult for researchers to verify online data in relation to 'real-world' reference points, so too anxieties relating to the loss of coherent physical identity in online environments (such as the dangers to children posed by unknowable others online) tend to centre on the absent body.

This is evident in the documentation of incidents of identity deception and individuals switching between personas (Turkle 1996a) in examples of 'identity masquerade,' and in cases where Internet researchers have themselves used disguise (White 2002). White (2002) uses Dibbell's description of a now infamous rape in cyberspace (Dibbell 1993, 1998) to demonstrate the 'ways that Internet characters do not correlate to a specific person' (White 2002, 261). The perpetuator in this case was revealed to be a group author, a collective identity made up of multiple participants. Similarly, Pearce and Artemesia (2009) describe a series of 'gender revelations' during their research, where friends they had come to know through their online avatars (and spoken to during in-world interactions) came out as having switched genders. Evidence of young people strategically placing false information and using pseudonyms in social networking sites also challenge the one-to-one relationship between online and offline identity. Lenhart and Madden (2007), for instance, suggest that nearly half of US teens who use social networking sites post at least some fake information about themselves online. These examples of identity play and masquerade remind researchers of the need to consider a question first posed by Sherry Turkle (1996b) and rephrased by TL Taylor: 'does it matter […] that you do not know all the identities/bodies a given participant has'? (Taylor 1999, no page nos.)

As descriptions of the potential instability and multiplicity of online identities suggest, the authorship of online utterances is often uncertain. This uncertainty is celebrated in sites that operate in different ways from those that unify contributions around distinctive, named handles. The website *4chan* (www.4chan.com), for example, does away with this signifier of apparently unified avatar identity by providing a default ‘anonymous2’ for posts.[4] The impact of this is that the individualising of members is replaced by the establishing of a group identity. Indeed, the site’s frequently asked questions establish this figure as a mythologised, reified creature:

> Who Is ‘Anonymous’?
> ‘Anonymous’ is the name assigned to a poster who does not enter text in to the [Name] field. Anonymous is not a single person, but rather, represents the collective whole of 4chan. He is a god amongst men. Anonymous invented the moon, assassinated former President David Palmer,[5] and is also harder than the hardest metal known to man: diamond. His power level is rumored to be over nine thousand. He currently resides with his auntie and uncle in a town called Bel-Air (however, he is West Philadelphia born and raised). He does not forgive. (http://www.4chan.org/faq)[6]

Although uploaded images can be used on the site to differentiate between the avatars of distinct ‘Anonymous’ posters, the use of this collective naming serves as a direct challenge to individualising moves that support the human subject model. To those more interested in forums where members are differentiated through their selection of names, a site like *4chan* unsettles expectations and reveals how traditional many sites are when it comes to the construction of online identity.

Text Approaches

The idea that online material constitutes human subjects has its detractors. Some scholars instead promote a contrasting focus on the textual rather than ‘human’ nature of online data and seek to unsettle the assumptions that underpin human subjects’ approaches. Default understandings of online activity as involving human subjects are challenged here, in favour of consideration of the formal, textual features of online environments. As Markham has argued, ‘text is a crucial discussion point in consideration of ethics in research of Internet culture’ in terms of ‘the presentation of identity’, ‘the building blocks of culture’ and the ‘interrelationship of researcher, participant, and readers of research’ (Markham 2003a, 51). A focus on textuality emphasises the constructed, performed, displayed nature of online activity, suggesting that our handling of online material should be informed by different frameworks to the human subjects model.

---

[4] *4chan* is, of course, not the only site that enables anonymous posting.

[5] Fictional president, from the television series *24*.

[6] The question of Anonymous’ identity has received growing attention during the writing of this book in the light of the Wikileaks event, in which Anonymous has been involved as a vocal, multiple participant/supporter (for newspaper coverage of this involvement, see Halliday and Arthur 2010).

Both White (2002) and Bassett and O'Riordan (2002) relate the confusion of representations and subjects to the way that the Internet is brought into being within the rhetoric surrounding new technologies, particularly via descriptions of online environments in spatial terms, as inhabitable places. In her discussion of 'the ways that Internet material is made into people' (White 2002, 260), White argues that work describing the Internet in such terms has been 'linked to guidelines for human subjects [as] representations get conflated with physical realities and people' (205). Bassett and O'Riordan (2002) suggest that the dominance of the metaphorical 'cloaking' of the Internet as a 'space' within this discourse has driven the 'blanket application' of the human subjects model to online research:

> The understanding of the Internet-as-a-space supports a conflation between activity carried out through this medium and the action of human actors in social space. Further, it leads to the argument that any manifestation of Internet activity should be regarded as a virtual person. (2002, 234)[7]

They argue that rather than ensuring the avoidance of harm to those involved, the non-differentiated application of a human subjects model to online research can actually lead to 'unethical' research practice (e.g. by preventing inquiry into certain types of activity (236)).

Like Herring's critique of ethical guidelines described in Chap. 2, Bassett and O'Riordan's stance is based on challenging the essentialising moves that suggest that the Internet is a uniform 'thing' (what they term the 'Internet-as-(community)-space' (235)). Their critique of these moves also challenges what is being privileged in this dominant, homogenising model of the Internet. It is not just that the Internet is a *space* that is significant, but that the Internet is seen to provide 'spaces' that are capable of supporting forms of life – that are *inhabited* and *inhabitable*. The dominance of this characterisation of the Internet is evident in Internet-related literature: in (as Bassett and O'Riordan note) Howard Rheingold's idea of the 'homestead', as well as in the title of Sherry Turkle's influential book *Life on the Screen* (1995) (and Annette Markham's *Life Online: researching real experience in virtual space* (1998)). It is also evident in everyday descriptions of the Internet – the use of phrases such as '"going somewhere" and "entering" […] when accessing web sites' (White 2002, 258).

This kind of rhetoric can be seen in the following description of the online community 'Cybercity' by Denise Carter:

> Cybercity is a virtual community on the Internet, a social world that is no less real for being supported by Internet technologies, with residents drawn from countries all over the world. With 1,062,072 registered inhabitants by June 2004, it is slightly larger than Dublin, Ireland and its design is similar to that of other large cities in the world. It also has many of the same amenities, for example, a plaza, a beach, a café, a funfair, a post office, an employment office, a jail and suburbs where the residents live, It is the city where I lived and worked for 3 years while engaging in ethnographic fieldwork. People visit the city by switching on their computers, logging onto the internet, and presenting their unique nickname and password at the city login page.
>
> (Carter 2005, 154)

[7] This resonates with White's position that 'the concept that people are alive on the Internet is supported by the way it is described as a place and space that allows them to congregate' (White 2002, 258).

Here, we have the rhetorical construction of an online environment as a 'real' place in which the researcher can 'live', one that is supported by the features of the environment which suggest its status as a 'city' and the way the site itself makes use of spatial codes (Carter 2005, 154) in the establishing of different locations (café, post office, plaza). This way of thinking about online environments can – critics suggest – lead to the expectation that human subjects are implicated in all the online actions that are observable to the researcher and the idea that informed consent should be obtained in order to prevent harm to these individuals.

Critics of such positions suggest that there are other ways of approaching web material. White, for example, argues that 'the visual and aesthetic aspects of avatars make it difficult to write about them solely as human subjects' (2002, 255), proposing that graphical avatars might instead be examined as art objects. For Bassett and O'Riordan (2002), spatial ontologising moves ignore the textual form of display which, they suggest, is an equally important way of thinking about the web. Rather than a home for subjects, they argue, the Internet should also be understood as a:

> [...] medium of publication, and significantly one where users can take control of the means of production, create their own cultural artefacts and intervene in the production of existing ones.
>
> (Bassett and O'Riordan 2002, 235)

These authors propose that, instead of adopting a blanket approach to online material, researchers should consider the particular nature of the site that is being observed and decide whether it is more appropriate to consider it via the use of spatial or textual metaphors.

What's interesting about Bassett and O'Riordan's argument is that their focus on textuality is tied to a particular type of online location, material positioned within the public domain. Talking about the way that activists participate within the political forum *IndyMedia.org* site (a hybrid site that includes email and forums), they describe how:

> [...] activists choose to make visible the political events in which they feel involved or which they consider important. They also make a decision about the level of their visibility by controlling the degree of their disclosure of identification. There is no sense in which the Independent Media Sites are private although they are highly 'sensitive'. They constitute a deliberate attempt to create a global public sphere through Internet use. (236)

They argue that due to this public nature:

> [...] there are a number of reasons for not treating this work as private and thus requiring deontological human subjects protections such as anonymity, seeking informed consent, etc. (236)

Whilst Bassett and O'Riordan argue that it is wrong to apply human subjects to all Internet activity, there is a suggestion here that the 'textual' nature of the Internet can be equated with online material published in the public domain (e.g. on websites). In contrast, 'private' interactions (on Listservs, forums of websites, etc.) are presented as demanding human subjects' protection. The distinction they make here implies that the Internet can be divided up into different types of settings, depending on whether their content is private or not and that this classification then has implications for whether the setting should be approached from a textual or human subjects' perspective.

In their discussion of the textuality of the Internet, Bassett and O'Riordan draw in work from literary studies, describing how authors such as George P. Landow, Vannevar Bush, and N Katherine Hayles have used textual metaphors to describe networked communication (236) and how this work challenges 'the dominance of a spatial paradigm by emphasising narrative as a way of understanding the Internet' (236). This emphasis suggests that research might be informed by scholarship within the arts and humanities, rather by human subjects frameworks developed in the context of medical and social science research. As White says:

> When Internet material is viewed as cultural production then the models for Internet research might be Art History and Visual Culture, English and Literary Studies, Film and Media Studies, Music and Sound Studies, and Theatre and Performance Studies. A more complete integration of these approaches into Internet Studies – either as a sole investigatory strategy or in tandem with other forms of inquiry – would change researchers' ethical questions. It would also change the ways that the material is seen and addressed because different academics and users understand Internet material through distinct lenses.
>
> (White 2002, 249)

A focus on the textual nature of the Internet emphases the *published* nature of online material, as equivalent to the circulation of films or books, put out on display and subject to the gaze of a viewing audience. The online utterance here becomes reconfigured as the published property of an author, rather than the inherent property of a human subject. Researchers might then approach these utterances as they would the work of an author or filmmaker. This focus on authorship raises legal concerns relating to copyright,[8] as well as bigger ethical questions relating to ownership and authorship – not least 'to whom do the posts belong?' (Sixsmith and Murray 2001)

In answering these questions, the researcher might consider other types of ethical frameworks than those typically used in social science research. White notes how researchers in the humanities, for example, are careful to 'identify the producer of a text, artist, or author by name' (2002, 253). Quoting the US Art Association's 'Guidelines for the Professional Practice of Art History', she describes how the guidelines insist that it:

> [...] is a maxim of scholarship that authors should be scrupulous in crediting sources, not only for ideas and textual material but also photographs and suggestions as to the location of documentation
>
> (White 2002, 253)

This guidance is clearly very different to the concern with anonymity and confidentiality in human subject frameworks. Whilst the naming of sources is common within humanities research, there is contestation here (the relationship between scholar and author is, for example, configured in different terms in the field of literary studies). Humanities approaches therefore do not offer unproblematic or unvarying

[8] For discussion of these issues, see Charlesworth (2008) and McKee (2008).

ethical codes, but instead a range of guidance that takes as its focus common questions and principles.

I have outlined above different ways that researchers can approach online material and contrasting ethical guidance that emphasises either the rights of the online subjects of research or the textual nature of online interactions. Researchers must position themselves in relation to these contrasting perspectives, deciding which guidance is more relevant to their own research. To a large extent, this depends on what they take their empirical data to be an instance of. A potentially legitimate case can then be made in either direction. But each will need to be defended and, as I will describe below, each may be challenged. Before considering the destabilisation of these stances I want to return to the challenges of verifying online data and the implications of these for research ethics.

Seeing Is Believing?

The discussion of human subjects and text approaches above raises an important methodological issue: whether the researcher needs to authenticate their understanding of online avatars in relation to real-world authors or not, and the challenges of establishing connections between online utterances and offline subjects if they decide they do.

Alongside the methodological question of whether researchers need to be able to confirm that their participants are who they say they are, the problem of verifying online data also has consequences for the maintenance of ethical positions. In Chap. 5, I explore the difficulty of maintaining ethical stances during the research process. My focus in that chapter is on moments in research that challenge researchers' ethical stances, including dilemmas that researchers have faced in offline research when using covert methods. When made aware of a threat of violence to an individual, for example, should the researcher intervene? If so, how? Such dilemmas can appear even more complex in online research due to the challenge of verifying online behaviour and assessing its relevance to offline activity.

Susannah Stern has explored this issue by examining Internet researchers' responses to 'distressing disclosure', including 'online users' announcements of suicide intentions, descriptions of self-destructive behaviours such as self-mutilation, or threats to kill, rape, or maim other person(s)' (Stern 2003, 250). Stern considers the extent to which researchers might be found liable in such situations should harm to an individual then occur. Making reference to cases where therapists were found liable for not passing on information about threats to a patient, she argues that the liability of online researchers is less clear because of the uncertain nature of the crises that may be faced.[9] She argues that online researchers' responsibilities to protect human subjects may be different to those working in offline environments:

[9] Stern argues that the fact that researchers may tend to approach online material as 'objects rather than subjects' (257) can make this even more problematic.

> [...] it is unlikely that any legal responsibility would be extended to online researchers [...] Two factors in particular suggest this. First, online researchers are significantly less able than offline researchers – and especially offline therapists – to verify the facts surrounding particular subjects. For example, medical records, family histories, and physical conditions often provide offline therapists with a content in which they can evaluate their patients. Online researchers do not have such environmental or contextual information available to them in order to determine the veracity of the distressing disclosure of those they study. Second, online communication is rife with possibility for misinterpretation.
>
> (Stern 2003, 254)

As Stern suggests, the challenge of interpreting ethical dilemmas – of recognising real threats of harm, for instance – may be increased when working in technologically mediated environments where there is a separation of author and utterance and where the researcher may have very limited contextual information about what they have observed.

This difficulty is not unique to Internet research, however. Scholars have raised similar issues about the uncertainty of direct experience when working in offline contexts. As Westmarland (2001) demonstrates, directly witnessing an event does not always provide a clear understanding of what has occurred. Reporting a 3-year ethnographic study of the British police force, she notes the difficulty of recognising moments of police brutality, of interpreting what constitutes violence or excessive force even when you see such actions with your own eyes. She suggests that these moments are not clear cut and that 'in the absence of any other reliable guidance it seems that personal moral judgements are the only resource available to decide whether force is "excessive" and the behaviour is violent or even "brutal"' (Westmarland 2001, 528). Here too, it is the responsibility of the researcher to make a judgement as to what they have observed and how they should now act.[10]

More importantly for the consideration of the ways that researchers approach online material, Stern's argument also suggests potential shifts in perspective. If we are taking a text approach, coming across a statement such as 'I am going to kill myself' might provoke a shift in objectification towards a subject-centred position, even if this contradicts the stance that has been developed previously. Stern herself suggests that distressing information can be involved in the 'personalising' of subjects (Stern 2003, 257). This may propel the researcher from a text approach to thinking about the subjects of research and how these subjects might be assisted or protected. The point here is that the objectification of the researched activity in respect of the subject/text distinction may be challenged, and the researcher's conceptual approach may shift. Whilst this may involve dramatic events, such change can also occur over time in more subtle ways, as my own experience of online research suggests.

[10] Westmarland suggests that 'such judgements usually rely upon understanding the motive behind the actors' behaviour' (Westmarland 2001, 528).

The Haunting

My study of COA and SHH approached posting activity as textual interactions rather than the utterances of human subjects. As described in Chap. 1, data was generated through observation of published, written posts. At no time did I meet or see any of the 'real' members of the site. I did not seek to connect these textual identities – these online avatars – to 'real' authors or draw conclusions about the motivations or experiences of users of the sites.[11]

The separation between text and subject that underpinned my stance reflected the focus of my research, which was concerned with producing an analysis of the strategies by which different relationships in these sites (between avatars, between fans and the fan objects, and between members and the sites) were maintained within the ongoing play of posting activity.[12] It also reflected the theoretical, deessentialised conceptualisation of identity that underpinned my work, a post-structuralist focus on the strategic moves that brought online avatars on these sites into being, involving a now common move away from essentialised notions of identity to a focus on the performance of identity (see Pelletier and Whiteman in press).

Because of the approach I was taking, there were many questions that I was unable to answer about the sites and their members. I could not verify the 'true' identities of the members of COA and SHH – I had no verifiable information about their ages or genders, for example. This was reflected in my presentation of data when I wrote up the study. I attempted to address the unknown directly by not using gendered pronouns in discussion of online members, although I sometimes found myself slipping into such gendering when talking about my project.[13] The lack of information I had about the 'real' members of COA and SHH sometimes appeared to annoy other people when I presented my work. When I was asked how I could draw conclusions about online activity when I did not know 'if these people are who

---

[11] My focus was similar to that outlined by Chin and Gray (2001), who described how their unannounced observation of Lord of the Rings fan communities:

> [...] may lay us open to charges of academic 'lurking' but must therefore stress that we were looking primarily at the text, and Tolkein fans' talk surrounding the text itself, not at how they use the Internet as a social apparatus [...]our aim is not to explain or theorise these viewers since it is not ethnography that we are concerned with, but an insight into how a pre-text takes form in the discussion of pre-viewers. (Chin and Gray 2001, no page nos.)

[12] Here, I am informed by Annette Markham's suggestion that although 'shoulds' are problematic in relation to Internet research, 'it should always come back to the question' (Markham 2004).

[13] Bronwyn Davies has described the challenge of escaping gendered pronouns: '[...] in attempting to reconceptualise the subject as process, we are limited by the images and metaphors we can find to create the new idea. Pronoun grammar is a good example of this. We cannot yet see how to do without it. We see the power of gendered pronouns, for example, to reconstitute the male/female binary every time we speak. We are frustrated to observe pronoun grammar re-creating the binary in the very language we use in our attempts to move beyond gender' (Davies 1997, 275).

they say they are', I argued that it did not matter if posters were misrepresenting their 'true' selves on the sites, as my interest was in their utterances. At the same time, had I interviewed participants I would not have moved nearer to the 'truth', I would merely have set up another research context.

Whilst I felt able to defend my decisions and approach to the material as text, during my research I became increasingly aware of the 'subjects' that I was starting to imagine through my engagement with the sites. Why did I start referring to online identities as 'he' or 'she' when speaking about the project, for example?

This imagining was partly shaped by the nature of the settings. Like other traditional bulletin boards, both COA and SHH demonstrated an assumed reliance upon the relatively stable and coherent nature of online avatars (despite some moments of identity confusion (see Whiteman 2007; Pelletier and Whiteman in press)). It also reflected my growing familiarity with these avatars, the distinct voices and personalities that I came to know through my prolonged observation of the sites. The repetition of recognisable linguistic and stylistic features made them appear like individuals, with distinct identities, and with this 'real' (see White 2002), but also lead to confusion when they behaved out of character. Members of the site appeared to struggle with similar problems (e.g. asking questions of new visitors who had taken the usernames of previous members to ascertain whether or not they were one 'person'). It was this familiarity that led me to believe that distinct usernames represented the same offline person. I continue to think that The Adversary and St Thomas were authored by the same individual, for instance, even though I have not formally verified this in any way.

There was, then, a tension between the theoretical position I was taking in my work and the way that I started to think and talk about the imagined subjects of these sites. The slippage from text to subjects I experienced in my relationship to COA and SHH suggests the difficulty of sustaining a properly post-structuralist performance when thinking and talking about data. The description of my research demonstrates my inability to produce an analysis of the ways that identities and relationships were constituted within the discursive practices of these sites without sliding into an imagining of the real-world persons involved in this activity (although these real-world persons did not enter into my analysis). I perhaps fell into the trap that Alison Jones (1997) suggests it is difficult for students and scholars to avoid, in deploying post-structuralist language whilst also 'seek[ing] to import the apparent solidity of the "real" person/girl into our writing and talk' (Jones 1997, 267).

Rather than this being a problem, we might consider what such tensions draw attention to. We might pay attention to the ways that the language of social science research implicates a (human) subject. We might perhaps acknowledge that research subjects are always illusory/imagined: that the subject is always fictional (Davies 1997, 272). Whilst in offline contexts this recognition can appear more difficult to accept due to the embodied nature of the individuals we face, within face-to-face research, the subjects of research can be seen to be 'imagined' by the researcher, as personas constructed from a multiplicity of offline 'posts' (spoken phrases, body language, dress, etc.). We might also consider the ways that textual approaches to conceptualising online activity are perhaps alienating in denying the subjects of research. Does this then make them more difficult to sustain? Finally, we might reflect upon the extent to which a growing identification with the subjects of research becomes significant in respect of the maintenance of the researcher's ethical stance. Should this change the methodological decisions we make? In my case, although it did not change my general approach to the collection of data from COA and SHH, my growing feelings towards the sites did reinforce my desire not to upset the settings (i.e. their members) and to ensure that my analysis and reporting was fair.

Conclusion

> [...] how can one invest emotionally, socially or 'materially' [...] with an other who might vanish, untraceably, at any moment, and whose identity claims are unverifiable?
>
> (Slater 2002, 233)

The literature explored in this chapter suggests the very different positions that researchers have established in respect of the relevance of the human subject to online research. As with the discussion of surveillance activity, this debate is key to whether we perceive certain methodological actions as constituting 'trespass to the person' (Marx 2002). The chapter has considered the separating/unifying moves between text and subject that underpin the different positions established in this work. As I have described, each position can be difficult to sustain as, in some ways, they can be seen to undermine each other. Just as textual approaches can be challenged by the growing sense of an authoring subject during the process of analysis (and we might, or might not, start to think this matters), so too approaches that regard online data as the embodiment of an offline subject can be undermined by the published, overtly textual nature of online material. At the same time, as I have described, the empirical characteristics of different online environments can both support and challenge the maintenance of these theoretical stances.

My intention here has not been to push one or another approach as 'right'. Researchers entering into online research for the first time need to establish a position, taking into account the issues explored in this chapter and the details of their own research projects. In some work, it may be appropriate to take a human subjects' approach, but the researcher needs to remember that different actions need to be appropriate to the context-attributing authorship may be as important as protecting anonymity. It is also possible to establish a stance that conceptualises material as text. However, if this stance denies the relevance of the human subject model to the research project, the researcher will need to be confident that they are able to justify and defend the decision not to seek consent. As Homan suggests, in the context of a 'professional consensus' that privileges informed consent, 'the principle of informed consent is that on which the self-respect and reputation of social research rest, and practitioners defy it at their peril' (Homan 2009, no page numbers).

In my own work, I was perhaps less than confident, falling instead between the two broad approaches I have examined in this chapter. My position was torn between the theoretical way I was defining the material on SHH and COA (as text) and my growing feelings of affiliation towards the imagined subjects represented by that text (which suggests a human subjects approach, a concern with harm and my lack of informed consent). This may relate to the amount of time I spent on these forums. But, more generally, it is perhaps impossible to escape what White has suggested is the alluring nature of online material, the way that the online avatar 'may seem like a direct imprint of some user that rests directly on the other side of the screen' (White 2002, 259) which appears 'to provide access into individual's personal domains and private thoughts' (260).

Whilst these issues might appear more relevant to research in pseudonymous online environments where the nature of the setting emphasises the constructed nature of 'human subjects', the unifying/separating moves between subject and utterance explored in this chapter are also visible within researchers' justifications of their ethical decisions in offline research. Subjects are brought into being in 'real-world' research, just as they are online. Whilst the authenticating subject seems more clearly defined in offline settings – as physical bodies that harm can be done to – both the online and offline subject might be regarded as an imagined projection, the product of a collection of utterances (whether online posts, interview transcripts, face-to-face interactions, or observed activities). Our consideration of the online subject might therefore provoke consideration of the construction of human subjects in offline research.

This task has already been taken up by a number of researchers who have responded to concerns about the verifiability of online data by challenging the distinction between on- and offline experience, undermining the idea that 'seemingly unproblematic, embodied encounters yield totally unambiguous information regarding personal identity' (Lyman and Wakeford 1999, 364). Judith Donath has noted that both online and offline, the researcher is involved in attributing unity, transforming 'fragmentary structure [...] into the completeness of an individuality' (Donath 2000, 303). Annette Markham notes that quandaries about identity and agency are 'apparent in any research context' (Markham 2003a), and (in respect of the potential for deception in online interviews) TL Taylor has noted that 'there are many things that in even an off-line interview we must take at the interviewee's word' (Taylor 1999, no page nos.). Taken to the extreme, it is the mythologised subject – the human author essentialised as having feelings and constructed from the multiplicity of posts – that can be betrayed by the researcher. The individual utterances have no feelings to hurt.

References

Bakardjieva, M., & Feenberg, A. (2001). Involving the virtual subject: Conceptual, methodological and ethical dimension. *Journal of Ethics and Information Technology, 2*(4), 233–248.

Bassett, E. H., & O'Riordan, K. (2002). Ethics of internet research: Contesting the human subjects research model. *Ethics and Information Technology, 4*(3), 233–247.

Berry, D. M. (2004). Internet research: Privacy, ethics and alienation: An open source approach. *Internet Research, 14*(4), 323–332.
Boehlefeld, S. (1996). Doing the right thing: Ethical cyberspace research. *The Information Society, 12*(2), 141–152.
Carter, D. (2005). Living in virtual communities: An ethnography of human relationships in cyberspace. *Journal of Information Communication and Society, 8*(2), 148–167.
Charlesworth, A. (2008). Understanding and managing legal issues in internet research. In N. Fielding, R. M. Lee, & G. Blank (Eds.), *The SAGE handbook of online research methods* (pp. 42–57). London/Thousand Oaks: SAGE.
Chin, B., & Gray, J. (2001). One ring to rule them all: Pre-viewers and pre-texts of the Lord of the Rings Film. *Intensities: The Journal of Cult Media, 2*. Available online: http://www.cult-media.com/issue2/Archingray.htm.
Crawford, S. P. (2004). Who's in charge of who I am? Identity and law online. *New York Law School Law Review, 49*, 211–229. Available online: http://scrawford.net/display/crawford%20identity.pdf. Last accessed 12 Sept 2010.
Davies, B. (1997). The subject of post-structuralism: A reply to Alison Jones. *Gender and Education, 9*(3), 271–283.
Dibbell, J. (1993, December 21). A rape in cyberspace. *Village Voice*, pp. 36–42. Available online: http://www.sla.purdue.edu/people/engl/blackmon/rape.html.
Dibbell, J. (1998). *My tiny life: Crime and passion in a virtual world*. New York: Holt Paperbacks.
Donath, J. (2000). Being real. In K. Goldberg (Ed.), *The robot in the garden: telerobotics and telepistemology in the age of the internet* (pp. 296–311). Cambridge: The MIT Press. Available online: http://smg.media.mit.edu/papers/BeingReal/BeingReal.html.
Economic and Social Research Council (ESRC) (2005). Research Ethics Framework. Available online http://www.esrc.ac.uk/ESRCInfoCentre/Images/ESRC_Re_Ethics_Frame_tcm6-11291.pdf.
Eysenbach, G., & Till, J. E. (2001). Ethical issues in qualitative research on internet communities. *British Medical Journal, 323*(10), 1103–1105.
Halliday, J., & Arthur, C. (2010, December 17 Friday). Known unknowns: Anonymous hierarchy emerges. *The Guardian*, p. 5. Available online: http://www.guardian.co.uk/media/2010/dec/16/wikileaks-anonymous-hierarchy-emerges?INTCMP=SRCH.
Herring, S. C. (1996). Linguistic and critical research on computer-mediated communication: Some ethical and scholarly considerations. *The Information Society, 12*(2), 153–168. Available online: http://ella.slis.indiana.edu/~herring/tis.1996.pdf.
Homan, R. (1980). The ethics of covert methods. *The British Journal of Sociology, 31*(1), 46–59.
Jones, A. (1997). Teaching post-structuralist feminist theory in education: Student resistances. *Gender and Education, 9*(3), 261–269.
Jordan, T. (1999). *Cyberpower*. London: Routledge.
Kendall, L. (1999). Recontextualising "Cyberspace": Methodological considerations for on-line research. In S. Jones (Ed.), *Doing internet research: Critical issues and methods for examining the net* (pp. 57–74). Thousand Oaks: SAGE.
Kendall, L. (2002). *Hanging out in the virtual pub: Masculinities and relationships online*. Berkeley: California University Press.
King, S. A. (1996). Researching internet communities: Proposed ethical guidelines for the reporting of results. *The Information Society, 12*(2), 119–128.
Konstan, J. A., Simon Rosser, B. R., Ross, M. W., Stanton, J., & Edwards, W. (2005). The story of subject naught: A cautionary but optimistic tale of Internet survey research. *Journal of Computer-Mediated Communication, 10*(2). http://jcmc.indiana.edu/vol10/issue2/konstan.html.
Lenhart, A., & Madden, M. (2007). *Teens, privacy & online social networks: How teens manage their online identities and personal information in the age of MySpace*. Washington, DC: Pew Internet & American Life Project. Available online: http://www.pewinternet.org/~/media//Files/Reports/2007/PIP_Teens_Privacy_SNS_Report_Final.pdf.pdf.
Lyman, P., & Wakeford, N. (1999). Introduction: Going into the virtual field. *American Behavioural Scientist, 43*(3), 359–376.

Markham, A. (1998). *Life online: Researching real experience in virtual space (ethnographic alternatives)*. Walnut Creek: AltaMira Press.
Markham, A. (2003a). Representation in online ethnographies: A matter of context sensitivity. In S. Chen, J. Hall, & M. Johns (Eds.), *Online social research: Theory, methods, and ethics* (pp. 131–145). New York: Peter Lang Publishers.
Markham, A. N. (2003b). Critical junctures and ethical choices in internet ethnography. In M. Thorseth (Ed.), *Applied ethics in internet research* (pp. 51–63). Trondheim: NTNU University Press.
Markham, A. (2004). Reconsidering self and other: Methods, politics, and ethics of representation in online ethnography. In N. Denzin & Y. Lincoln (Eds.), *Handbook of qualitative research* (pp. 793–820). London: SAGE.
Marks, A. (2007). Drug detection dogs and the growth of olfactory surveillance: Beyond the rule of law? *Surveillance & Society, 4*(3), 257–271.
Marks, A. (2008, March 31). Smells suspicious. *The Guardian*. http://www.guardian.co.uk/science/2008/mar/31/internationalcrime.
Marx, G.T. (2002). 'What's new about the 'new surveillance'? Classifying for change and continuity', Surveillance & Society 1(1): 9–29. http://www.surveillance-and-society.org/articles1.whatsnew.pdf.
McKee, H. A. (2008). Ethical and legal issues for writing researchers in an age of media convergence. *Computers and Composition, 25*, 104–122.
Miller, D., & Slater, D. (2001). *The internet: An ethnographic approach*. Oxford: Berg.
Pearce, C., & Artemesia. (2009). *Communities of play: Emergent cultures in multiplayer games and virtual worlds*. Cambridge: The MIT Press.
Pelletier, C., & Whiteman, N. (in press). Affiliation in the construction of fan identity: A comparison of face-to-face and virtual settings. In Ching, C. C., & B. J. Fdey (Eds.) *Constructing the self in a digital world*. To be published by Cambridge University Press.
Rutter, J., & Smith, G. (1999). *Presenting the off-line self in an everyday, online environment*. Paper presented at Identities in Action, University of Wales.
Sixsmith, J., & Murray, C. D. (2001). Ethical issues in the documentary data analysis of internet posts and archives. *Qualitative Health Research, 11*(3), 423–432.
Slater, D. (2002). Making things real: Ethics and order on the internet. *Theory, Culture & Society, 19*(5/6), 227–245.
Stern, S. R. (2003). Encountering distressing information in online research: a consideration of legal and ethical responsibilities. *New Media & Society, 5*(2), 246–266.
Taylor, T. L. (1999). Life in virtual worlds: Plural existence, multimodalities, and other online research challenges. *American Behavioral Scientist, 43*(3), 436–449.
Taylor T.L. (2002). Living Digitally: Embodiment in Virtual Worlds. In: Ralph Schroeder (ed), The Social Life of Avatars: Presence and Interaction in Shared Virtual Environments. London, Springer-Verlag, pp. 400–462.
Taylor, T. L. (2006). *Play between worlds: Exploring online game culture*. Cambridge: The MIT Press.
Turkle, S. (1995). *Life on the screen: Identity in the age of the Internet*. New York: Simon & Schuster.
Turkle, S. (1996a). Constructions and reconstructions of the self in virtual reality. In T. Druckery (Ed.), *Electronic culture: Technology and visual representation*. Romford: Aperture.
Turkle, S. (1996b, January). Who am we? *Wired* (4.01), pp. 148–152.
Westmarland, L. (2001). Blowing the whistle on police violence. *British Journal of Criminology, 41*, 523–535.
White, M. (2002). Representations or people? *Ethics and Information Technology, 4*(2), 249–266.
Whiteman, N. (2007). *The establishment, maintenance and destabilisation of fandom: A study of two online communities and an exploration of issues pertaining to internet research*. Unpublished Ph.D. thesis, Institute of Education, University of London. Available online: http://homepage.mac.com/paulcdowling/ioe/studentswork/whiteman(2007).pdf.
Wolfendale, J. (2007). My avatar, my self: Virtual harm and attachment. *Ethics and Information Technology, 9*, 111–119.

Chapter 5
Unstable Relations: Observational Methods and Ethical Instability

Abstract This chapter moves from a focus on the production of ethics in research towards an interest in the *undoing* of ethical positions, the challenging of ethical stances that can arise from the unpredictable and contingent nature of research. Drawing from the accounts of scholars who have engaged in observation-based studies of online and offline environments, the chapter explores the nature of 'participation' in fieldwork-based research and how contingent events and ethical dilemmas may lead researchers to change the nature of their involvement with their empirical settings. The chapter examines the shifting affiliations and modes of participation that researchers may experience during research and returns to one of the key questions introduced in Chap. 2: to what extent can, and should, researchers align their ethics with those of the setting?

In October 2005, when I attempted to visit the forums at SHH, I found that they no longer existed. In place of the site's familiar homepage, I found the following announcement:
HaCKeD BY Yusuf:: [Turkish Team]- =
HaCKeD@web.com = – –
Information:
Sorry, but this board is currently unavailable. Please try again later
I had had problems accessing the site in the past, and experienced moments of 'downtime,' but these had only ever been temporary. On this occasion, the absence of the forums was more significant. The hacking of the site by 'Yusuf' had emptied the forums of content, removing the posting history of the site; over 64,000 posts had been deleted.
Days after the site went down a notice appeared on SHH saying that the forums should soon be returning. At the beginning of November they were back online, but in a somewhat altered form. Whilst they retained the same formal structure and organisation, and the same segregation of topics for discussion

N. Whiteman, *Undoing Ethics: Rethinking Practice in Online Research*,
DOI 10.1007/978-1-4614-1827-6_5, © Springer Science+Business Media, LLC 2012

within different boards, the forums now had a new url address and looked slightly different following the introduction of new header artwork.

They were also strangely empty. The hacking had emptied the forums of content, deleting the posting history of the site and of individual members. Whilst individual post counts remained, the contents of these posts had been lost. This loss was severe, but did not prove fatal: by 6th November 2005 there were already 1,475 posts on the site; the process of re-building had begun.

Introduction

In a preface to their *Ethical Guidelines for Good Research Practice* (1999), the Association of Social Anthropologists of the UK and Commonwealths (ASA) underline the challenges of research. They describe how:

> Anthropologists, like other social researchers, are faced increasingly with competing duties, obligations and conflicts of interest, with the need to make implicit or explicit choices between values and between the interests of different individuals and groups.

They then go on to note that 'ethical and legal dilemmas occur at all stages of research' and to remind researchers that they 'have a responsibility to anticipate problems and insofar as is possible to resolve them without harming the research participants or the scholarly community'.[1] As the extract implies, the value of this guidance reaches beyond the field of anthropology. All researchers need to try to anticipate potential ethical problems that may arise in respect of their work. Yet, as my description of the hacking of SHH in 2005 above suggests, it is impossible to predict all the unexpected and contingent events that may occur during research.

The hacking of SHH was a terrible event for the members of the site (one which temporarily lead to the setting up of a 'refugee camp' on another *Silent Hill* fan site[2]). The event also raised a significant ethical question for me. I had been archiving material from the site – should I now break with my nonparticipation and offer my archive to the community? More broadly, what was my relationship to a site that I had been covertly visiting almost daily for over a year? By provoking consideration of these questions, the hacking of SHH led me to reflect on my own 'competing duties, obligations, and conflicts of interest' and unsettled the position I had established in relation to the site up until this point.

The previous two chapters have considered the way that specific stances might be established and maintained in respect of key issues: whether one regards a setting as public or private and whether one regards online material as text or subject. Here, rather than focusing on the *production* of ethical stances, I want to explore in more detail the *undoing* of such positions, the destabilisation of ethical stances that can arise from the unpredictable and contingent nature of research. This destabilisation

[1] http://www.theasa.org/ethics/guidelines.shtml.

[2] See Whiteman (2007) for discussion of the immediate aftermath of the hacking.

has been suggested in the previous chapters in my discussion of the ways that the contexts of research and researcher/researched relationships may shift and develop over time (e.g. how one might start to identify with textual material). Here, however, ethical destabilisation is my focus.

As I described in Chap. 1, researchers typically face institutional pressures to fix the methodological and ethical groundwork of their studies before embarking on research. Such fixing is evident in the ethics approval process – which tends to be structurally front-loaded[3] – and in the explanation of research design in proposals and funding bids. Yet, as the ASA suggests, the experience of actually doing research often challenges such fixing, presenting dilemmas and contingent events that can unsettle the stances that researchers have established in advance of their fieldwork.[4] As the consideration of observational research in this chapter will suggest, once the researcher enters the field making and enacting decisions becomes a more complex endeavour, revealing the maintenance of an ethical stance to be a dynamic and continuous activity. Drawing from the accounts of researchers who have engaged in observation-based research, the chapter examines the shifting affiliations and ethical challenges that researchers may experience. In exploring these, I return to one of the key questions introduced in Chap. 2: to what extent can, and should, researchers align their ethics with those of the setting?

Observation Online

The Internet and new media technologies present researchers with different ways of experiencing empirical phenomena. These can be seen to correspond with those available to researchers working in offline environments, but also present researchers with unique viewing positions and forms of embodiment and interaction.

Some sites, including public forums, blogs, websites, and some social networks (such as *Myspace*), enable researchers to lurk invisibly, to generate data without being represented within the setting and with participants therefore being unaware of the researcher's presence. Offline, such research would likely involve deception or adopting a covert position, with the researcher making a concerted effort to shield their research intentions from those inhabiting the environment. In many online environments, however, lurking is a normal state of being. Visitors to such sites are invisible, only coming into the public gaze of other visitors if and when they make an utterance. The suggestion that lurking is problematic because it is akin to spying in the 'real world' – seen in the following criticism of unannounced research – therefore appears misplaced as, in such sites, *everyone* is hidden unless they post a contribution to the site:

[3] It is worth noting that institutions are increasingly incorporating ongoing review/surveillance processes into the ethics review process.

[4] I am using the term fieldwork broadly to refer to empirical data collection.

> While we seem willing to accept a researcher openly taking notes on interaction in a public park from a bench, we might have more concerns about them doing so while hidden in a bush.
>
> (Smith 2004, 230)

Although taking an unannounced position will need to be defended and justified (for the reasons discussed in Chaps. 3 and 4), lurking in public settings does not equate with spying in offline domains because shared invisibility is a natural state of engagement in these environments. The researcher may or may not be able to defend their use of data from such sites, but is not 'hidden in a bush'.

Other online environments are more demanding, forcing the researcher to be directly present within the setting. As Cecilia Pearce and Artemesia (2009) suggest, in order to view and experience the activity contained within virtual worlds (such as MMORPGS and environments such as *Second Life*), a representation of the researcher must enter these domains. For technical reasons, the researcher 'cannot observe a virtual world without being *inside* it, and in order to be inside it, you have to be "embodied"' (Pearce and Artemesia 2009, 196). Here, the generation of data can only take place through, and in relation to, the avatar of the researcher. It is not possible to lurk invisibly in such settings, although the intentions of the researcher may be hidden from other inhabitants.[5] The researcher could, of course, rely on documentary evidence of activity, such as video capture of interactions made by others, but this would be equivalent to the use of secondary data, rather than direct experience. As in the lurkable settings described above (as well as in offline environments), the nature of the researcher's involvement in a site such as *Second Life* is therefore constrained/enabled by the affordances of the environment, whilst also being dependent on the extent to which the researcher wishes to adopt an open, visible presence in the setting.

There are, then, similarities and differences between the forms of embodiment and presence that researchers can adopt when working in online and offline environments. Although the empirical settings they study may have very different characteristics, online researchers are faced with the same essential questions about the nature of their research approach as those faced by offline researchers. A key question, which relates to both the presence and visibility of the researcher, is the extent to which the researcher participates in the activity or remains a more distant observer.[6] Will they seek to obtain an insider perspective or carry out their work from 'outside' the activity? As I suggested in Chap. 3, answers to such questions

---

[5] The possibilities for deception are founded on the separation of avatar and subject, as discussed in Chap. 4 – although it is important to remember that similar deceptions can also occur in face-to-face environments.

[6] There are, of course, many other facets to the researcher/researched relationship aside from the extent to which one is an observer or participant. As Marlane de Laine (2000) describes, the role of the researcher may be defined along multiple dimensions. This may include the extent to which the subjects of research are involved in the research projects as participants (and with this, the extent to which expertise is transferred from researcher to researched, 107), the extent to which the researcher obtains an insider perspective, the degree of disclosure of the research activity the researcher makes, and the extent to which they intrude in the settings (de Laine 2000, 102–109).

are likely to have significant ethical implications, affecting the relationship that researchers establish in respect of the empirical contexts of research. At the same time, it is likely that these answers will be challenged by those who might argue that other observational stances might be more productive or more appropriate.

Participant or Observer?

This distinction between participation and observation suggests that contrasting observational positions are available to the researcher. In the teaching of research methods, these are often presented in terms of the different roles that researchers might inhabit. The decision I made to lurk within SHH and COA – to be a nonparticipant observer – might, for example, be seen to push my observational stance towards one end of Gold's (1958) classic typology of observational positions.[7] That is, towards the 'complete observer' and away from the explicit membership role of the 'complete participant', where the researcher becomes an active and legitimate member of the setting (whose other members may, however, be unaware of the researcher's research intentions).

The marking out of different modes of academic engagement in this way rests upon certain interpretations of what it means to be a 'participant' or 'observer'. Each term suggests an orientation to the researched activity, implying either distance (in terms of the observer) or closeness (in terms of the participant).[8] Such positioning is particularly evident in the ways that the strengths and limitations of different observational methods are discussed in research methods writing. Unobtrusive observation, for example, is presented as having certain benefits in preventing the researcher from 'muddying the waters' and, Scott and Usher suggest, in providing a distanced position that can protect the researcher from being influenced by 'the agendas of participants' (1999, 101). Yet, this distance is also configured as a limitation. Robson, for example, suggests that 'virtual total detachment can come across as anti-social and itself cause reactions from those observed' (Robson 2002, 311), whilst others argue that this distance leads to an impoverished understanding of empirical situations as 'to remain an observer is to remain distant from the experience of being-in-culture' (Markham 2004, 145).

Those who call for more directly engaged forms of participation often present such methods as enabling researchers to gain understandings of empirical phenomena that cannot be obtained via more distanced positions. The sociologist Loïc Wacquant, for example, describes the importance of embodied initiation into an

---

[7] See also Junker's early description of observational roles (1952, 1960).

[8] As Bryman points out, Gold's schema of participant observer positions 'can be arrayed on a continuum of degrees of involvement with and detachment from members of the social setting' (Bryman 2008, 410).

activity as providing a research perspective that cannot be gained from the outside. The value of such initiation, he argues, is that it allows scholars to:

> [...] probe into the makeup of habitus by studying not its products but its production; not the regulated strategies it informs but the coordinated techniques and patterned relations that form it.
>
> (Wacquant 2005, 466)

In contrast to the more clinical distance of observation, it is suggested, getting directly involved in the messy micro-level details of activity can be rewarding.

Different methodological vulnerabilities are identified here, however. Most notably, the participant-researcher faces the danger of 'going native'. This, we are warned, involves the researcher overidentifying with the setting and, in so doing, losing their research perspective (Robson 2002), or as Jackson puts it, '"going-native" to the extent that [the researcher's] observational acuity is reduced' (Jackson 1983, 41). A second danger relates to the assumption that an insider perspective necessarily leads to academic enlightenment. As Wacquant notes, the fact that one has acquired membership status via involvement in an activity does not *automatically* result in the production of authoritative knowledge:

> [...] membership in a category or collective does not by itself make one a good anthropologist of it. At best it might make one an informant about it; at worst, it invites a descent into moral subjectivism, a parroting of the folk sociology of members [...]. (Wacquant 2005, 457)

For this reason, some distance is required. This suggests, perhaps, that it is not enough for the researcher to be observer or participant, the researcher must instead enter into a dialogue between these perspectives.

Whether or not the researcher is persuaded by the arguments for or against the use of different observational methods, it is clear that in designing observation-based projects, certain warnings must be heeded. If the researcher stands too far from the researched contexts, they may fail to gain understanding. Stand too close and the academic gaze of the observer may be lost. This distance/involvement is assessed in relation to different perspectives: that of the researcher, engaged in academic endeavour, and that of the member-insider, engaged with the activity of the setting.[9]

The researcher can therefore be seen to be faced with 'divided loyalties' (Scheper-Hughes 2000), needing to satisfy the aims and procedures of research, whilst also taking into account the empirical contexts of their study. This division is suggested in Gold's definition of the fieldwork role as being 'at once a social interaction device for securing information for scientific purposes and a set of behaviours in which an observer's self is involved' (Gold 1958, 218). This tension between roles and interests

---

[9] Arguing for the need for membership roles in fieldwork, for example, Adler and Adler (1987) distinguish between detached outsider/wallflower positions vs. membership based on varying degrees of insider affiliation (Adler and Adler 1987, 8). They make reference to the ways that researchers 'are often compelled to put aside their academic or other everyday life roles' (8) during the practice of research.

can be experienced whatever methods are being used (whether observation, survey, interview, etc.). In coming into direct contact with researched individuals/contexts, the researcher enters into a dialogue between their academic interests and the ethics of their own behaviour within, and in relation to, the settings of research. As I now want to explore, these different concerns can be seen to produce ethical tensions in research and also have implications for the maintenance of observational positions.

Observational Shifts and Ethical Destabilisation

Although it provides a neat marker of different modes of engagement, the distinction between observation and participation is difficult to sustain when the researcher actually moves into the field. The difficulty of maintaining specific roles is acknowledged in writing on observational methods, where the purity of different observational viewpoints is undermined by reference to the idea that perspectives might merge or be moved between. Jackson (1983), for example, notes that rather than extremes of participation/observation, researchers will more usually deploy 'some combination of these extremes: the "participant-as-observer" for example or the "observer-as-participant"' (Jackson 1983, 41). Adler and Adler (1987) describe how 'shifts' in the researcher's relationship to the setting can occur, with events leading the researcher to become more or less involved during research.[10] This work suggests that the role of the researcher is constantly in progress. It does not stay still but develops and changes as the research goes on and as different 'pulls and pushes' (Van Maanen et al. 1987, 5) lead researchers to engage more/less directly with their empirical setting(s).

Why might the researchers' relationship to the setting change? On one level, the lifecycle of a research project itself suggests a developing observational identity. The researcher may start out as an observer, deciding to enter into a setting (or settings) in order to carry out research and then, through engagement with the setting, achieve membership status. Moving in the other direction, if the researcher starts out as a member of the researched activity, they may begin from a position of similarity and close proximity to the setting. Once the setting becomes part of their academic gaze, however, another domain presses, and there is likely to be a necessary distancing from the setting or the researcher will be unable to produce an analysis that moves beyond the summarising of empirical concepts.

Shifts may also arise as a result of events that present a challenge to the researcher's approach, provoking distancing or affiliating moves to the different contexts of research. Such moments of 'crisis' can pitch the researcher out of the relative comfort of an established ethical position, or methodological approach, by introducing a condition of instability to the research endeavour that must be resolved. The nature

[10] Whilst they are talking about shifts within membership roles based on participation, we see similar moves in more observational roles, where researchers may feel their own pulls towards greater participation in a setting – I will return to this later in the chapter.

of this destabilisation may vary. We might be faced with an ethical dilemma or contingent event that raises particular questions about how we should (and need to) act, for example. As a result, we might shift our mode of engagement with the researched activity, perhaps distancing ourselves from our research settings, removing ourselves from them completely, or drawing closer to them.

Ethical crises might not just involve exceptional events or distinct ethical 'dilemmas'; they can also arise as a result of what Guillemin and Gillan (2004) refer to as 'ethically important moments': 'the difficult, often subtle, and usually unpredictable situations that arise in the practice of doing research' (262). In their view, such moments are central to the consideration of 'ethics in practice' (264). They suggest that:

> There can be all sorts of ethically important moments: when participants indicate discomfort with their answer, or reveal a vulnerability; when a research participant states that he or she does not want to be assigned a pseudonym in the writing up of the research but wants to have his or her real name reported; or the case described by Orb et al. (2001) of interviewing victims of violence where the researcher has to decide how far to probe a participant about a difficult and distressing experience.
>
> (Guillemin and Gillam 2004, 265)

These moments – 'where the approach taken or the decision made has important ethical ramifications, but where the researcher does not necessarily feel himself or herself to be on the horns of a dilemma. [...]' (265) – are less dramatic than the ethical crises that I am going to explore in the rest of this chapter. Nevertheless, they present similar destabilising challenges to researchers and are, Guillemin and Gillan write, key to the consideration of 'the day-to-day ethical issues that arise in the doing of research' (264). The 'importance' of such moments, they argue, is that they raise questions about how ethics are practiced in research (because it is in the day-to-day management of ethical issues that 'the researcher's ethical competence comes to the fore' (269)).[11]

Whether they involve dramatic incidents, or the more subtle ethical complexities of data collection/dissemination, destabilising events constitute points of crisis if they serve to unsettle the stance that the researcher has established. In order to think about these potential challenges, I want to return to the scheme that I introduced in Chap. 2. There, I introduced four domains of ethics as a framework for thinking about the construction and articulation of ethical stances in research. Now, rather than thinking about the ethical discourses within these domains as potential resources for the production of an ethical identity, I am interested in thinking about them as sites of potential destabilisation, destabilisation that is not always negative and is necessary for development and growth, but can be uncomfortable.

The second and third columns of Fig. 5.1 show the strongly and weakly institutionalised forms of ethical mediation which might be the focus of the researcher's attention in the design and conduct of research. As I have suggested above, the researcher needs

[11] 'By this we mean the researcher's willingness to acknowledge the ethical dimension of research practice, his or her ability to actually recognize this ethical dimension when it comes into play, and his or her ability to think through ethical issues and respond appropriately' (Guillemin and Gillam 2004, 269).

	ETHICAL DISCOURSE	
ETHICAL DOMAIN	**I-**	**I+**
Researcher	**Personal Contingencies** A personal epiphany.	**Personal codes** The researcher's political affiliations
Researched (empirical field)	**Setting contingencies** Act of violence in the setting, members of community react negatively to presence of researcher	**Setting codes** Agreements on rights/values – as expressed in rules of use for example
Academy (theoretical field)	**Academic contingencies** An unsettling question at a Q+A at a conference, or in informal feedback to writing	**Academic codes** Research ethics frameworks, guidance in journal articles
Institution	**Official contingencies** The university announces an edict, ethics committee intervention	**Official codes** University code of ethics

Fig. 5.1 Four domains of research ethics (destabilisation) (Adapted from Whiteman 2010, Fig. 1)

to move between these domains in research. If they position themselves solely in relation to the ethics of the researched, they risk going native and being unable to speak to the academy. If they focus solely on their own ethics, then they risk being alienated from both the setting and the academy, isolated and unable to speak about (or to) either.

I suggested in Chap. 2 that these domains, and the different ethical discourses they present, can be recruited in the construction of an ethical stance. Here, I am claiming that the researcher's stance can be *destabilised* from any position within this framework. Such destabilisation can be anticipated to some extent as long as one focuses on the strongly institutionalised discourses (shown in the third column of Fig. 5.1). It is likely that the researcher will familiarise themselves with the codes of different domains before entering the field as part of the early scoping and planning activity. They will need to get to grips with these in order to give their work a grounding in the empirical and theoretical contexts of their research, as well as the official requirements of their institutions. If they fail to do this, they are likely to be challenged, perhaps at viva or thesis defence, perhaps at publication. However, because they are codified areas, these codes can still provoke destabilisation. Contrasting interpretations, shifting readings, and wider exposure or discovery can unsettle the researcher's stance.

In advance of the research, the researcher's focus may be on the strongly institutionalised discourses of these domains. From then on, however, their attention is likely to shift to the local contingencies presented in the second column of Fig. 5.1. These are unpredictable developments that cannot be completely anticipated in the planning of research. Local contingencies are challenging precisely because-although we might expect to be able to anticipate the general *sorts* of legal and ethical challenges we might face in the conduct of research (and this will depend on the nature of the activity/environment[12]), the contingencies we *actually* experience cannot be predicted with certainty. They introduce the unexpected and can hence be destabilising.[13] It is for this reason that the researchers' ability to deal with ethical problems comes to the fore in the face of local contingencies.

John Edward Campbell's (2004) book *Getting It On Online: Cyberspace, Gay Male Sexuality and Embodied Identity* presents an example of a personal contingency. Here, Campbell describes the 'mixture of disbelief coupled with bewilderment' (154) he felt when a man with whom he had developed a relationship on the Internet Relay Chat channel #gaymuscle revealed himself not to be the 'bodybuilder of immense size and physical strength' (152) that he had portrayed online, but instead a man living with his mother who 'viewed himself as considerably obese and physically unattractive' (153). This event is presented in the context of an academic discussion of hierarchies of beauty within the setting, but is memorable for the troubling revelation that Campbell appears to fear that it suggests about himself and his own relationship to the setting:

> How was it that I had been so utterly convinced by Younghung's performance? Did this mean that what I had come to view as a cherished online friendship was itself an illusion? Did his affirmations that I was an attractive man suddenly carry less weight? [...] Though Britannic[14] and I experienced an initial sense of betrayal, we also agreed that there was something understandable in Younghung's enactment of virtual body bending. After all, would I have been so eager to become Younghung's friend if I had known he was an out-of-shape security guard still living at his mother's house in the first place? [...] Perhaps I so readily accepted his performance because I was so enamoured with the notion that someone possessing such a physique should find me (a man in his late twenties with an average build and gut) attractive. (154)

[12] Research into sensitive topics or potentially dangerous environments, for example, might alert us to the need for caution in respect of particular interactions.

[13] This destabilisation may occur in direct response to, or later reflection upon, these local contingencies.

[14] Another member of the list.

In Campbell's expression of his reactions to this revelation, it is not Younghung's deception itself that is presented as destabilising, but instead the personal questions that Campbell's belief in this constructed identity raises about himself. His focus is turned inwards to consider his own position, affiliations, and potential prejudices; the personal ethics of the researcher are the local source of destabilisation here.

As Campbell's experience suggests, contingencies can arise within the empirical contexts of research. It was, after all, Younghung's revelation that triggered the sudden personal realisation described in the example above. Reports of fieldwork often contain descriptions of such setting contingencies, unexpected events that demonstrate how local developments relating to the contexts of research can unsettle researchers' observational positions and methodological actions.

Romance on a Global Stage (2005) – a study of Internet dating and mail order marriages – provides one example. Here, the author, Nicole Constable, describes an aborted attempt to enter an online setting for research. With the approval of moderators of the group, and after lurking for a while, Constable introduced herself to an Internet List where she hoped to carry out research into correspondence relationships between American men and Filipina women. She describes the response of the site's membership to her post in the following way:

> There were three main responses to my presence: friendly, challenging, and hostile. At first most were very friendly. Many members welcomed me as they do all new members and encouraged me to participate. [...] Some other members' responses were more challenging, although not hostile. They explicitly and repeatedly called on me to explain and defend my research goals. [...] When I checked my email a few hours later, there were many more messages, including several that were far more hostile. These came from four members, two of whom were especially outspoken and angry. [...] Other members accused the critics of paranoia, noting possible positive outcomes of having a researcher on the list, and observing that other researchers could already be on the list but not have been so honest to say so. [...] The four outspoken critics remained adamantly opposed to my presence. Two of them sent me private messages demanding that I leave. (pp. 48–49)

The destabilising challenge in this case emerges during the negotiation of entry into the setting, a result of Constable's openness of approach and the negative response of some members of the List to her study. The moment presents a question: what is the best – or 'most ethical' way – to respond to the hostility of these members? To remain within the site and carry out the research in light of the support she had received from the majority of respondents (defying the criticism of a small number of potential subjects and ignoring the possibility that she might disrupt the setting further)? Or to withdraw from the setting, losing the opportunity that she had been given by the official gatekeepers of the List and, indeed, denying her supporters on the site the potential benefit that they envisaged? In this case, Constable was unable to accommodate the negativity. Her response was to withdraw from the setting.

Within the academic domain, alongside the coding of ethical discourse, academic contingencies can also arise in the informal exchanges that academics have with each other. In an example from my own work, a senior colleague, having read a lengthy defence of my own observational stance in respect of COA and SHH – one which was at the time based largely on the normalcy of lurking within these settings[15] – pointed out quite sharply that, just because lurking was an acceptable mode of participation in the setting, it did not mean that it was necessarily ok for a *researcher* to lurk within the site. This comment was unsettling because it revealed a weakness in the stance I had established. Whilst it did not cause me to change my observational approach to COA and SHH, this warning provoked a necessary reflection upon the weighting I gave to this argument in my presentation of my research design and writing up of the work. It also led me to reflect more clearly on what it might mean to be an *academic lurker*, providing a timely reminder that the interests of researcher and researched are not the same.

Finally, we might also consider the official contingencies that researchers may face, those that emerge from within the institutional settings of research and in relation to those with bureaucratic responsibility for the regulation and supervision of research ethics. Carol Rambo's (2007) description of an IRB's decision to deny approval for the publication of an autoethnographic account she had written provides one example. Rambo describes her Departmental Chair's strong reaction to her work, which explored issues relating to abuse and the staff/student relationship:

> I'm going to give it to you straight and be blunt. This manuscript should never see the light of day – ever. If it were mine, I'd bury it under the nearest rock-deep. [The departmental chair stabs the manuscript repeatedly with an index finger.] (356)

Rambo was instructed to submit the paper to the Institutional Review Board of her institution and, upon doing so, was informed that the work would not be approved. Exploring the stated reasons for the IRB's decision, Rambo states that 'as a result of [the board members] performance, I have been silenced' (365). Her response in this case was to produce a different paper examining the incident and its ethical implications (including a consideration of what exactly the Board might understand by 'research').

We can, then, consider the ways that the weakly institutionalised contingencies and strongly institutionalised codes of the ethics of the researcher, researched, academy, and institution might unsettle and destabilise the researcher's ethical stance. Our attention might then shift to how researchers react to this destabilisation.

Rupturing and Suturing Identification

As I have described above, the researcher's ethical stance can be challenged in relation to antagonisms that can arise in respect of each ethical domain of research. Responses to such moments are revealing because, in forcing efforts to reconstruct the researcher's ethical stance, they often provoke reflections upon, and reassessment of, the researcher's methods and ethics. It may be possible to assimilate the disruption and proceed largely as the researcher had done before the event occurred. Alternatively, a destabilising event may lead the researcher to adapt or even substantially transform their stance. Yet, if they are unable to accommodate the disruption,

[15] See Chap. 3.

it may halt the research, as Constable and Rambo's cases demonstrate (the former involving the researcher withdrawing from the setting, the latter leading to the original paper being abandoned).

Researchers' accounts of such crises demonstrate the internal conflict resolution involved in maintaining an ethical stance and with it, the ongoing configuration and reconfiguration of a coherent and 'ethical' research identity that can be presented to public audiences and institutional bodies. This identity emerges in descriptions of the ethical disruptions that researchers have faced and is also evident in their responses to these disruptions. I discussed in Chap. 2 how the legitimacy of research actions is often established via appeals to different ethical resources and how these are used to explain and justify researchers' ethical and methodological decision-making. We can extend awareness of these moves via a consideration of the responses of researchers to destabilising events. Specifically, where does the researcher position their allegiance during research and what triggers provoke disruption?

I want to suggest that we can identify strategic *suturing* and *rupturing* moves in researchers' responses to destabilising events. This is a conceptual distinction that I developed during my study of SHH and COA (see Whiteman 2007). Then, I was interested in the ways that fans of serial forms of entertainment maintained their identification to their 'loved objects' (e.g. specific videogames and television programmes) over time and how this identification was challenged by destabilising events (such as the release of new material that disappointed them or even that they hated).[16] This involved a consideration of the strategic actions involved in fans' expressions of their allegiances to, and identification with, the objects of their fan interest, how these were secured within posting activity (e.g. what was cited when fans described what they loved about *Silent Hill* in contrast to other videogames) and the developments that marked a break in their identification to the text (what changes displeased them and why?). I argued that these suturing and rupturing moves were key to the configuration of fan identities within these sites because they tended to emphasise competing affiliations/dislikes in the maintenance of fans' identification to their favoured texts. Now, I am interested in exploring similar moves in a very different context – research activity, rather than fan activity. Specifically, how are researchers' identifications articulated within their accounts of research practice and what suturing and rupturing moves do they establish in relation to the ethical discourses of different domains?

Castellano (2007) has suggested that one way of dealing with ethical issues that arise from role conflicts in participant observation-based research is via the use of 'anchoring' and 'distancing' moves. This is a distinction that she takes from Emerson and Pollner (2001), where 'anchoring involves deepening participation in fieldwork settings, and distancing refers to negotiating withdrawal from member culture' (Castellano 2007, 705). Such moves are strategic because they are used to protect

[16] For a discussion of suturing and rupturing in relation to media fans identifications with fan objects and cultures online, see Whiteman 2007.

the researcher, who can anchor and distance themselves from both their researcher and participant roles (706/77). Castellano describes how:

> [...] distancing from the researcher role refers to underplaying or minimizing data activities. Anchoring to the researcher role refers to openly engaging in research tasks for purposes of collecting data. (707).

Castellano illustrates different ways that distancing/anchoring moves might be seen to be used in the process of fieldwork in respect of her own study of the criminal justice system and the dilemmas she faced working in correctional facilities in the USA. She describes how, not feeling comfortable 'pulling inmates' from their cells for interviews, she negotiated an exemption from this task, first in reference to her IRB restrictions and later by telling her co-worker that she felt she did not have the experience to do this safely (716). She notes that this withdrawal from participation 'involved anchoring to my researcher role and distancing myself from my participant role' (716).[17]

I am using the terms suturing and rupturing in a similar way to describe the actions that, respectively, establish researcher's allegiances to specific ethical domains (anchoring them to different domains, so to speak) and those that mark a break from them (asserting distance from particular positions). This involves a consideration of the identifications that researchers develop during research and how allegiances to different domains of ethics are evident in the presentation of research activity. Different suturing/rupturing moves are clearly possible in respect of the same reference points. Attention to both the rupturing and suturing moves evident in researcher's accounts of such crises is important because the ethical significance of these moments is only partly about the nature of the destabilising occurrence itself. More significant – if we are interested in how researchers negotiate the ethics of their practice – are the affiliations that are implicated in the researchers' inability to accept the destabilising event and what it represents. Like the fans on COA and SHH, the regularity of certain affiliating moves/referents can be seen to be involved in the dynamic establishing of the researcher's ethical identity.

To take one of the contingent events introduced above, for example, the destabilising event in Constable's study can be seen to arise from the open hostility of a small number of members of the List (from Constable's account, this was by no means the majority of the site's membership). Their response produced a rupture, became problematic, because Constable was unwilling to deny the legitimacy of their concerns or to proceed with her research without their acceptance. If she did not care, or felt she could ignore their voices, their reaction would not have proved disruptive.

Constable explains her decision to withdraw from the List and to locate a different research site via reference to the subjects of research. She suggests that she could

[17] 'Initially, I anchored to my researcher role by declining the task on the basis of ethical limitations set up by the IRB. Because this explanation caused confusion, I was pressed to directly confront the situation. I then reframed the problem by talking about how my limited experience prevented me from doing the task safely. The strategy of seeking an exemption illustrates that multiple techniques can be deployed consecutively to resolve a fieldwork dilemma' (Castellano 2007, 716).

not remain within a setting where participants were hostile to her presence as 'I had never knowingly forced myself on research subjects before and had no intention to do so now' (49). This response is thus established in relation to the ethics of the researcher – a notion of herself as a researcher who maintains a specific type of relationship to the subjects of research. In this example, both the rupturing and the suturing moves relate to a privileging of the (human) research subject. This is what the ethical stance is fixed in relation to. We might imagine different outcomes of course where the researcher might instead feel that she could accommodate the disruption and continue with her work. Such a decision could be explained in relation to her own interests, or guidance in an academic paper, or by making a case for the legitimacy of doing such work via reference to authorisation the researcher may have obtained from an ethics committee, or indeed in reference to the ethics of the setting in a different way (perhaps drawing on the fact that she had the support of most members of the site, or on the authority of the moderators who had granted her permission for her work). These justifications might be easier/harder to defend depending on the audience.

Moving between examples of online and offline research, the rest of this chapter examines researchers' responses to setting contingencies. My focus on the destabilising events that occur in the empirical contexts of research is due to my interest in observational methods in this chapter; it is contingencies that arise within the field that are perhaps most likely to disrupt during research. As I have suggested, however, these events cannot be separated from the other elements of the schema. Setting contingencies can be disruptive precisely because of their relation to the other discourses that inform the production of the researcher's ethical stance. In exploring this disruption, I am going to consider how ruptures in researchers' identifications to domains of research ethics can shift those engaged in observational work in different directions, motivating them to adopt more or less directly engaged modes of observation. In examining these moves, I am also interested in the ways that attention to researchers' identifications with different domains can reveal the practical and theoretical complexity of 'observation' and 'participation'.

From Participant to Observer?

I want to start by looking at a number of cases where researchers have experienced difficulties sustaining insider positions in research based on covert participant observation. Any researcher engaged in such work faces the need to 'act in line with subject norms over the entire period of research if s/he wishes to retain trust and access' (Pearson 2009, 248). However, crises can arise when researchers embedded within an environment are confronted by setting contingencies that challenge their continued participation within the research contexts. Difficulties here can relate to the challenges of operating within the setting and 'acclimating to member culture' (Castellano 2007) – challenges that can produce ethical questions about the types of activity that researchers will and will not participate in. Roger Homan (1980), for example, describes different kinds of 'ethical problem at the individual level' that can be experienced during covert research (52), problems that he suggests emerge in relation to 'individual morality'.[18] Drawing from his own research experience, he describes the 'crisis of conscience' that he experienced during covert research within Pentecostal churches, documenting the activities he took part in (such as participation in the breaking of bread, 53) and those he 'eschewed' ('I could not offer myself for baptism: somehow these measures seemed inordinately fraudulent' (53)).

Work on covert research into illicit and criminal activities has presented numerous, often dramatic examples of researchers being confronted with setting contingencies and needing to decide where they will draw the line in terms of what actions they will and will not engage in (or indeed what they should report to external authorities). Pearson's (2009) work on violent football supporters describes the demands of researching contexts in which criminal activity of varying degrees of severity regularly takes place, including:

> [...] drink and drug offences, ticket touting, breaches of the Football (Offences) Act 1990 (invading the pitch, throwing missiles, indecent or racialist chanting), disorderly and threatening behaviour, assault and actual bodily harm, theft and criminal damage [...] riot, affray, violent disorder, robbery and assault occasioning grievous bodily harm.
>
> (Pearson 2009, 246)

Pearson describes the resulting pressure he faced to undertake criminal acts as 'a refusal to commit crimes on a regular basis would have aroused suspicions and reduced research opportunities' (Pearson 2009, 246). Significantly, he also identifies more extreme criminal acts that he refused to participate in, including racist chanting.[19] In these cases, 'personal ideas of ethics and morality' impinged (Pearson 2009, 249). Similarly, the researcher in a study by Winlow et al. of bouncing and the night time economy (2001) is described as being able to 'grudgingly put up with brawling groups of men who occasionally directed violence at him' (2001, 545), but as being shaken by moments such as the glassing[20] of a young girl (545–546). Schacht's (1997) covert study of rugby culture describes the author's 'considerable anguish' at observing a woman being drunkenly tormented by a gang of men and women holding her aloft and 'serenading' her with a vile, misogynistic song as she became increasingly upset, attempted to escape, and began to cry. He reflects on his involvement in the setting: by observing without intervening, he 'neither encouraged nor condemned' the event yet was complicit in it due to his presence and noninterference.

---

[18] 'Concern here is with the ethical code which the fieldworker adopts in his personal life which may render unacceptable or uncongenial some of the expectations made of him either directly by supervisors or indirectly as a consequence of a tradition or fashion for particular methodologies in his discipline' (Homan 1980, 52).

[19] '[...] I refused to indulge in racist chanting, even though in the eyes of the law this is considered less serious than other offences I committed. Practical pressures meant that I also avoided other offences, particularly when my crowd observations were combined with interviews with police officers and football officials who were present on the ground' (2009, 249).

[20] In this case, this involved an individual being attacked with an empty beer bottle.

Like Pearson, Schacht also describes where he drew the line: refusing to take part in the 'singing of rugby songs or other blatantly misogynist activities' (Schacht 1997, no page nos.).

In these examples, researchers adopting a membership role based on participation within different settings found the nature of their involvement challenged by unsettling events. Such descriptions of where researchers 'draw the line' focus attention on the 'self-regulation' of ethical conduct (Calvey 2008, 913) in contexts where the ethics (and interests) of the researcher meet, and are in conflict with, the (deviant) ethics of the researched. In the examples above, it is acts of violence and humiliation that mark the researcher/researched as dissimilar and that produce a rupture in the researcher's identification with the setting, nudging them towards observational distance rather than identification with the activity. Confronted by actions that may be alien to how the researcher sees themself as an 'ethical' individual, these accounts signal the need to maintain a stance that the researcher feels they can justify in respect of their own ethics struggling against the desire to remain within the setting to continue their research. The result is a wrangling over what the researcher personally will or will not do and the extent to which they align with the ethics of the researched. As I suggested earlier, such wrangling might not just occur directly in response to an event but can also emerge later in reflection after the event, leading to a reevaluation of previous research actions.

How do these researchers justify their responses to these setting contingencies? Both Schadt (rugby club study) and Winlow et al. (study of bouncing) explain their decision-making by placing an emphasis on continuing the study for the greater good, even if this means going against ones values. In Schacht's rugby club study, the researcher describes becoming 'sylph-like',[21] distancing himself in a pragmatic way away from his personal beliefs, friends, and academic colleagues. He justifies this in relation to the importance of his research, implying in his feelings of being 'morally compelled to illuminate the activities of this setting to others' (1997)[22] a

[21] 'My solution to this outsider within status and the alienation I experienced from it during the fieldwork portion of the study was to temporarily become a sylph – a being without a soul. [...] I do not believe that my initially becoming a sylph was the result of a conscious decision; rather, it was perhaps the only pragmatic way that I could survive the overwhelming feelings of self-estrangement I was experiencing at the time. As my alienation from both inside and outside of the setting increased, I slowly but very definitely took on this researcher role. As my time in the field increased [...] I did begin to consciously recognize that I was trying to control and repress – but not ignore – my feelings about the research I was undertaking. Since the only other realistic alternative would have been for me to withdraw from setting (something that I did consider on numerous occasions) this seemed at the time to be a reasonable way to continue the research' (Schacht 1997).

[22] This argument is reminiscent of the anthropologist Peter Kloos's description of becoming a 'non-person' in research, where the researcher must suppress their own values:

When I went in the Carib village, I was a vegetarian (as I am now); but since such a dietary restriction would have been extremely burdensome there (for instance, in the case of feasts or gifts), I suspended my principle for the duration of the fieldwork. Likewise I talked in a racist manner with the Caribs, who are prejudiced in this respect (to say it in a neutral way) – loathsome behaviour, I realise. (1969, 511).

greater good, the idea that the ends, though unpleasant, justified the means. He describes how separating himself from his (feminist) values and personal feelings was a methodological necessity – the only way to continue the study – but that this had repercussions, alienating him from those both outside of the study (such as his feminist friends who voiced their discomfort with his work) and those within the setting.

Winlow et al. (2001) establish a slightly different stance, arguing that when researching empirical worlds infused by violence, distancing moves are potentially dangerous. These authors suggest that the researcher cannot afford, or risk, switches from participation to observation. Instead, the researcher needs to maintain a participatory engagement and identification with the site, even if this involves taking part in violent action. The conclusion these authors reach is that adherence to the ethics of the setting, rather than a distanced position underpinned by concern with the ethics of the academy or institution, is the only way to survive:

> Complying with formal academic ethical codes when we seek to understand the complex interaction of social worlds that do not acknowledge such bourgeois conceits is an unrealistic tactic, in particular for ethnographers. This is not to say that ethnography is inherently unethical, but rather that if the ethnographer can comply with the normative behaviour and moral code of the researched culture, and if these forms of behaviour do not contrast too sharply with one's own ethical considerations, then so be it [...] .
>
> (Winlow et al. 2001, 547)

Despite the different arguments that Schadt, Calvey, and Winlow et al. present, the emphasis in each case is on the continuation of the study. There is a prioritising of the value of the research, with the decisions established in relation to the importance of extending knowledge within the academy. Each is very different to Constable's privileging of her concern for her research participants.

Pearson's (2009) paper on football fans displays different suturing and rupturing moves in justifying his decision to commit a number of 'minor offences' during his research (participating in pitch invasions, consuming alcohol on 'football specials', engaging in threatening behaviour towards the supporters of rival teams). The legitimacy of these acts is asserted via reference to different domains of ethics. Firstly, Pearson's breaching of 'normal' ethics is explained in deference to methodological requirements: broadly, a concern with being accepted in the culture, but also more specifically in acquiring specific learnings. The pitch invasion 'enabled me to pick up the mood of the supporters involved in the "charge"' (246). Consuming alcohol 'proved to be an important method of encouraging social interaction, which in turn led to increased opportunities for data collection' (247). He also relates his actions to his own personal ethical codes, defending his breaking the law by drinking alcohol on public transport in relation to his developing criticism of:

> [...] the provisions of the Sporting Events (Control of Alcohol etc.) Act 1985, considering it badly drafted, rushed legislation that caused more public order problems than it solved (Pearson 2000). As a result, I had no moral qualms about breaching this statute, and found little criticism from my academic peers. However, that is not to say that such activity was therefore justifiable, or would have been considered acceptable by my institution. (248)

Finally, he defends his actions in relation to the academic field and the importance of the research itself, the gathering of data 'from a closed field which over the years has been much misunderstood, and from research subjects who have been subject to serious injustices and maltreatment by those in authority' (249).

The destabilising events described in these examples were not so severe as to jettison the researcher from the contexts of their inquiry or to halt their studies. In each case, the researcher instead accommodated the challenges to their ethical positions, sidestepping those actions that they felt they could not go along with. In each case, however, this involved distancing moves away from the settings, a partial rupturing of identification with the research contexts.

From Observer to Participant?

I am going to now turn to two studies where researchers establish very different relationships to their research contexts than those described above. Here, rather than looking at projects that involve distancing moves away from affiliation to the settings (as in the case of the studies where the ethics of the researched are marked as different from those of the researcher), I want to consider two cases where scholars move towards greater involvement in, and identification with, the sites of research. In approaching these texts, my focus is on the difficulty of sustaining a *distanced* rather than insider position. In each case, in looking at suturing/rupturing moves, I also want to think about the nature of participation that is implied in these studies.

I am going to look at destabilising events described in two books: Sudhir Venkatesh's description of fieldwork with gang members in the south side of Chicago *Gang Leader for a Day* (2008) and Celia Pearce and Artemesia's (the name of Pearce's online avatar[23]) description of 18 months ethnographic fieldwork in virtual worlds and online games *Communities of Play* (2009). Each study is characterised by research designs that involved the researcher's presence within the research environment. However, in each case, the researcher is described as being initially distanced from the activity, engaged in observation rather than participation. In each case, this position is unsettled by contingent events that directly involve the researcher.

Gang Leader for a Day – an account of 10 years participant observation within gang culture in a high-rise housing project in Oakland, Chicago (Venkatesh 2008) – is, at heart, a description of an ongoing struggle to maintain an ethical stance during research. The book describes Venkatesh's developing relationship with residents of the projects and members of the Black Kings gang, particularly his relationship with a gang leader J.T. and his growing relationship with the 'building

[23] See Chap. 4 for discussion of this joint authorship.

president for the Local Advisory Council', Ms. Bailey (146). As Venkatesh describes his research experience, we follow his entry into the setting. He starts as a novice researcher with little clue as to what he is doing: hanging out and making up his research approach as he goes along, learning along the way and on the job. His stated aim is to obtain a richer understanding of these environments than that presented by survey research by obtaining direct experience of the lives of those living within the environment and by observing gang life. This aim leads Venkatesh into a number of challenging situations that he reflects upon in the book as he works through the role conflicts he experienced as a researcher operating within this environment; the full title of the book is *Gang Leader for a Day: A Rogue Sociologist Crosses the Line*.

For much of his account, Venkatesh appears to perceive himself as primarily an observer, engaged in generating data through observation and interviews – a recording instrument which is present within the setting but does not influence events. Despite his growing affinity for those within the setting, his focus, as he admits several times, is on obtaining the information needed for his study. This distanced mode of engagement appears to dominate, yet, as he reports, maintaining this position is troublesome. The book describes a number of moments where Venkatesh considers his position, role, and responsibility to the site's residents, reflecting on contingent events that occurred within the setting.[24] This includes moments when he intervenes in the observed activity, stepping further into the action because he feels he has to. Most notably, during a shooting, he helps drag a gang member to safety (for which he seems to obtain kudos within the gang). On another occasion, he buys food for the apparently neglected children of a local woman (Ms. Bailey later warns him against being exploited).

Venkatesh's book contains one particularly memorable scene, where the reader, observing his observations, is party to a moment of short-sightedness that creeps up horribly, revealing Venkatesh to be (as he later admits and discusses) blinkered by a naive understanding of his potential impact on the site. The event occurs when Venkatesh starts to explore the diverse economies that operate within the high rises via a series of interviews that are enabled by J.T. and Ms. Bailey, who act as gatekeepers. The reader has earlier been informed that both J.T. and Ms. Bailey feel it their right to tax those earning money within the blocks through the exchange of goods or labour.[25] With this knowledge, the reader is perhaps taken aback by the

[24] Venkatesh also discusses contingent events arising in his institutional context. He describes an example of academic contingency: 'during a casual conversation with a couple of my professors, in which I apprised them of how J.T.'s gang went about planning a drive-by-shooting – they often sent a young woman to surreptitiously cosy up to the rival gang and learn enough information to prepare a surprise attack – my professors duly apprised *me* that I needed to consult a lawyer. Apparently the research I was doing lay a bit out of bounds of the typical academic research' (Venkatesh 2008, 185).

[25] 'If you occasionally cut hair in your apartment, it was probably a good idea to give Ms. Bailey a free styling once in a while. In these parts Ms. Bailey was like the local IRS – and probably a whole lot more successful at collecting her due' (192).

report of a scene in which Venkatesh, following a successful day's interviewing, is 'summoned to Ms. Bailey's office' (199), whereby J.T. and Ms. Bailey enquire as to how his research is going and what he has learned, and he proceeds to report the full details of his findings to them:

> For the next three hours, I went through my notebooks and told them what I'd learned about dozens of hustlers, male and female. There was Bird, the guy who sold license plates, Social Security cards, and small appliances out of his van. Doritha the tax preparer, Candy, one of the only female carpenters in the neighbourhood, Prince, the man who could pirate gas and electricity for your apartment. J.T. and Ms. Bailey rarely seemed surprised, although every now and then one of them perked up when I mentioned a particularly enterprising hustler or a woman who has recently started taking in boarders. I finally left, riding the bus home to my apartment. I was grateful for having had the opportunity to discuss my findings with two of the neigborhood's most formidable power brokers.
>
> (Venkatesh 2008, 200)

A few weeks later, Venkatesh returns to the high rises to find himself shunned by the residents, the information that he had provided to J.T. and Ms. Bailey having led to individuals being taxed and, in some cases, beaten. He is confronted with the sudden realisation that he had failed to 'anticipate the consequences of [his] actions. After several years in the projects, I had become attuned to each and every opportunity to get information from the tenants' (206).

Venkatesh's affiliation to J.T. enabled him to continue his work within the high-rise, and its residents appeared to be forgiving. However, there is a sense that this event changed his relationship to the setting forever:

> I eventually came back to the building to face the tenants. No one declined to speak with me outright, but I didn't exactly receive a hero's welcome either. [..] Perhaps the best indicator of my change in status was that I wasn't doing much of anything casual – hearing jokes, sharing a beer, loaning someone a dollar. (207)

Venkatesh later initiates a creative writing class for young women from the area, a decision that is in part attributed to his mistake: 'I was also still reeling from the fact that I had alienated so many people around J.T.'s territory. I was feeling guilty, and I needed to get people back on my side again' (211). Although the classes are attended by a group of women from the projects, they result in increased hostility when Venkatesh is called to a meeting by Ms. Bailey to defend his actions: 'people had seen me picking up the young women and driving away with them. Apparently they thought I was sleeping with them, or maybe pimping them out' (218). It is not until Ms. Bailey comes to his rescue ('He's trying to tell you that he's just helping them out with homework!') that the residents calm down. Venkatesh notes his hurt at their response: 'why weren't any of the women from the workshop in attendance? Why hadn't anyone come to defend me, to tell the truth?' (218).

Pearce and Artemesia's *Communities of Play* (2009) is similarly based on prolonged fieldwork, albeit in online rather than face-to-face environments. This study explores intergame immigration in online worlds, following the closure of the massively multiplayer online game *Uru: Ages Beyond Myst* and the migration of a group of *Uru* players (The Gathering of Uru) to other virtual worlds once the 'plug was pulled' (85) on their home. This study of the 'Uru Diaspora' (88) is ethnographic in nature, based on Pearce/Artemesia's 'in-world fieldwork' (199) in a number of online environments including the 3-D virtual world *there.com*, *Until Uru* (a *Uru* game hosted on player-run servers), and *Koalanet* (a player-run forum for The Gathering's members to meet after the closure of *Uru: Ages Beyond Myst*). Like Venkatesh, Pearce/Artemesia describes her movement into her research sites, her developing relationships with participants, and the changing nature of her involvement with the empirical contexts of her research. Not least, how she was to find it 'impossible not to play along' (196).

The destabilising event that I want to focus on in this study arises when Pearce/Artemesia is already accepted as a researcher within the setting. Friction arises as a result of an interview that she gives to a local newspaper reporter. The resulting article is then posted on the forums of there.com, prompting strong responses on the site ('Jeeze, what did you WRITE about us?') and 'a firestorm of postings' on *Koalanet*, most of which are negative:

> The posts are flaming. They accuse me of 'dumbing down' my research into sound bites for the journalist and distorting facts to support my own bias. One says if she were my Ph.D. professor, she'd send me back to the drawing board. Another critique is that my 'arm's-length' approach has given me little insight into TGU, let alone online gaming, and that 'my' article showed my ignorance of the subject. (228).

This is then followed by a period during which Pearce/Artemesia endeavours to reestablish her relationship with members of the *Uru* Diaspora. She makes a couple of attempts to 'connect with *Uru* people' (229), explaining to one that 'the article, by a journalist, is her interpretation of what she and I talked about, not my words, and certainly not my report' (228). Finally, managing to speak to Lynn, one of the leaders of the group, she is given a few home truths: Lynn's anger at Pearce/Artemesia using text rather than voice to communicate within the environment and her belief that Pearce/Artemesia is 'observing from afar' (230) and should start posting on Koalnet (230). Accused of focusing on documenting rather than participating within the setting, Pearce/Artemesia describes how this event 'precipitated a complete reassessment and overhaul of my research approach' (231), a reassessment that involved moves towards legitimate membership by participating in game-related activity.

This description of Pearce/Artemesia's shunning is then followed by a number of events that provided Pearce/Artemesia with opportunities to enter into a 'deeper engagement' (231) with the researched activity. One of these involved her participation in a game of 'Buggy Polo' in *there.com*. Pearce/Artemesia starts out riding in a buggy, but then puts on a 'hoverpack' in order to take photographs of the proceedings from the air. Here is her description of the incident that follows:

> I am flying around, taking pictures of the chaos below, listening to the chat box banter, when I notice that the orb-ball, now empty, has somehow managed to get itself lodged into the upper branches of one of the trees by the soccer field. It is one of those moments where a series of clues add up. First I notice the ball has landed in the tree. Then I notice that everyone is grouping below, looking up from their buggies, trying to figure out what to do. At that moment, I have a startling revelation: because I am on my hoverpack, I am in the *air*, so I could actually get the ball. Apparently everyone else had the same thought at the same

> time, because I suddenly hear (and see) people yelling, 'Arte, get the ball! Get the ball!' At the same moment I am yelling, 'Hey, I can get it; I'm on my hoverpack!' I keep flying toward it, bumping it and trying to knock it out of the tree, but I cannot get it to move. Then someone says, 'Pick it up, Art.' So I drag my cursor over to the little blue circle (the primary interface to objects in *there.com*), and click on it, and before I know what has happened, I am instantly sucked inside the ball.
>
> At this point I stop taking pictures because I am too caught up in the moment [...] but I realize very quickly that the orb is drivable, so I use my arrow keys to roll it out of the tree back onto the playing field, position myself, take my hands off the arrow keys, and prepare myself for an all-out assault. It is in this way that I become the ball for the remainder of the Buggy Polo game. [...] Afterward, a whole group gathers around me and we excitedly discuss what transpired. This is a turning point. I have finally gotten in on the action and *played* with them. This is the beginning of my shift from participant observation to participant *engagement*. (234, her emphasis)

This rather joyful description of acceptance and inclusion is memorable because it involves such a dramatic shift in position from the response to the earlier disruptive event. The moment positions Pearce/Artemesia literally in the middle of things, moving towards acceptance and membership in the activity.

Despite the differences between these studies – not least the very different locations in which fieldwork took place – similarities can be identified between the events described in these two works. In each case, despite their physical presence or material representation within the setting, the researcher initially established a distanced observational position, one that is presented as being detached from the inhabitants of the environments. Each is then faced with an unexpected event, which arises as a result of their presence in the setting, negating any claim that their presence does not have an impact on the sites. This then challenges the relationships that they had established within the sites, relationships they need to sustain in order to continue their work.

In each study, there is also an earnest identification with the settings, and their inhabitants. The shock each researcher experiences involves a misplaced identification with their project and a failure to recognise the implications of their actions for the setting. In each, the researcher then reassesses their position and research activity, deciding that they need to become more directly engaged, moving towards what Pearce/Artemesia refers to as 'participant engagement'. In *Gang Leader for a Day*, this sees Venkatesh setting up his literacy classes for young women, giving something back to the site, rather than just taking. In *Communities of Play*, this sees Pearce/Artemesia starting to play rather than simply observe, stating that the right thing to do is to go along with the desires of the participants (the basis for this stance is not stated explicitly).

Yet, the nature of the participation that each author moves towards is markedly different. This difference can perhaps be illuminated through reference to a distinction between 'pedagogic' and 'exchange' modes of action (Dowling 2007, 2009). In the former, pedagogic modes, the speaker in an interaction seeks to maintain control over the principles of evaluation, 'themselves retaining control over the principles of evaluation of their acts and utterances' (Dowling 2007, 13). In contrast, in exchange modes, 'the principles of evaluation of an act or utterance are located with the audience rather than the author of the act or utterance' (Dowling 2007, 9). Venkatesh's involvement in his research setting is based upon the establishing of a pedagogic relationship to its members. It involves an attempt to withdraw the participants from the setting (e.g. by increasing their literacy) and maintains his difference from them (as 'teacher' rather than fellow resident). This involves an assertion of the authority implied in the nickname that Venkatesh was given by residents of the site – 'Mr. Professor'. Pearce/Artemesia was also known as a researcher within the game environments she studied. In contrast to Venkatesh, however, her move towards greater involvement is based on an exchange mode of interaction with the sites' participants. She adopts a similar position to them, one that is informed by the feedback she receives from the sites' members. By becoming a player within the setting (whilst continuing to operate as a researcher), she breaks down her previously distanced position in respect of the sites.

These differences suggest that we might problematise the notion of 'participation' by posing the question, participation on whose terms? Venkatesh, in a move that is perhaps consistent with his earlier naivety, retains control over the principles of just what constitutes appropriate activity (hence, perhaps, the continuing hostility to his presence within the setting). Pearce/Artemesia realises that these principles are, in terms of actions impacting on the setting, properly under the control of the participants (and as a result of her new participation becomes accepted within the setting). Whilst both move towards greater 'participation', the authors can therefore be seen to establish contrasting relationships to their researched settings, which are based on the attributing of authority in different ways, attempting to assert it (in Venkatesh's case) and locating it in the settings (in Pearce/Artemesia's case). Whilst Venkatesh's stance appears to privilege his own ethical commitments (as well as the ethics of the academy in the value of doing the work), Pearce/Artemesia's stance appears more centrally informed by the ethics of the researched.

Conclusion

I suggested at the beginning of this chapter that the production of ethics in research involves a tension between the researcher's need to fix the groundwork of their research project and their need to deal with the developmental and contingent nature of the different contexts that inform the production of research. This chapter has explored the resulting destabilisation of ethical stances that can arise as a result of this contingency, returning to the scheme introduced in Chap. 2, but here focusing on the dismantling rather than construction of ethical stances.

My focus in this chapter has been on setting contingencies, ethical destabilisation arising from the contexts of empirical research. More specifically, I have looked at the ways that changes within the setting can unsettle the maintenance of observational positions. It is in deeper involvement with our research settings that such destabilising might be expected. However, as I have illustrated in this chapter, responses to such events may impose upon the other domains represented in Fig. 5.1.

At the same time – as the examples of local contingencies presented in this table suggest – the genesis of such destabilising may also arise in the contexts of the researcher, academy, and institution.

It is possible to identify, in the descriptions of moments of crisis, different kinds of 'triggers' that can provoke ethical destabilisation and reflection in research. An angry response from potential research subjects, religious quandaries, violent actions or vulnerable participants, and so forth. Such moments illustrate the ways that researchers stand at the intersection of very different interests and different contexts in which ethics are constituted – professional, personal, empirical, and institutional. They remind us that the domains of ethics that researchers can use to build their ethical stances can also be sources of disruption.

If we are interested in the strategies by which researchers maintain and justify their ethics in research – and with it the nature of the positions we ourselves establish – the nature of these destabilising events is perhaps the least significant aspect of these accounts. This is not to say that description of such events has no value in helping the researcher to try to preempt or think through potential challenges they might face when working in different types of research contexts. Of greater interest, however, are the ways that researchers respond to such destabilisation, their moves to stabilise ethical positions during the research process and how these are defended/explained in accounts of research. Researchers' efforts to deal with ethical destabilisation- to stabilise their position by grasping onto particular resources- are revealing because they speak of the ethical identities that researchers construct both for themselves and for the consumption of public audiences. I have suggested that in order to get a sense of these identities, we might look at the patterning of researcher's identification to, and alienation from, different domains of ethics in the maintenance, adaptation, and articulation of their ethical stances.

I began this chapter with a description of the hacking of Silent Hill, the most dramatic ethical crisis that occurred during my study of COA and SHH. The question that I posed – whether or not, in the light of the hacking and my archive of the site's forums, I should break with my previous nonintervention, contact the site, and offer a copy of my archive – was, in practice, not a difficult question to answer. I was in a position to help and decided to try to do so. In terms of the production of my research, this decision was also relatively easy to make. As the data collection stage of the project was nearly over, if members of the site had reacted negatively to my continued presence in the setting, I could have made the decision to withdraw without it being detrimental to my study.

More importantly, however, the decision was based on my personal feelings for those involved in the setting. This event drew to the foreground an aspect of my own ethical commitments that had been submerged up until this point. My personal affiliation to the sites and their fan interests had developed during the study. I had started out as a fan of *Silent Hill* and *Angel* and had come to know the sites and their 'members' during my project. This affiliation had informed my desire to be confident in the ethical stance I was establishing, particularly in respect of the observational approach that I was adopting. There was no conflict here between my personal feelings and methodological approach, as I felt I could defend the decision to be a lurker on the forums for the reasons described in Chaps. 3 and 4. Now, however, this identification influenced my decision to try to help the site and their members. They therefore provoked a recognition of my identification with the members of the site that involved a shift in the constitution of my ethical stance (see Whiteman 2010). I contacted one of the owners of SHH, notified them of my study and my archive of the material from the site, and offered them a copy. We exchanged a few emails and then I did not hear from them again. I did not chase them because I felt it was up to them if they wanted to continue the interaction. I was later informed that the owner had not received the last email I had sent to them.

I am aware in describing this event that the nature of my intervention sounds (particularly in contrast to Pearce/Artemesia's account of her research) somewhat half-hearted. This is something that I still struggle with when I reflect back on my response to this event. My position remained more similar to that established by Venkatesh in his work; in making an 'offer' to the site, I remained distant and positioned as researcher rather than potential participant in the setting. Yet, this fits with my observational role. Unlike Pearce/Artemesia, I was not seeking participant status. At the same time, unlike Venkatesh, the relationship I established was not pedagogic. Instead, it set up a relationship based on a potential exchange that was not realised. This was to be extended, however, when I later sent a copy of my completed Ph.D. thesis to the site and it was taken up and examined by its members, an event which I will discuss in the chapter that follows.

References

Adler, P., & Adler, P. (1987). *Membership roles in field research* (Qualitative research methods series 6). London/Newbury Park: Sage.

Association of Social Anthropologists of the UK and Commonwealths. (1999). *Ethical guidelines for good research practice*. http://www.theasa.org/ethics/guidelines.shtml.

Bryman, A. (2008). *Social research methods* (3rd ed.). Oxford/New York: Oxford University Press.

Calvey, D. (2008). The art and politics of covert Research: Doing 'situated ethics' in the field. *Sociology, 42*(5), 905–918.

Campbell, J. E. (2004). *Getting it on online: Cyberspace, gay male sexuality and embodied identity*. New York: The Harrington Park Press.

Castellano, U. (2007). Becoming a nonexpert and other strategies for managing fieldwork dilemmas in the criminal justice system. *Journal of Contemporary Ethnography, 36*(6), 704–730.

Constable, N. (2005). *Romance on a global stage: Pen pals, virtual ethnography and 'mail order' marriages*. Berkeley/London: University of California Press.

de Laine, M. (2000). *Fieldwork, participation and practice: Ethics and dilemmas in qualitative research*. London/Thousand Oaks: Sage.

Dowling, P. (2007, September). Organising the social. *Philosophy of Mathematics Education Journal, 21*. Available online: http://people.exeter.ac.uk/PErnest/pome21/Dowling%20Organising%20the%20Social.doc.

Dowling, P. (2009). *Sociology as method: Departures from the forensics of culture, text and knowledge*. Rotterdam: Sense.

Emerson, R. M., & Pollner, M. (2001). Constructing participant/observation relations. In R. M. Emerson (Ed.), *Contemporary field research: Perspective and formulations* (2nd ed.). Prospect Heights: Waveland Press.

Gold, R. L. (1958). Roles in sociological field observations. *Social Forces, 36*(3), 217–223.
Guillemin, M., & Gillam, L. (2004). Ethics, reflexivity and 'ethically important moments' in research. *Qualitative Inquiry, 10*(2), 261–280.
Homan, R. (1980). The ethics of covert methods. *The British Journal of Sociology, 31*(1), 46–59.
Jackson, P. (1983). "Principles and problems of participant observation" *Geografiska Annaler*, Series B. *Human Geography, 65*(1), 39–46.
Junker, B. (1952). Some suggestions for the design of field work learning experiences. In E. C. Hughes et al. *Cases on Field Work* (hectographed by The University of Chicago, 1952), Part III-A.
Junker, B. H. (1960). *Field work: An introduction to the social sciences*. Chicago: University of Chicago Press.
Kloos, P. (1969). Role conflicts in social fieldwork. *Current Anthropology, 10*(5), 509–511.
Markham, A. (2004). Reconsidering self and other: Methods, politics, and ethics of representation in online ethnography. In N. Denzin & Y. Lincoln (Eds.), *Handbook of qualitative research* (pp. 793–820). London: Sage.
Orb, A., Eisenhauer, L., & Wynaden, D. (2001). Ethics in qualitative research. *Journal of Nursing Scholarship, 33*(1), 93–96.
Pearce, C., & Artemesia. (2009). *Communities of play: Emergent cultures in multiplayer games and virtual worlds*. Cambridge: The MIT Press.
Pearson, G. (2000). Legislating for the football hooligan: A case for reform. In S. Greenfield, G. Osborn (Eds.) *Law and sport in contemporary society*, (pp. 82–200). London and New York: Routledge.
Pearson, G. (2009). The researcher as hooligan: Where 'participant' observation means breaking the law. *International Journal of Social Research Methodology, 12*(3), 243–255.
Rambo, C. (2007). Handing IRB an unloaded gun. *Qualitative Inquiry, 13*(3), 353–367.
Robson, C. (2002). *Real world research: A resource for social scientists and practitioner-researchers* (2nd ed.). Oxford: Blackwell.
Schacht, S. P. (1997). Feminist fieldwork in the misogynist setting of the rugby pitch: Temporarily becoming a sylph to survive and personally grow. *Journal of Contemporary Ethnography, 26*(3), 338–363.
Scheper-Hughes, N. (2000). Ire in Ireland. *Ethnography, 1*(1), 117–140.
Scott, D., & Usher, R. (1999). *Researching education: Data, methods and theory in educational enquiry*. London and New York: Continuum.
Smith, K. M. C. (2004). 'Electronic eavesdropping': The ethical issues involved in conducting a virtual ethnography. In M. D. Johns, S. Chen, G. Jon Hall (Eds.), *Online social research: Methods, issues, & ethics* (pp. 223–238). New York: Peter Lang.
Van Maanen, J., Manning P. K., & Miller, M. L. (1987). *Editors' introduction* in Patricia A. Adler and Peter Adler (1987) *Membership roles in field research,* Qualitative research methods series 6 (p. 5). London/Newbury Park: Sage.
Venkatesh, S. (2008). *Gang leader for a day: A rogue sociologist crosses the line*. London/New York: Penguin.
Wacquant, L. (2005). Carnal connections: On embodiment, apprenticeship, and membership. *Qualitative Sociology, 28*(4), 445–471.
Whiteman, N. (2007). The establishment, maintenance and destabilisation of fandom: A study of two online communities and an exploration of issues pertaining to internet research. Unpublished PhD thesis, Institute of Education, University of London.
Whiteman, N. (2010). Control and contingency: Maintaining ethical stances in research. *International Journal of Internet Research Ethics, 3*(1), 6–22.
Winlow, S., Hibbs, D., Lister, S., & Hadfield, P. (2001). Get ready to duck: Bouncers and the realities of ethnographic research on violent groups. *British Journal of Criminology, 41*, 536–548.

Chapter 6
Undoing Ethics

Abstract The concluding chapter draws out the key themes explored in the book and presents a consideration of the moves between the general and local that underpin the preceding chapters. The chapter considers the continuities between online and offline research, the constructed rather than natural status of research ethics, and the interrelationship between the ethics of researcher and researched. The chapter ends with a consideration of the dissemination of research.

Introduction

The previous chapters have examined a range of ethical issues, questions, and challenges relating to the practice of research in online domains and have considered the diverse ways that researchers have responded to these. In this concluding chapter, I want to draw out some of the underlying themes explored in the book and signal the main points that might, I hope, be taken from the discussion. I am particularly interested in reflecting here upon the nature of the 'localisation' that I have argued is key to the production of ethical stances in research and in thinking about the questions that we might ask when considering the production of our own stances, as well as when interrogating the work of others. In the final part of the chapter, I return to the issues raised in the preface to this book, where I described the journalistic invasion of an Internet-based fansite and the site's responses to this. Here, however, my focus is closer to home, involving a consideration of the way that members of SHH responded to my study (of them). Before this, I want to cast a gaze back over the previous chapters, starting with a return to the current state of ethical regulation and the challenges that this presents to researchers. I am therefore going to begin this ending by restating the value of concerning ourselves with the debates that I have explored throughout the book.

N. Whiteman, *Undoing Ethics: Rethinking Practice in Online Research*,
DOI 10.1007/978-1-4614-1827-6_6, © Springer Science+Business Media, LLC 2012

Research Ethics Under Surveillance

> Until about 1800, ethics, especially professional ethics, was about character, honour and dishonour, virtue and vice. Ethics had nothing to do with formal codes of conduct. A true professional, being a gentleman, needed no written instruction in how to behave.
>
> (Baker 1999, no page nos.)

As I described in Chap. 1, social science researchers today inhabit a period of increasing ethical surveillance, one in which institutional regimes oversee and regulate research activity and in which ethical guidance is set down in frameworks and codes of practice. This surveillance is felt in different ways, from the attention now given to the obtaining of ethics approval for research projects at undergraduate as well as post-graduate levels, to the involvement of lawyers in the introduction of research ethics review procedures in some academic institutions.

In light of these developments, the focus of research ethics has moved increasingly away from the expertise of the individual, towards the authority of the institution. This institutional framing of research conduct presents different challenges. It demands that researchers be able to articulate and 'display' their ethical identities in a way that satisfies external assessments and interests, emphasising the significance of argumentation in the practice of 'ethical' research. Pressures also arise in relation to the interpretation of ethical codes and the manner by which these are seen to shape researchers' actions. Here, scholars have recognised the need for a balance between guidance and instruction. This is because, as May (2001) has argued:

> [..] rigid and inflexible sets of ethical rules for social research [...] could leave us with undesirable consequences. Going so far down this ethical road, we might also conclude that 'the only safe way to avoid violating principles of professional ethics is to refrain from doing research altogether' [...] On the other hand, a loose and flexible system involving 'anything goes' so easily opens the door to the unscrupulous; to those who regard such considerations as a luxury or irrelevance in the face of assertion of a self-interested pursuit of ends. (61)

Scholarly attention to the embedded nature of ethical practice, described in the previous chapters, can be contrasted with the idea of 'research ethics' that underpins some of the models of research that have influenced the formation of the new ethical surveillance. In a paper on the 'evils' of ethical regulation, for example, Martyn Hammersley has suggested that regulation, and the model of research that it is based on, neglects the embedded and ongoing decision-making involved in research:

> The image of the research process built into the rationale for ethical regulation neglects the unavoidable role of relatively autonomous, situated decision-making by researchers: right action cannot be produced by some process of pseudocalculation; guidelines can only be guidelines not algorithmic rules that govern behaviour; and, as a result, there is always scope for reasonable disagreement about what is and is not, was or was not, acceptable behaviour in the circumstances.
>
> (Hammersley 2009, 215)

In criticising these models, Hammersley makes the point that it would be misguided to regard ethical decisions as clear-cut and separate from other methodological and practical questions:

> It is quite wrong to suggest that researchers are faced with ethical decisions per se. Rather, they make practical decisions which involve ethical considerations, but also considerations of other types, both prudential and methodological [...] One effect of recognizing this is that the ethics of any particular research project is inseparable from the other considerations that researchers must take into account. Once this is acknowledged, the brief of ethics committees would need to become, in effect, the whole process of doing research; it would incorporate the field of methodology as well.
>
> (Hammersley 2009, 215)

Hammersley here suggests the complex nature of the considerations that researchers take into account when carrying out research, arguing that these are ill-aligned with the conceptualisation of research underpinning some regulatory regimes. The making of 'practical decisions' is presented as the result of numerous considerations, rather than clear-cut 'ethical' decisions. The activity of doing research ethics, Hammersley argues, is intertwined in the complex and multifaceted nature of research practice.

Rather than the institution, it is the researcher who finds themselves positioned within this mess. As I have described, despite their growing influence in the shaping of research guidance and overseeing of research practice, the institutions in which researchers work constitute only one of the sites that are involved in the production of research ethics. Even with the move towards the institution, the individual researcher retains the primary responsibility for ensuring that research is carried out 'ethically' and (as a number of scholars I have discussed in this book have argued) researchers remain the agents of the actual practice of research ethics. Because institutions are unable to control what goes on in the field,[1] the researcher constitutes the fundamental site of ethical negotiation during research. This negotiation is established in relation to different contexts and interests that can (as I discussed in Chap. 5) leave researchers torn between different concerns.

Negotiating Local and General Ethical Discourses

> It has been said (perhaps apocryphally) that there are two ways of losing oneself: in the universal and in the particular.
>
> (Guyer 1999, 30)

The focus on the local production of ethics over the application of general doctrines suggested by Hammersley and developed in this book involves a warning against a sanitising of research and an understanding of research ethics as dynamically configured in, and in relation to, different practices, contexts and interests. Rather than applying ethical principles, this focuses attention on how, in designing and carrying out research, individuals think through 'the relations between principles and particularity' (McNamee 2001, 314), how they consider general aspirations or

[1] A fact reflected in institutional moves towards the continual assessment of ethical review rather than just at the front end of research.

statements about what constitutes good research practice, whilst also taking into account the specificities and contingencies of the local contexts in which they operate.

The manoeuvring between 'principles and particularity' – or more broadly between general ethical statements that are taken to have implications beyond specific contexts, and local instantiations of ethical behaviour – has been a key focus of this book in pursuing an examination of embedded, contingent, and emergent research ethics. As I described in Chap. 1, the conceptual move to the local reaches beyond the interests of research ethics writing. As Turnbull (2000) puts it, increasingly:

> In physics, ecology, history, feminist theory, literary theory, anthropology, geography, economics, politics and the sociology of science the focus of attention has been the specific, the contingent, the particular, be it a text, reading, culture, population, site, region, an electron or a laboratory. (39)

Turnbull describes how different disciplines have noted 'the necessity of focusing on the particular conditions at specific sites and times rather than losing that specificity in unlocalised generalizations' (40). He also suggests, however, the danger of losing one's perspective by focusing in a blinkered sense on either the local *or* the general. In his view, '[…] we should not be too easily seduced by the apparently liberatory effects of celebrating the local, since it is all too easy to allow the local to become a "new kind of globalising imperative"' (45). Instead, he says, 'we have to maintain the local and the global in dialectical opposition to one another' (45). Why? Because otherwise we risk falling into different traps: either losing the specificity of local contexts in a global perspective or finding local perspectives leading to a fragmentation in understanding and approaches – a 'proliferation of ghettos and dogmatic nationalisms' (45).

Although Turnbull is here discussing the local/general distinction in relation to issues of post-colonialism, it is perhaps easy to imagine the proliferation of 'ghettos' in respect of ethical guidance through a loss of sight of general principles in the move towards localised ethics. Although the previous chapters have emphasised localisation in the doing of research ethics, I have not argued for the rejection of general aims (or indeed against the institutional overview of research practice). As I suggested in Chap. 1, there are ideas about research, ethical expectations, that have been normalised and present common frameworks – broad principles regarding aspirations (first principles?). Take, for example, the six key ethical principles of the Economic and Social Research Council which I introduced in Chap. 4:

1. Research should be designed, reviewed and undertaken to ensure integrity, quality and transparency.
2. Research staff and participants must normally be informed fully about the purpose, methods and intended possible uses of the research, what their participation in the research entails and what risks, if any, are involved. […]
3. The confidentiality of information supplied by research participants and the anonymity of respondents must be respected.
4. Research participants must take part voluntarily, free from any coercion.

5. Harm to research participants must be avoided in all instances.
6. The independence of research must be clear, and any conflicts of interest or partiality must be explicit.[2]

These principles are able to speak to/across multiple contexts because of their relative abstraction (words like harm, quality, transparency, coercion, and independence are all broad placeholders for a range of ideas/values). Yet at a local level, deciding what research actions are appropriate in specific contexts and in relation to these principles may be debatable. What might be meant by 'harm', for example; what might constitute coercion; and what exceptions are there to the 'normal' need for informed consent?[3] This uncertainty – which I have attempted to unpick in the previous chapters – arises in the move from these general statements to the methodological operationalisation of our research projects. As I described in Chaps. 3 and 4, for example, we might agree with the idea that we should respect the rights of subjects, but this does not necessarily mean that we should always seek informed consent from those whom our research might touch upon. The applicability of this particular requirement (to obtain informed consent) suggests an equivalence between research settings/contexts/methods that might not be relevant to settings/actions that can be seen to be exempt from this demand. Here, we find the need for openness in ethical guidance that May argues for.

The space between general and local discourses therefore opens up questions and problems that must be reflected upon as we seek to 'adhere' to the ethical principles of funding bodies and institutions. In this way, our moves between the local and general – and the space that this opens up for contrasting actions – can be seen to be crucial to the production of ethical stances in research. Whilst my focus has been on localising moves, the discussion has not, I therefore hope, lost sight of the general concerns that researchers have or the generalisable principles, aspirations, and aims that can unite researchers as participants within a professional community (one of the arguments for the value of regulation in social science research might be seen to relate to the ways that the production of ethical codes helps to articulate these). Instead, it is the moves that we make between the local and general in the construction of our ethical stances that we need to reflect upon when doing research.

Doing Ethics, Online or Offline

This book has attempted to organise the complex nature of 'doing ethics' by introducing a framework for conceptualising the localised production of ethical stances in research. I have promoted a way of thinking about the doing of ethics that goes beyond narrow definitions of 'research ethics' to consider (as Hammersley suggests)

[2] http://www.esrc.ac.uk/_images/Framework_for_Research_Ethics_tcm8–4586.pdf.

[3] The ESRC document provides information in respect of this question.

the different considerations that may inform our ethical manoeuvring throughout the research process, but also the ways that ethics are enacted and articulated in different domains of practice. The illustrations that I have introduced throughout the book – including researchers' accounts of their experiences working in different contexts and descriptions of ethics in different online domains – demonstrate the diverse nature of these ethical discourses and the distinct ways that researchers have responded to the challenges of doing research 'ethically'. In considering the move from generalised ethical rules to localised ethical perspectives, I have attempted to undermine the notion of 'an' ethical approach to research in favour of the establishment of an informed ethical stance. The four domains that I introduced in Chap. 2 – the ethics of the academy, institution, researcher and researched – constitute points of potential authority in respect of this production. Generating an informed ethical stance involves engaging with ethical discourses 'conducted at various levels of abstraction' from 'ethical theories, principles, rules or norms, codes, and judgements' (Sieber 2006, no page nos.) and from within both academic and nonacademic domains. It also involves recognising the different locations in which ethics are constituted and the aspects of these that might shape our own actions.

As well as interrogating the local production of ethics, the previous chapters have presented a number of conceptual resources for interrogating and reflecting upon this production. The central element of this is the general framework that I have proposed for conceptualising the relational production/destabilisation of ethics in research – the 'four domains' of research ethics which, as I described in Chap. 2, arises from a development of Dowling and Brown's conceptualisation of the research process. The framework I have proposed signals the diverse ethical discourses that may influence the achievement of the researcher's ethics, raising questions about how these are reconciled (or not), which domains are privileged/prioritised in the achievement of ethics, and the implications of this for the configuration of the researcher's ethical identity. The researcher may feel that as long as they do what their authorising institution signs off on, they are safe. However, as the examples introduced in my discussion of the ethics of the institution in Chap. 2 demonstrated, scholars have argued for the importance of going beyond institutional guidance, and others have suffered because they did not establish their own positions. The strongly and weakly institutionalised discourses within these domains, I have suggested, present the possibility of control, but also the unexpected of contingent events (see Whiteman 2010 for further discussion of this).

Elsewhere, I have drawn attention to other theoretical distinctions that might assist in the way that researchers understand their research settings and own research practice. The strongly/weakly codified expression of privacy/publicness in online environments presented in Chap. 3, for example, provides a focus for reflection on the construction of private/public definitions, and the textualising moves involved in the ways that online environments orient themselves in relation to the public/private distinction. Similarly, the modality of suturing/rupturing identification described in Chap. 5 provides one way of reflecting on researchers' allegiances and affiliations and how these emerge in accounts of research practice.

Because they are analytical, these schemas/distinctions stand apart from local contexts; these resources can be used whatever the research interest or focus. This is important because it enables a comparison/contrasting of different accounts of research practice and different online environments. This is what theory does, enabling us to speak about different objects, settings, and processes in consistent ways. In revealing qualities in our own practice, such conceptual resources therefore also provide a way of approaching the positioning of others.

So, quite deliberately, this book does not offer prescriptions for how research *should* be conducted. Instead, I have presented a consideration of contrasting approaches to the achievement of ethics which places the responsibility on the reader (to consider this in relation to their own research actions and their own reading). However, alongside the introduction of these conceptual resources, a number of key points have been presented in my consideration of the formation and maintenance of ethical stances which perhaps signal other more generalisable contributions arising from the previous discussion.

Continuities Between Online and Offline Research

There are, of course, differences between online and offline research. Sometimes, these differences are used to fuel the generation of a dichotomy between research in online and offline domains. In a report entitled 'Online versus Offline Research', for example, Gunter et al. (2002) compare the use of online and offline questionnaires, arguing that, despite the growing popularity of Internet-based methods, 'it is important to recognise that online and offline research are not the same', setting out these differences in relation to technical features relating to the design of survey research (response rates, sampling, and 'quality' of data collection (Gunter et al. 2002)). Such work catalogues contrasting characteristics, quantifying differences between online and offline research in relation to instrumental markers, and reductively generalising online and offline practice by platform rather than taking into account local details of content and theme.

Others – and, as I have described, those promoting qualitative methodological approaches have been influential here – have approached this relationship somewhat differently, opening up and undermining the 'versus' to consider the common features between the concerns, questions and challenges of research in online and offline environments. This work suggests that, rather than seeing Internet research as something that is different from work in offline domains, we should acknowledge the commonalities between online/offline research practices and question the assumptions that our understandings of 'real-world' research are based upon.

This book has explored a number of these shared features: the uncertainty of the meaning or significance of observed behaviour in technologically mediated *and* physically embodied environments (Chap. 4); the constructed nature of the public/private distinction and research subject in online and offline research (Chaps. 3 and 4, respectively); and the allegiances and shifting observational positions that Internet researchers, as well as those working in the 'real world', may develop and inhabit (Chap. 5). These themes suggest that shared concerns, uncertainties and challenges are felt wherever one is carrying out research, and that affiliations can develop in relation to textual material as well as physically embodied beings.

In examining these commonalities, I have positioned my approach in alliance with other researchers who have argued that in all contexts the researcher is faced with performances and in opposition to those who argue that those who engage in 'real-world' research are closer to an empirical 'truth' than those working online. Whilst identifying a number of the particular difficulties of online research, I have demonstrated how the issues faced are similar to those encountered by researchers working within physically embodied environments. More broadly, I have argued that the production of research ethics is the same essential activity whether one is carrying out online or offline research, it is just that the researcher is faced with different sorts of empirical phenomena. Whilst my focus throughout the book has been on the use of qualitative methods, as I hope to have demonstrated, these similarities are also felt and need to be considered by those using quantitative methods.

The recognition of the continuities between research in online and offline domains is significant because it warns against the impulse to rely on, or mythologise, the apparently concrete nature of face-to-face data. It suggests that it is wrong to celebrate 'the real' as an authentic marker of identity, or more broadly, as a source of 'truth'. In some ways, the emergence of the Internet and new media technologies has been rejuvenating, causing scholars to reflect back on the nature of qualitative inquiry in face-to-face environments and the uncertainties that we experience when we engage with, or observe, activity in offline domains. As Baym and Markham have argued, 'the challenges of internet research have [...] prompted its researchers to confront, head-on, numerous questions that lurk less visibly in traditional research contexts' (Baym and Markham 2008, 8). This inversion (turning the tables onto the offline world(s)) suggests the value of seeing the familiar as strange and the productivity of 'misperceiving', being jolted out of, and moving outside of, our assumptions (Turnbull 2000, 44).

We are left, then, with the idea that online and offline domains may not be so different. As the author William Gibson has noted, '[...] my guess has always been that the thing our grandchildren will find quaintest about us is that we made the distinction between here and the Internet' (Gibson, quoted in Grossman 2010).[4]

Ethical Destabilisation as Well as Construction

As well as emphasising the localised nature of the production of ethical stances, the previous chapters have also explored the emergent, dynamic, and contingent nature of this production. I have described how, throughout the research process, researchers

[4] Thanks to a different Will Gibson for pointing me towards this quote.

must be responsive to changing situations and may find themselves engaged with stabilising (research) activity in the face of unexpected developments and challenges. This is both in relation to general research design issues and more specific ethical questions. This reminds us that the researcher is engaged in the production of their ethical stance throughout their research, that this is only 'achieved' when the work is finished and that, even then, this achievement may be undone by reflection upon, and challenges to, the decisions made previously.

My consideration of this destabilisation has drawn from accounts of ethical dilemmas experienced by researchers working in diverse environments. I have also made reference to my own first-hand experience of this destabilisation. In explaining my methodological and ethical decision-making during my study of COA and SHH, I have explored how I worked through issues in the construction of my own ethical stance – the achievement of my ethics. In each chapter, my emphasis has also been on how these decisions were challenged: my need to reestablish my research field and definition of COA and SHH as 'public' in the light of the shifting nature of these sites (Chap. 3); how my growing identification with, and imagining of the members of COA and SHH unsettled my stance (Chap. 4); and my hesitant moves towards SHH during my research (Chap. 5). These examples – and the points of instability they suggest – demonstrate the way that the ethical stances that we produce can come undone and the stabilising efforts required when engaging with empirical research. Whilst the unexpected events which occurred during my study underline the uncertainties involved in engaging with online environments, such contingencies are similar to those arising in offline research, where the researcher (whether using qualitative or quantitative methods) is likely to face their own challenges and surprises.

The Constructed Rather Than Natural Status of Ethical Practice

Just as challenging our assumptions regarding the certainties of offline research can be productive, so too finding our ethical decisions challenged by unexpected events can provoke learning, demanding that we step back and reassess our actions (see Whiteman 2010). The emphasis on the contingent and dynamic nature of ethical decision-making is also important because it undermines the idea that there might, in fact, be 'right' answers that can be fixed upon and guide our practices. Instead, recognition of the unstable nature of research ethics draws attention to the shaping of our production of these answers.

In emphasising the localised production of ethical stances, the previous chapters have argued for recognition of the constructed, rather than natural, status of ethical decision-making. They have highlighted the agency involved in the construction of ethical stances, rather than thinking about ethics as involving a taking on, or application, of ethical rules. If we are trying to understand our own agency, recognition of this manoeuvring is vital. Our stances need to be understood as constructed rather than natural outcomes of moves made in relation to different discourses. This construction perhaps seems more obvious in the move to the Internet, which appeared to unsettle the methods of research by destabilising expectations, challenging norms established in the contexts of offline research, and thus drawing attention to researchers' attempts to construct 'good practice'. But, as I have argued, this is something that should also be remembered in the context of offline research.

I have also considered how different approaches to the objectification of empirical phenomena (as public/private, or text/subject, for instance) have become attached to attitudes towards the acceptability of using certain types of methods – the ways that the naturalising of assumptions often involves the attribution/denial of moral value to specific methodological actions. I have been particularly interested in arguments relating to the use of covert methods and have argued against those who seek to present some methods as inherently ethical and some as not. My perspective here aligns with Denzin's claim: 'my position holds that no areas of observation are in an a priori fashion closed to the sociologist, nor are any research methods in a priori fashion defined as unethical' (Denzin 1968, 502). In this paper, Denzin calls for decisions based on the empirical nature of our research contexts, with judgements about which methods are ethical, dangerous, or disruptive, being made in relation to this. Whilst it may be legitimate to criticise the methodological decisions that researchers make (and my own use of covert methods might be deemed unacceptable by some), we need to consider the suitability of research methods in respect of their use in particular contexts and in relation to specific research questions.

A Sociological Approach to Research Ethics

Throughout the book, I have recruited a range of theoretical resources, including research ethics frameworks, accounts of anthropological and sociological research, textbooks and papers on research ethics, and literature on the ethics of online research practice. The field of Internet research ethics writing has developed considerably since I started working on my Ph.D. in 2004. This development has involved the publication of new edited collections, papers, and monographs on the ethics of online research as well as the launch of the *International Journal of Internet Research Ethics.*[5] Shared objects of interest have also led to the production of specialist guidance for Internet researchers who have mutual concerns (such as the ethics of studying social networking activity[6]). Just as ethical guidance has built around shared objects/interests/methods in the context of 'real-world' research (e.g. the ethics of covert research and the ethics of research involving children), increasingly complex territories of guidance are now developing in relation to the ethics of online research practice.

---

[5] http://ijire.net.

[6] See Wilkinson and Thelwall (2011), and Bruckman et al. (2010), for discussion of the ethics of such research.

My interest in these resources is perhaps most obvious in Chap. 2, in my engagement with Susan Herring's paper on ethics, and in Chap. 5, in my discussion of researchers' expressions of their identification to objects of interest in accounts of research. Elsewhere throughout the book, however, I have recontextualised accounts of research as pedagogic resources in the presentation of my argument, using examples to illustrate the strategic construction of positions in respect of key ethical issues. I have marked out continuities and discontinuities between different perspectives/voices and tried to point to the diverse ways that the ethics of the academy might inform our research actions. Throughout, I have focused on the published utterances of researchers, rather than speaking to scholars directly about their experiences of research.[7]

My engagement with this work – and exploration of the textual negotiation of research ethics in this literature – has been fuelled by an interest in the rhetorical moves involved in the articulation of ethical positions, the strategies that scholars have developed for dealing with ethical and methodological questions/problems, and the formation of ethical identities in the reporting of research. In establishing our own ethical stances, I would argue, our engagement with these moves needs to be critical, involving an analytical approach to the reading of the work of others rather than, say, a collector approach to gathering ethical guidance as it emerges.

The approach to ethics I have taken in this book can perhaps be considered as sociological, rather than philosophical, in that it has explored the ethical positioning of other researchers, their strategic manoeuvring as they present and seek to defend/assert the legitimacy of their actions. In some ways, I have shifted from exploring moves within one type of activity (media fandoms – my focus of interest during my study of COA and SHH) to another (research and scholarship.) In each case my focus has been on their practices and relationships to objects of interest. Despite their differences, in both cases, participants are involved in the construction of identities as ethical agents, and in both cases, this articulation is framed and understood within particular audiences/contexts. The task is to then get a sense of our own identities/audiences in the conduct of our own work.

The Interrelationship Between the Ethics of the Researcher and the Ethics of the Researched

As well as looking to the theoretical ethics of the academy, the previous chapters have also discussed the ethics of the empirical contexts in which researchers work – drawing in a range of different online and offline settings. My concern has been less on the ethics of these settings. This is an area of investigation that presents its own extremely interesting questions and interests, and one that is being explored by a range of scholars (e.g. Langford 2000; Slater 2002; Spinello and Tavani 2004; Craft

[7] For an example of the latter approach, see McKee and Porter's (2009) book on Internet research ethics.

2007; Drushel and German 2011). Rather, I have been interested in the interrelationship between these ethics and our own. Specifically, how does the objectification of our research settings shape researchers' actions or, in the terms I have introduced, how do the ethics of the researched relate to the ethics of the researcher?

I have described how researchers' actions can be shaped and influenced by the nature of the environments that they study and by the demands and expectations of the inhabitants of these environments. The potential for the ethics of the researched to influence those of the researcher was evident in a number of examples discussed in earlier chapters. These include the ways that Internet users' perceptions of privacy might inform the researcher's objectification of the public/private status of online environments (discussed in Chap. 3) and Pearce and Artemesia's moves towards greater participation in their study of online worlds (described in Chap. 5). In these examples, researchers can be seen to establish an earnest position in relation to their research settings, aligning their ethics with those of the researched. Other scholars I have introduced (such as Herring in Chap. 2 and the scholars of deviant and criminal acts in Chap. 5) have positioned themselves in opposition to the ethics of their research settings, either because they were unacceptable to them personally or because they sought to take a more critical stance.

When considering the relationship between the ethics of the researcher/researched, the issue is not just about the extent to which the ethics of the setting can inform or destabilise the researcher's ethics, but also how the ethics of the researcher can destabilise those of the research settings. Burgess (1984) provides one example of this. In a discussion of the challenges of dissemination he describes Nancy Scheper-Hughes' description of how the focus of her 1979 study *Saints, Scholars and Schizophrenics*, the town 'Ballybran', had been changed by her work. Burgess notes how:

> [...] the study had challenged the local people's interpretations of the meanings of events and of their lives. In her study, Scheper-Hughes had reported on a woman giving up a disapproved love match to care for her widowed father and unmarried brothers. Before publication [of her study] this had been locally regarded as a moral 'Christian' thing to do but was now openly challenged. There were alternative views of pity and of questioning her attachment to her study [...]. However, there were also benefits to her study. Hitherto unspoken issues were now discussed: problems of the aged, problems of family and marriage and new insights about their lives.
>
> (Burgess 1984, 204–205)

As this account suggests, researcher's activities can unsettle and influence the ethical behaviour of the researched. This potential for influence, and possibility for bringing about change, means that scholars must take particular care in the dissemination and publication of their work.

The interrelationship between the ethics of researcher and researched therefore operates in two directions. Researchers can be influenced by their settings, and settings can change as a result of the activities of researchers. Aligned with this, the researcher and researched can adopt very different positions in respect of one another – accepting or distancing from each other. I have also suggested that, despite the moves that researchers may make towards their research settings, some distance is necessary if the researcher is not simply to present the voice of the setting. At the same time, without looking towards the setting, researchers risk speaking only from a position outside the setting, which may not be sensitive to the local concerns and interests of the researched.

From 'Me' to 'Them' to 'You'

The previous chapters have traced different concerns relating to the localised production of ethics. Initially, in Chaps. 1 and 2, my focus was on a priori consideration of doing good – conceptualising the production of an ethical stance, led by the researcher's concern with the construction of 'my' ethics as defined in relation to distinct domains and discourses. I then shifted attention in Chaps. 3 and 4 onto the ways that researchers might generate a sense of the ethics of the researched (how we might objectify 'them'). In Chap. 5, I moved into the field, focusing on the challenge of dealing with in situ responses and how 'they' can influence 'my' ethics. In closing, I want to think about what might happen when we address 'them' as 'you' – the move towards sharing our work with the researched settings and the uncertainty/unease that may surround our ethical manoeuvring.

In 2007, I emailed my Ph.D. thesis to the owner of SHH, with whom I had earlier had some limited correspondence in the aftermath of the hacking of the site. Subsequently (with my permission), a link to my thesis was posted on a thread on one of the forums of SHH. In the days following the post, around 30 members of the site responded to my study and discussed my work. The reactions of the site's members to my study were quite balanced – not overly positive and not overly negative. Some engaged in a close interrogation of my analysis, highlighting in particular my analysis of key personalities on the forum. Some mocked the academic nature of my study – the fact that a student would be so interested in their activities and spend so much time on the forums. Others recalled and asked about moments and events described in the thesis. Reactions also included a range of responses to the methods of my study, including the expression of unease at having been put under the microscope, and the posting of reminders by others that the site was, after all, in the public domain. During this time, I posted my first of two messages onto the boards, confirming that I had not been a participant on the forums (in response to a poster who had queried this) and explaining my research design further.

In some ways, sharing my study with the site provided a test of the stance that I had established and the justifications that I had made during my study against the opinions of some of those most closely involved in the activity. SHH was different from COA, which had closed its forums by the time I had finished my study and with which I had had no interactions. Whilst I felt that I could justify and defend the decisions I had made, I have to admit that I was nervous about what the reaction of SHH members might be. This was partly because my study was different from many of the studies of online communities that I had read at that time, studies of online sites that had adopted more participatory approaches. Despite commonalities in our aims (in taking a qualitative approach towards the study of online cultures and seeking to understand the workings of online settings over time), my more distanced observational stance, and lack of correspondence with the sites' members, meant that I could not obtain reassurance from recognising a family resemblance with other qualitative studies of life online.

At the very start of this book, I described the intervention of journalists into the activities of *Avatar* fans. How different was my engagement with, and academic 'invasion' of, COA and SHH from the activity of these journalists? Unlike the journalistic coverage of *Avatar Forums,* my Ph.D. thesis (and the subsequent dissemination of my research at conferences, in journal articles, and in this book) brought relatively little additional visibility to the site because of the limited readership of my work (in contrast to that of the *Metro* paper, for instance, which in 2010 was reported to have a circulation of 1.3 million nationwide[8]). My work was therefore different in terms of both the manner of its publication and its publicness, and did not draw the site into the public domain in the same way as news reports would have done. Yet I was still an invader. I still do not have a clear sense of whether my research unsettled SHH or its members. Perhaps it has caused at least one member of the site to think differently about their posting activity, or about the audience that might be observing them. As I argued in Chap. 3, this might not be a bad thing. Yet it was a source of unease then and remains one now in my reflections back on my study from a more distanced vantage. I would still defend the decisions that I made during my project, but I am also aware of the tensions that developed during the study and in my reflections since completing it.

This unease is perhaps inescapable. The achievement of ethics is, as I have described in this book, a messy and complicated business. If we decide that it is not appropriate to cling to the lifebuoys of ethical rules and focus our attention instead on negotiating the localised production of ethical positions, positions which must be established in relation to other possible positions, and if we take into account competing interests, audiences, and parties, we move into an ongoing reflection upon our responsibilities and actions. As these parties, positions, interests, and contexts change, we may well find ourselves challenging, even losing faith in this earlier achievement. Inevitably, perhaps, the researcher will look back on their earlier self and say 'if only I had done it this way!' When all is said and done, research ethics are perhaps more local than we would like to think.

References

Baker, R. (1999). *Code of ethics: Some history*. Available online: http://ldysinger.stjohnsem.edu/ThM_580_Bioethics/03_Hist_2_15-19c/06_percival.htm.

Baym, N. K., & Markham, A. N (2008). Introduction: Making smart choices on shifting ground. In A. N. Markham & N. K. Baym (Eds.), *Internet inquiry: Conversations about method.* Thousand Oaks: Sage.

[8] http://www.pressgazette.co.uk/story.asp?storycode=45139.

Bruckman, A., Karahalios, K., Kraut, R. E., Poole, E. S., Thomas, J. C., & Yardi, S. (2010). *Revisiting research ethics in the facebook era: Challenges in emerging CSCW research*. http://research.microsoft.com/en-us/um/redmond/groups/connect/CSCW_10/docs/p623.pdf.

Burgess, R. G. (1984). *In the field: An introduction to field research*. London: George Allen & Unwin.

Craft, A. J. (2007). Sin in cyber-eden: Understanding the metaphysics and morals of virtual worlds. *Ethics and Information Technology, 9*, 205–217.

Denzin, N. (1968). On the ethics of disguised observation. *Social Problems, 115*, 502–504.

Drushel, B. E., & German, K. (2011). *Ethics of emerging media: Information, social norms, and new media technology*. London/New York: Continuum International Publishing Group.

Grossman, L. (2010). William Gibson serves up zero history. *Time.com,* Saturday, September 18 2010, http://www.time.com/time/magazine/article/0,9171,2015775-2,00.html.

Gunter, B., Nicholas, D., Huntington, P., & Williams, P. (2002). Online versus offline research: Implications for evaluating digital media. *ASLIB Proceedings, 54*(4), 229–239.

Guyer, J. (1999). Anthropology: The study of cultural and cultural originality. *African Sociological Review, 3*(2), 30–53.

Hammersley, M. (2009). Against the ethicists: On the evils of ethical regulation. *International Journal of Social Research Methodology, 12*(3), 211–225.

Langford, D. (2000). *Internet ethics*. London/Basingstoke: Macmillan Press.

May, T. (2001). *Social research: Issues, methods and process*. Buckingham: Open University Press.

McKee, H. A., & Porter, J. E. (2008). *The ethics of digital writing research: A rhetorical approach*. Available online: www.writing.ucsb.edu/wrconf08/Pdf_Articles/McKee_Article.pdf.

McKee, H. A., & Porter, J. E. (2009). *The ethics of Internet research: A rhetorical, case-based process*. Oxford: Peter Lang.

McNamee, M. (2001). Introduction: Whose ethics, which research? *Journal of Philosophy of Education, 35*(3), 309–327.

Sieber, J. E. (2006). Ethical principles. *The Sage dictionary of social research methods*, Research Methods Online, http://srmo.sagepub.com/

Slater, D. (2002). Making things real: Ethics and order on the internet. *Theory, Culture & Society, 19*(5/6), 227–245.

Spinello, R. A., & Tavani, H. T. (2004). *Readings in cyberethics*. Sudbury: Jones and Bartlett Publishers.

Turnbull, D. (2000). *Masons, tricksters and cartographers: Comparative studies in the sociology of scientific and indigenous knowledge*. London/New York: Routledge.

Whiteman, N. (2010). Control and contingency: Maintaining ethical stances in research. *International Journal of Internet Research Ethics, 3*(1), 6–22.

Wilkinson, D., & Thelwall, M. (2011). Researching personal information on the public web: Methods and ethics. *Social Science Computer Review, 29*(4), 387–401.

Index

DOI 10.1007/978-1-4614-1827-6, © Springer Science+Business Media, LLC 2012

MIX
Papier aus verantwortungsvollen Quellen
Paper from responsible sources
FSC® C105338

If you have any concerns about our products,
you can contact us on
ProductSafety@springernature.com

In case Publisher is established outside the EU,
the EU authorized representative is:
Springer Nature Customer Service Center GmbH
Europaplatz 3, 69115 Heidelberg, Germany

Printed by Libri Plureos GmbH
in Hamburg, Germany